Microsoft® Official Academic Course

Networking Fundamentals, Exam 98-366

Credits

EDITOR	Bryan Gambrel
DIRECTOR OF SALES	Mitchell Beaton
DIRECTOR OF MARKETING	Chris Ruel
MICROSOFT SENIOR PRODUCT MANAGER	Merrick Van Dongen of Microsoft Learning
EDITORIAL PROGRAM ASSISTANT	Jennifer Lartz
CONTENT MANAGER	Micheline Frederick
SENIOR PRODUCTION EDITOR	Kerry Weinstein
CREATIVE DIRECTOR	Harry Nolan
COVER DESIGNER	Jim O'Shea
TECHNOLOGY AND MEDIA	Tom Kulesa/Wendy Ashenberg

Cover photo: Credit: © Dwight Nadig/iStockphoto.

This book was set in Garamond by Aptara, Inc. and printed and bound by Bind Rite Graphics.
The cover was printed by Phoenix Color.

Microsoft, ActiveX, Excel, InfoPath, Microsoft Press, MSDN, OneNote, Outlook, PivotChart, PivotTable, PowerPoint, SharePoint, SQL Server, Visio, Visual Basic, Visual C#, Visual Studio, Windows, Windows 7, Windows Mobile, Windows Server, and Windows Vista are either registered trademarks or trademarks of Microsoft Corporation in the United States and/ or other countries. Other product and company names mentioned herein may be the trademarks of their respective owners.

The example companies, organizations, products, domain names, e-mail addresses, logos, people, places, and events depicted herein are fictitious. No association with any real company, organization, product, domain name, e-mail address, logo, person, place, or event is intended or should be inferred.

The book expresses the author's views and opinions. The information contained in this book is provided without any express, statutory, or implied warranties. Neither the authors, John Wiley & Sons, Inc., Microsoft Corporation, nor their resellers or distributors will be held liable for any damages caused or alleged to be caused either directly or indirectly by this book.

ISBN 978-0-470-90183-0

Printed in the United States of America

10 9 8 7 6 5 4

Foreword from the Publisher

Wiley's publishing vision for the Microsoft Official Academic Course series is to provide students and instructors with the skills and knowledge they need to use Microsoft technology effectively in all aspects of their personal and professional lives. Quality instruction is required to help both educators and students get the most from Microsoft's software tools and to become more productive. Thus our mission is to make our instructional programs trusted educational companions for life.

To accomplish this mission, Wiley and Microsoft have partnered to develop the highest quality educational programs for Information Workers, IT Professionals, and Developers. Materials created by this partnership carry the brand name "Microsoft Official Academic Course," assuring instructors and students alike that the content of these textbooks is fully endorsed by Microsoft, and that they provide the highest quality information and instruction on Microsoft products. The Microsoft Official Academic Course textbooks are "Official" in still one more way—they are the officially sanctioned courseware for Microsoft IT Academy members.

The Microsoft Official Academic Course series focuses on *workforce development*. These programs are aimed at those students seeking to enter the workforce, change jobs, or embark on new careers as information workers, IT professionals, and developers. Microsoft Official Academic Course programs address their needs by emphasizing authentic workplace scenarios with an abundance of projects, exercises, cases, and assessments.

The Microsoft Official Academic Courses are mapped to Microsoft's extensive research and job-task analysis, the same research and analysis used to create the Microsoft Technology Associate (MTA) and Microsoft Certified Information Technology Professional (MCITP) exams. The textbooks focus on real skills for real jobs. As students work through the projects and exercises in the textbooks they enhance their level of knowledge and their ability to apply the latest Microsoft technology to everyday tasks. These students also gain resume-building credentials that can assist them in finding a job, keeping their current job, or in furthering their education.

The concept of life-long learning is today an utmost necessity. Job roles, and even whole job categories, are changing so quickly that none of us can stay competitive and productive without continuously updating our skills and capabilities. The Microsoft Official Academic Course offerings, and their focus on Microsoft certification exam preparation, provide a means for people to acquire and effectively update their skills and knowledge. Wiley supports students in this endeavor through the development and distribution of these courses as Microsoft's official academic publisher.

Today educational publishing requires attention to providing quality print and robust electronic content. By integrating Microsoft Official Academic Course products, *WileyPLUS*, and Microsoft certifications, we are better able to deliver efficient learning solutions for students and teachers alike.

Bonnie Lieberman

General Manager and Senior Vice President

Preface

Welcome to the Microsoft Official Academic Course (MOAC) program for Networking Fundamentals. MOAC represents the collaboration between Microsoft Learning and John Wiley & Sons, Inc. publishing company. Microsoft and Wiley teamed up to produce a series of textbooks that deliver compelling and innovative teaching solutions to instructors and superior learning experiences for students. Infused and informed by in-depth knowledge from the creators of Microsoft products, and crafted by a publisher known worldwide for the pedagogical quality of its products, these textbooks maximize skills transfer in minimum time. Students are challenged to reach their potential by using their new technical skills as highly productive members of the workforce.

Because this knowledge base comes directly from Microsoft, creator of the Microsoft Certified IT Professional (MCITP), Microsoft Certified Technology Specialist (MCTS), and Microsoft Certified Professional (MCP) exams (www.microsoft.com/learning/certification), you are sure to receive the topical coverage that is most relevant to students' personal and professional success. Microsoft's direct participation not only assures you that MOAC textbook content is accurate and current; it also means that students will receive the best instruction possible to enable their success on certification exams and in the workplace.

■ The Microsoft Official Academic Course Program

The *Microsoft Official Academic Course* series is a complete program for instructors and institutions to prepare and deliver great courses on Microsoft software technologies. With MOAC, we recognize that, because of the rapid pace of change in the technology and curriculum developed by Microsoft, there is an ongoing set of needs beyond classroom instruction tools for an instructor to be ready to teach the course. The MOAC program endeavors to provide solutions for all these needs in a systematic manner in order to ensure a successful and rewarding course experience for both instructor and student—technical and curriculum training for instructor readiness with new software releases; the software itself for student use at home for building hands-on skills, assessment, and validation of skill development; and a great set of tools for delivering instruction in the classroom and lab. All are important to the smooth delivery of an interesting course on Microsoft software, and all are provided with the MOAC program. We think about the model below as a gauge for ensuring that we completely support you in your goal of teaching a great course. As you evaluate your instructional materials options, you may wish to use the model for comparison purposes with available products.

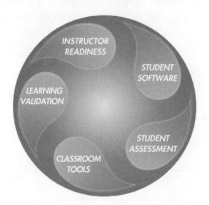

▪ Pedagogical Features

The MOAC textbook for Networking Fundamentals is designed to cover all the learning objectives for that MTA exam 98-366, which is referred to as its "objective domain." The Microsoft Technology Associate (MTA) exam objectives are highlighted throughout the textbook. Many pedagogical features have been developed specifically for *Microsoft Official Academic Course* programs.

Presenting the extensive procedural information and technical concepts woven throughout the textbook raises challenges for the student and instructor alike. The Illustrated Book Tour that follows provides a guide to the rich features contributing to *Microsoft Official Academic Course* program's pedagogical plan. Following is a list of key features in each lesson designed to prepare students for success as they continue in their IT education, on the certification exams, and in the workplace:

- Each lesson begins with a **Lesson Skill Matrix**. More than a standard list of learning objectives, the Domain Matrix correlates each software skill covered in the lesson to the specific exam objective domain.

- Concise and frequent **Step-by-Step** instructions teach students new features and provide an opportunity for hands-on practice. Numbered steps give detailed, step-by-step instructions to help students learn software skills.

- **Illustrations:** Screen images provide visual feedback as students work through the exercises. The images reinforce key concepts, provide visual clues about the steps, and allow students to check their progress.

- **Key Terms:** Important technical vocabulary is listed with definitions at the beginning of the lesson. When these terms are used later in the lesson, they appear in bold italic type and are defined. The Glossary contains all of the key terms and their definitions.

- Engaging point-of-use **Reader Aids**, located throughout the lessons, tell students why this topic is relevant (*The Bottom Line*), provide students with helpful hints (*Take Note*). Reader Aids also provide additional relevant or background information that adds value to the lesson.

- **Certification Ready** features throughout the text signal students where a specific certification objective is covered. They provide students with a chance to check their understanding of that particular MTA objective and, if necessary, review the section of the lesson where it is covered. MOAC offers complete preparation for MTA certification.

- **End-of-Lesson Questions:** The Knowledge Assessment section provides a variety of multiple-choice, true-false, matching, and fill-in-the-blank questions.

- **End-of-Lesson Exercises:** Competency Assessment case scenarios, Proficiency Assessment case scenarios, and Workplace Ready exercises are projects that test students' ability to apply what they've learned in the lesson.

■ Lesson Features

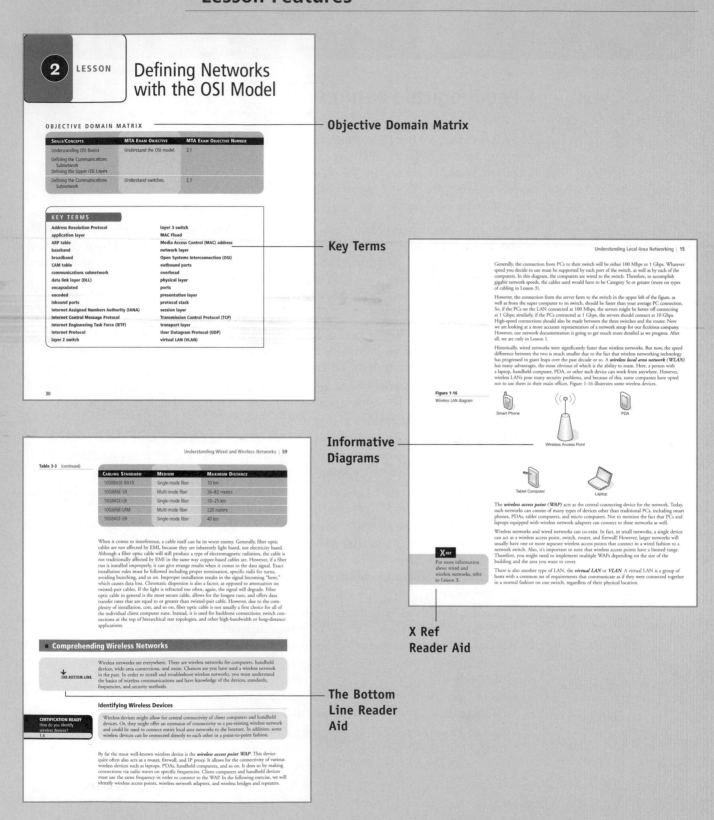

Objective Domain Matrix

Key Terms

Informative Diagrams

X Ref Reader Aid

The Bottom Line Reader Aid

Download Reader Aid

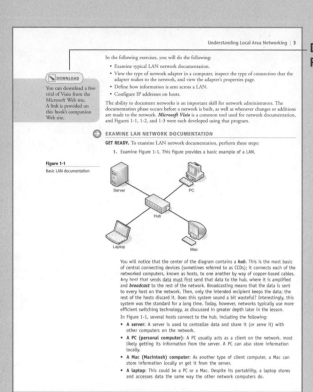

Understanding Local Area Networking | 3

In the following exercises, you will do the following:

• Examine typical LAN network documentation.
• View the type of network adapter in a computer, inspect the type of connection that the adapter makes to the network, and view the adapter's properties page.
• Define how information is sent across a LAN.
• Configure IP addresses on hosts.

The ability to document networks is an important skill for network administrators. The documentation phase occurs before a network is built, as well as whenever changes or additions are made to the network. **Microsoft Visio** is a common tool used for network documentation, and Figures 1-1, 1-2, and 1-3 were each developed using that program.

EXAMINE LAN NETWORK DOCUMENTATION

GET READY. To examine LAN network documentation, perform these steps:

1. Examine Figure 1-1. This figure provides a basic example of a LAN.

Figure 1-1
Basic LAN documentation

You will notice that the center of the diagram contains a **hub**. This is the most basic of central connecting devices (sometimes referred to as CCDs); it connects each of the networked computers, known as hosts, to one another by way of copper-based cables. Any host that sends data must first send that data to the hub, where it is amplified and **broadcast** to the rest of the network. Broadcasting means that the data is sent to every host on the network. Then, only the intended recipient keeps the data; the rest of the hosts discard it. Does this system sound a bit wasteful? Interestingly, this system was the standard for a long time. Today, however, networks typically use more efficient switching technology, as discussed in greater depth later in the lesson.

In Figure 1-1, several hosts connect to the hub, including the following:

• **A server:** A server is used to centralize data and share it (or *serve* it) with other computers on the network.
• **A PC (personal computer):** A PC usually acts as a client on the network, most likely getting its information from the server. A PC can also store information locally.
• **A Mac (Macintosh) computer:** As another type of client computer, a Mac can store information locally or get it from the server.
• **A laptop:** This could be a PC or a Mac. Despite its portability, a laptop stores and accesses data the same way the other network computers do.

Easy-to-Read Tables

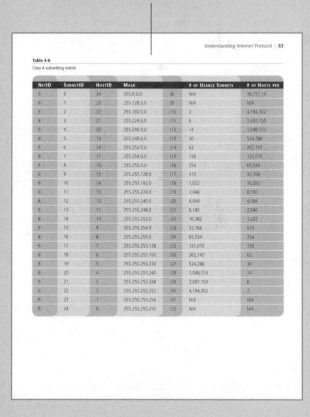

Understanding Internet Protocol | 83

Table 4-6
Class A subnetting matrix

NetID	SubnetID	HostID	Mask		# of Usable Subnets	# of Hosts per
8	0	24	255.0.0.0	/8	N/A	16,777,14
8	1	23	255.128.0.0	/9	N/A	N/A
8	2	22	255.192.0.0	/10	2	4,194,302
8	3	21	255.224.0.0	/11	6	2,097,150
8	4	20	255.240.0.0	/12	14	1,048,574
8	5	19	255.248.0.0	/13	30	524,286
8	6	18	255.252.0.0	/14	62	262,142
8	7	17	255.254.0.0	/15	126	131,070
8	8	16	255.255.0.0	/16	254	65,534
8	9	15	255.255.128.0	/17	510	32,766
8	10	14	255.255.192.0	/18	1,022	16,382
8	11	13	255.255.224.0	/19	2,046	8,190
8	12	12	255.255.240.0	/20	4,094	4,094
8	13	11	255.255.248.0	/21	8,190	2,046
8	14	10	255.255.252.0	/22	16,382	1,022
8	15	9	255.255.254.0	/23	32,766	510
8	16	8	255.255.255.0	/24	65,534	254
8	17	7	255.255.255.128	/25	131,070	126
8	18	6	255.255.255.192	/26	262,142	62
8	19	5	255.255.255.224	/27	524,286	30
8	20	4	255.255.255.240	/28	1,048,574	14
8	21	3	255.255.255.248	/29	2,097,150	6
8	22	2	255.255.255.252	/30	4,194,302	2
8	23	1	255.255.255.254	/31	N/A	N/A
8	24	0	255.255.255.255	/32	N/A	N/A

Certification Ready Alert

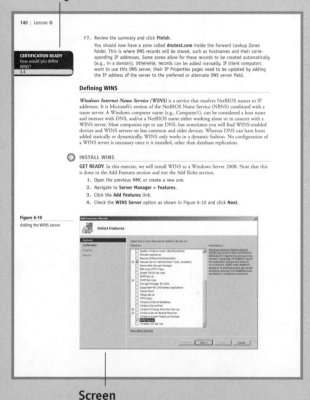

140 | Lesson 6

CERTIFICATION READY
How would you define WINS?
3.4

17. Review the summary and click **Finish**.

You should now have a zone called **dnstest.com** inside the Forward Lookup Zones folder. This is where DNS records will be stored, such as hostnames and their corresponding IP addresses. Some zones allow for these records to be created automatically (e.g., in a domain). Otherwise, records can be added manually. If client computers want to use this DNS server, their IP Properties pages need to be updated by adding the IP address of the server to the preferred or alternate DNS server field.

Defining WINS

Windows Internet Name Service (WINS) is a service that resolves NetBIOS names to IP addresses. It is Microsoft's version of the NetBIOS Name Service (NBNS) combined with a name server. A Windows computer name (e.g., Computer1), can be considered a host name and interact with DNS, and/or a NetBIOS name either working alone or in concert with a WINS server. Most companies opt to use DNS, but sometimes you will find WINS-enabled devices and WINS servers on less common and older devices. Whereas DNS can have hosts added statically or dynamically, WINS only works in a dynamic fashion. No configuration of a WINS server is necessary once it is installed, other than database replication.

INSTALL WINS

GET READY. In this exercise, we will install WINS to a Windows Server 2008. Note that this is done in the Add Features section and not the Add Roles section.

1. Open the previous MMC or create a new one.
2. Navigate to **Server Manager > Features.**
3. Click the **Add Features** link.
4. Check the **WINS Server** option as shown in Figure 6-10 and click **Next**.

Figure 6-10
Adding the WINS server

Screen Images

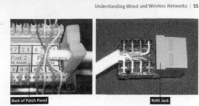

Photos

Take Note Reader Aid

Step-by-Step Exercises

Skill Summary

SKILL SUMMARY

IN THIS LESSON, YOU LEARNED:

• How to differentiate between the Internet, intranets, and extranets.
• How to set up a virtual private network with Windows Server 2008 and with a typical SOHO four-port router.
• About firewalls and how to initiate port scans on them to see whether they are locked down.
• About other perimeter devices and zones, such as proxy servers, Internet content filters, NIDS, NIPS, and the DMZ.

Knowledge Assessment

Knowledge Assessment

Multiple Choice

Circle the letter that corresponds to the best answer.

1. You have been tasked to set up an authentication server on a DMZ that will allow only users from a partner company. What kind of network are you configuring?
   a. Internet
   b. Intranet
   c. Extranet
   d. World Wide Web

2. You are in charge of setting up a VPN that allows connections on inbound port 1723. What tunneling protocol are you going to use?
   a. PPTP
   b. PPP
   c. L2TP
   d. TCP/IP

3. Proseware, Inc., wants you to set up a VPN server. What service in Windows Server 2008 should you use?
   a. FTP
   b. DNS
   c. RRAS
   d. IIS

4. The IT director has asked you to install a firewall. Which of the following is not a type of firewall?
   a. NAT filtering
   b. DMZ
   c. ALG
   d. Stateful packet inspection

5. You suspect an issue with one of the ports on the firewall. You decide to scan the ports. Which of the following is the appropriate tool to use?
   a. PPTP
   b. Protocol analyzer
   c. NMAP
   d. NIDS

Case Scenarios

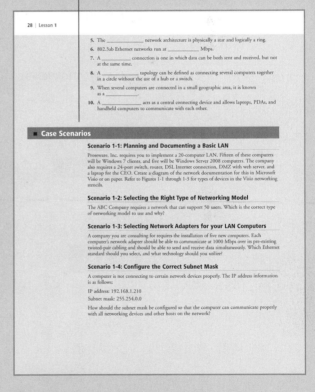

5. The _____ network architecture is physically a star and logically a ring.

6. 802.3ab Ethernet networks run at _____ Mbps.

7. A _____ connection is one in which data can be both sent and received, but not at the same time.

8. A _____ topology can be defined as connecting several computers together in a circle without the use of a hub or a switch.

9. When several computers are connected in a small geographic area, it is known as a _____.

10. A _____ acts as a central connecting device and allows laptops, PDAs, and handheld computers to communicate with each other.

Case Scenarios

Scenario 1-1: Planning and Documenting a Basic LAN

Proseware, Inc. requires you to implement a 20-computer LAN. Fifteen of these computers will be Windows 7 clients, and five will be Windows Server 2008 computers. The company also requires a 24-port switch, router, DSL Internet connection, DMZ with web server, and a laptop for the CEO. Create a diagram of the network documentation for this in Microsoft Visio or on paper. Refer to Figures 1-1 through 1-3 for types of devices in the Visio networking stencils.

Scenario 1-2: Selecting the Right Type of Networking Model

The ABC Company requires a network that can support 50 users. Which is the correct type of networking model to use and why?

Scenario 1-3: Selecting Network Adapters for your LAN Computers

A company you are consulting for requires the installation of five new computers. Each computer's network adapter should be able to communicate at 1000 Mbps over its pre-existing twisted-pair cabling and should be able to send and receive data simultaneously. Which Ethernet standard should you select, and what technology should you utilize?

Scenario 1-4: Configure the Correct Subnet Mask

A computer is not connecting to certain network devices properly. The IP address information is as follows:

IP address: 192.168.1.210

Subnet mask: 255.254.0.0

How should the subnet mask be configured so that the computer can communicate properly with all networking devices and other hosts on the network?

2. Set up daily ping tests to a server with the same IP that will consist of one hundred 1,500 byte ICMP packets.

3. Configure these so that they run every day and are output to a text file.

Workplace Ready

Workplace Ready

TCP/IP Command Table

TCP/IP commands are a huge part of a network administrator's life. The ability to use them quickly and efficiently depends on the knowledge of the user. Memorization of the commands, and especially the various command options, is imperative. Proper and smart use of the command prompt is also vital.

Research the commands listed after the following table and create your own table that describes them and each of their options (e.g., ping –t). In your table, include a column that describes why the command (and its option) would be used.

EXAMPLE	SOLUTION		
Ping	–t	Pings a remote computer continuously.	Used to determine long-term connectivity. Works well with cabling tests.
Ipconfig	/all	Shows in-depth information about a network adapter.	Can help find details such as the MAC address, DNS server, and so on.

FTP
Ipconfig
Nbtstat
Net command
Netsh
Netstat
Nslookup
Pathping
Ping
Route
Telnet
Tracert

Note that navigation in Windows can be slightly different in different versions. Once you are finished assembling your table, spend some time working with each of the commands on as many of the following operating systems that you can:

-Windows 7
-Windows Vista
-Windows XP
-Windows Server 2008 or 2003

Conventions and Features Used in This Book

This book uses particular fonts, symbols, and heading conventions to highlight important information or to call your attention to special steps. For more information about the features in each lesson, refer to the Illustrated Book Tour section.

CONVENTION	MEANING
↓ THE BOTTOM LINE	This feature provides a brief summary of the material to be covered in the section that follows.
CLOSE	Words in all capital letters indicate instructions for opening, saving, or closing files or programs. They also point out items you should check or actions you should take.
CERTIFICATION READY	This feature signals the point in the text where a specific certification objective is covered. It provides you with a chance to check your understanding of that particular MTA objective and, if necessary, review the section of the lesson where it is covered.
TAKE NOTE*	Reader aids appear in shaded boxes found in your text. *Take Note* provides helpful hints related to particular tasks or topics.
DOWNLOAD	Download provides information on where to download useful software.
X REF	These notes provide pointers to information discussed elsewhere in the textbook or describe interesting features of Windows Server that are not directly addressed in the current topic or exercise.
Alt + Tab	A plus sign (+) between two key names means that you must press both keys at the same time. Keys that you are instructed to press in an exercise will appear in the font shown here.
Example	Key terms appear in bold italic.

Instructor Support Program

The *Microsoft Official Academic Course* programs are accompanied by a rich array of resources that incorporate the extensive textbook visuals to form a pedagogically cohesive package. These resources provide all the materials instructors need to deploy and deliver their courses. Resources available online for download include:

- The **MSDN Academic Alliance** is designed to provide the easiest and most inexpensive developer tools, products, and technologies available to faculty and students in labs, classrooms, and on student PCs. A free 3-year membership is available to qualified MOAC adopters.

  Note: Microsoft Windows 2008 Server, Microsoft Windows 7, and Microsoft Visual Studio can be downloaded from MSDN AA for use by students in this course.

- The **Instructor's Guide** contains Solutions to all the textbook exercises and Syllabi for various term lengths. The Instructor's Guide also includes chapter summaries and lecture notes. The Instructor's Guide is available from the Book Companion site (http://www.wiley.com/college/microsoft).

- The **Test Bank** contains hundreds of questions in multiple-choice, true-false, short answer, and essay formats, and is available to download from the Instructor's Book Companion site (www.wiley.com/college/microsoft). A complete answer key is provided.

- A complete set of **PowerPoint presentations and images** are available on the Instructor's Book Companion site (http://www.wiley.com/college/microsoft) to enhance classroom presentations. Approximately 50 PowerPoint slides are provided for each lesson. Tailored to the text's topical coverage and Skills Matrix, these presentations are designed to convey key concepts addressed in the text. All images from the text are on the Instructor's Book Companion site (http://www.wiley.com/college/microsoft). You can incorporate them into your PowerPoint presentations, or create your own overhead transparencies and handouts. By using these visuals in class discussions, you can help focus students' attention on key elements of technologies covered and help them understand how to use it effectively in the workplace.

- When it comes to improving the classroom experience, there is no better source of ideas and inspiration than your fellow colleagues. The **Wiley Faculty Network** connects teachers with technology, facilitates the exchange of best practices, and helps to enhance instructional efficiency and effectiveness. Faculty Network activities include technology training and tutorials, virtual seminars, peer-to-peer exchanges of experiences and ideas, personal consulting, and sharing of resources. For details visit www.WhereFacultyConnect.com.

MSDN ACADEMIC ALLIANCE—FREE 3-YEAR MEMBERSHIP AVAILABLE TO QUALIFIED ADOPTERS!

The Microsoft Developer Network Academic Alliance (MSDN AA) is designed to provide the easiest and most inexpensive way for universities to make the latest Microsoft developer tools, products, and technologies available in labs, classrooms, and on student PCs. MSDN AA is an annual membership program for departments teaching Science, Technology, Engineering, and Mathematics (STEM) courses. The membership provides a complete solution to keep academic labs, faculty, and students on the leading edge of technology.

Software available in the MSDN AA program is provided at no charge to adopting departments through the Wiley and Microsoft publishing partnership.

As a bonus to this free offer, faculty will be introduced to Microsoft's Faculty Connection and Academic Resource Center. It takes time and preparation to keep students engaged while giving them a fundamental understanding of theory, and the Microsoft Faculty Connection is designed to help STEM professors with this preparation by providing articles, curriculum, and tools that professors can use to engage and inspire today's technology students.

*Contact your Wiley rep for details.

For more information about the MSDN Academic Alliance program, go to:

http://msdn.microsoft.com/academic/

Note: Windows Server 2008, Windows 7, and Visual Studio can be downloaded from MSDN AA for use by students in this course.

■ Important Web Addresses and Phone Numbers

To locate the Wiley Higher Education Rep in your area, go to http://www.wiley.com/ college and click on the "*Who's My Rep?*" link at the top of the page, or call the MOAC Toll Free Number: 1 + (888) 764-7001 (U.S. & Canada only).

To learn more about becoming a Microsoft Certified Technology Specialist and exam availability, visit www.microsoft.com/learning/mcp/mcp.

Student Support Program

▪ Additional Resources

Book Companion Web Site (www.wiley.com/college/microsoft)

The students' book companion site for the MOAC series includes any resources, exercise files, and Web links that will be used in conjunction with this course.

Wiley Desktop Editions

Wiley MOAC Desktop Editions are innovative, electronic versions of printed textbooks. Students buy the desktop version for up to 50% off the U.S. price of the printed text, and get the added value of permanence and portability. Wiley Desktop Editions provide students with numerous additional benefits that are not available with other e-text solutions.

Wiley Desktop Editions are NOT subscriptions; students download the Wiley Desktop Edition to their computer desktops. Students own the content they buy to keep for as long as they want. Once a Wiley Desktop Edition is downloaded to the computer desktop, students have instant access to all of the content without being online. Students can also print out the sections they prefer to read in hard copy. Students also have access to fully integrated resources within their Wiley Desktop Edition. From highlighting their e-text to taking and sharing notes, students can easily personalize their Wiley Desktop Edition as they are reading or following along in class.

▪ About the Microsoft Technology Associate (MTA) Certification

Preparing Tomorrow's Technology Workforce

Technology plays a role in virtually every business around the world. Possessing the fundamental knowledge of how technology works and understanding its impact on today's academic and workplace environment is increasingly important—particularly for students interested in exploring professions involving technology. That's why Microsoft created the Microsoft Technology Associate (MTA) certification—a new entry-level credential that validates fundamental technology knowledge among students seeking to build a career in technology.

The Microsoft Technology Associate (MTA) certification is the ideal and preferred path to Microsoft's world-renowned technology certification programs, such as Microsoft Certified Technology Specialist (MCTS) and Microsoft Certified IT Professional (MCITP). MTA is positioned to become the premier credential for individuals seeking to explore and pursue a career in technology, or augment related pursuits such as business or any other field where technology is pervasive.

MTA Candidate Profile

The MTA certification program is designed specifically for secondary and post-secondary students interested in exploring academic and career options in a technology field. It offers students a certification in basic IT and development. As the new recommended entry point for Microsoft technology certifications, MTA is designed especially for students new to IT and software development. It is available exclusively in educational settings and easily integrates into the curricula of existing computer classes.

MTA Empowers Educators and Motivates Students

MTA provides a new standard for measuring and validating fundamental technology knowledge right in the classroom while keeping your budget and teaching resources intact. MTA helps institutions stand out as innovative providers of high-demand industry credentials and is easily deployed with a simple, convenient, and affordable suite of entry-level technology certification exams. MTA enables students to explore career paths in technology without requiring a big investment of time and resources, while providing a career foundation and the confidence to succeed in advanced studies and future vocational endeavors.

In addition to giving students an entry-level Microsoft certification, MTA is designed to be a stepping stone to other, more advanced Microsoft technology certifications, like the Microsoft Certified Technology Specialist (MCTS) certification.

Delivering MTA Exams: The MTA Campus License

Implementing a new certification program in your classroom has never been so easy with the MTA Campus License. Through the one-time purchase of the 12-month, 1,000-exam MTA Campus License, there's no more need for ad hoc budget requests and recurrent purchases of exam vouchers. Now you can budget for one low cost for the entire year, and then administer MTA exams to your students and other faculty across your entire campus where and when you want.

The MTA Campus License provides a convenient and affordable suite of entry-level technology certifications designed to empower educators and motivate students as they build a foundation for their careers.

The MTA Campus License is administered by Certiport, Microsoft's exclusive MTA exam provider.

To learn more about becoming a Microsoft Technology Associate and exam availability, visit www.microsoft.com/learning/mta.

▪ Activate Your FREE MTA Practice Test!

Your purchase of this book entitles you to a free MTA practice test from GMetrix (a $30 value). Please go to www.gmetrix.com/mtatests and use the following validation code to redeem your free test: **MTA98-366-2F8AD70A331A.**

The **GMetrix Skills Management System** provides everything you need to practice for the Microsoft Technology Associate (MTA) Certification.

Overview of Test features:

- Practice tests map to the Microsoft Technology Associate (MTA) exam objectives
- GMetrix MTA practice tests simulate the actual MTA testing environment
- 50+ questions per test covering all objectives
- Progress at own pace, save test to resume later, return to skipped questions
- Detailed, printable score report highlighting areas requiring further review

To get the most from your MTA preparation, take advantage of your free GMetrix MTA Practice Test today!

For technical support issues on installation or code activation, please email support@gmetrix.com.

Acknowledgments

■ MOAC MTA Technology Fundamentals Reviewers

We'd like to thank the many reviewers who pored over the manuscript and provided invaluable feedback in the service of quality instructional materials:

Yuke Wang, University of Texas at Dallas

Palaniappan Vairavan, Bellevue College

Harold "Buz" Lamson, ITT Technical Institute

Colin Archibald, Valencia Community College

Catherine Bradfield, DeVry University Online

Robert Nelson, Blinn College

Kalpana Viswanathan, Bellevue College

Bob Becker, Vatterott College

Carol Torkko, Bellevue College

Bharat Kandel, Missouri Tech

Linda Cohen, Forsyth Technical Community College

Candice Lambert, Metro Technology Centers

Susan Mahon, Collin College

Mark Aruda, Hillsborough Community College

Claude Russo, Brevard Community College

David Koppy, Baker College

Sharon Moran, Hillsborough Community College

Keith Hoell, Briarcliffe College and Queens College— CUNY

Mark Hufnagel, Lee County School District

Rachelle Hall, Glendale Community College

Scott Elliott, Christie Digital Systems, Inc.

Gralan Gilliam, Kaplan

Steve Strom, Butler Community College

John Crowley, Bucks County Community College

Margaret Leary, Northern Virginia Community College

Sue Miner, Lehigh Carbon Community College

Gary Rollinson, Cabrillo College

Al Kelly, University of Advancing Technology

Katherine James, Seneca College

Brief Contents

Contents

Understanding Local Area Networking

LESSON 1

OBJECTIVE DOMAIN MATRIX

SKILLS/CONCEPTS	MTA EXAM OBJECTIVE	MTA EXAM OBJECTIVE NUMBER
Examining Local Area Networks, Devices, and Data Transfer	Understand local area networks (LANs).	1.2
Identifying Network Topologies and Standards	Understand network topologies and access methods.	1.5

KEY TERMS

8P8C
broadcast
centralized computing
client-server
CSMA/CA
CSMA/CD
computer telephony integration (CTI)
CTI-based server
data transfer rate
database server
demilitarized zone (DMZ)
distributive computing
Ethernet
file server
frames
full duplex
half duplex
host
hub
IEEE 802.3
IP address
local area network (LAN)
medium dependent interface (MDI)
mesh topology

messaging server
Microsoft ISA Server
Microsoft Visio
multistation access unit (MAU)
network adapter
network controller
network documentation
network operating systems
network topology
peer-to-peer (P2P)
perimeter network
print server
ring topology
RJ45
serial data transfer
star topology
subnet mask
switch
transceive
unicast
virtual LAN (VLAN)
web server
wireless access point (WAP)
wireless LAN (WLAN)

1

Local area networks (LANs) are used by just about every organization, and today, many homes have them as well. In this first lesson, we will refer to a fictitious company named Proseware, Inc., that wants to implement a new LAN that will serve approximately 20 users in a brand-new office. The company requires an extremely quick network that can transfer many different types of data. It wants the most cost-effective layout possible without losing speed or efficiency! As in all such situations, the network engineer's job responsibilities include selecting the right equipment, making sure this equipment is compatible, and getting everything installed on time. Also, the network engineer should have a thorough understanding of technologies such as Ethernet and switching, because they will be critical in designing and implementing the network. Therefore, in this chapter, we will cover all of the concepts necessary for confidently installing the network that Proseware desires. Then, as the book progresses, we will build on this scenario and add many more networking technologies to the company's infrastructure.

■ Examining Local Area Networks, Devices, and Data Transfer

THE BOTTOM LINE

Simply stated, a "network" is two or more computers that exchange data. A *local area network (LAN)* is a group of these computers that are confined to a small geographic area, usually one building. Setting up a LAN requires computers with network adapters, central connecting devices to connect those computers together, and a numbering scheme (such as IP addresses) to differentiate from one computer to the next. Set-up might also include servers, some type of protective device (such as a firewall), and connections to perimeter networks that are adjacent to the LAN.

Defining a LAN

As mentioned, a LAN requires computers with network adapters, central connecting devices, and some type of medium to tie it all together, be it cabled or wireless connections. These elements must be connected in some way to facilitate data transfer. When creating a LAN, it is important to define how these items are connected, as well as how they actually transmit data.

CERTIFICATION READY
How do you define local area networks?
1.2

Earlier, we mentioned that networks are used to exchange data. But what are the *real* reasons that organizations need networks? These reasons can be divided into four categories:

- **Sharing:** Networks permit the sharing of files, databases, and media.
- **Communication:** Networks are critical for email, instant messaging, and faxing capabilities.
- **Organization:** Networks centralize data and make it more accessible, which increases the efficiency and speed with which this information can be accessed.
- **Money:** A network should ultimately save a company money, often by aiding in the budgeting process and/or increasing productivity.

Some people would also place security in this list of categories, but unfortunately, many networks, devices, and operating systems are insecure when they are fresh out of the box. Merely having a network doesn't ensure security. Rather, you must take numerous steps to implement a secure network.

In order to understand LANs better, it helps to write out the structure of a LAN—in other words, to *document* it. **Network documentation** is any information that helps describe, define, and otherwise explain how computers are connected in a physical and logical way. For example, the physical connection could involve cables, and the logical connection could involve the various IP addresses used by the devices on the network.

In the following exercises, you will do the following:

- Examine typical LAN network documentation.
- View the type of network adapter in a computer, inspect the type of connection that the adapter makes to the network, and view the adapter's properties page.
- Define how information is sent across a LAN.
- Configure IP addresses on hosts.

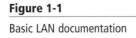

You can download a free trial of Visio from the Microsoft Web site. A link is provided on this book's companion Web site.

The ability to document networks is an important skill for network administrators. The documentation phase occurs before a network is built, as well as whenever changes or additions are made to the network. *Microsoft Visio* is a common tool used for network documentation, and Figures 1-1, 1-2, and 1-3 were each developed using that program.

 EXAMINE LAN NETWORK DOCUMENTATION

GET READY. To examine LAN network documentation, perform these steps:

1. Examine Figure 1-1. This figure provides a basic example of a LAN.

Figure 1-1

Basic LAN documentation

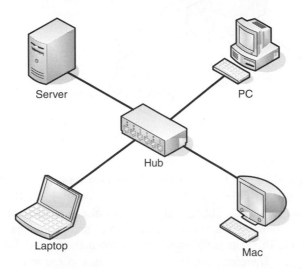

You will notice that the center of the diagram contains a *hub*. This is the most basic of central connecting devices (sometimes referred to as CCDs); it connects each of the networked computers, known as hosts, to one another by way of copper-based cables. Any host that sends data must first send that data to the hub, where it is amplified and *broadcast* to the rest of the network. Broadcasting means that the data is sent to every host on the network. Then, only the intended recipient keeps the data; the rest of the hosts discard it. Does this system sound a bit wasteful? Interestingly, this system was the standard for a long time. Today, however, networks typically use more efficient switching technology, as discussed in greater depth later in the lesson.

In Figure 1-1, several hosts connect to the hub, including the following:

- **A server:** A server is used to centralize data and share it (or *serve* it) with other computers on the network.
- **A PC (personal computer):** A PC usually acts as a client on the network, most likely getting its information from the server. A PC can also store information locally.
- **A Mac (Macintosh) computer:** As another type of client computer, a Mac can store information locally or get it from the server.
- **A laptop:** This could be a PC or a Mac. Despite its portability, a laptop stores and accesses data the same way the other network computers do.

2. Now, examine your own network and jot down your observations. Use Visio if possible; otherwise, draw out your own network documentation on paper. Whether you are at home or at a school or business, chances are that you are connected to a LAN. Try to identify any hosts on the network (PCs, laptops, servers, etc.). Then, identify the central connecting device that ties everything together. This could be a basic hub, a switch, or a router or multifunction network device.

3. Examine Figure 1-2. This is an intermediate example of a LAN.

Figure 1-2

Intermediate LAN documentation

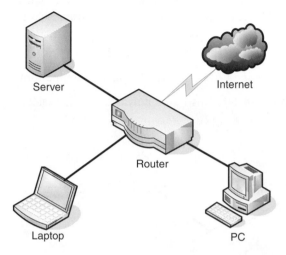

In Figure 1-2, we have replaced the hub with a basic 4-port router; these are also referred to as SOHO (small office–home office) routers. The router acts as a central connecting device, but it also has a special communications link to the Internet, thereby allowing the hosts to send data to and receive data from computers on the Internet. This communications link between the router and the Internet is where the LAN ends. Therefore, the PC, laptop, server, and router are part of the LAN, but anything beyond the router is considered outside the LAN.

4. Examine your own LAN again. If possible, identify any routers and connections to the Internet (or other networks). Add these to your written or Visio documentation.

5. Examine Figure 1-3. This is a slightly more advanced example of a LAN.

Figure 1-3

Advanced LAN documentation

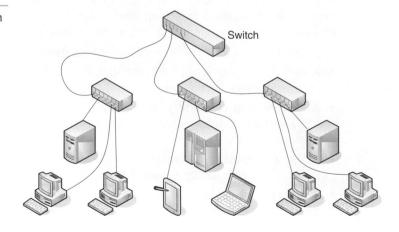

In Figure 1-3, we have added more central connecting devices. Instead of connecting hundreds of devices to a single central connecting device, we can break up the network in a hierarchical fashion. For example, on the left side of the figure, there are two PCs and one server connected to a hub. Let's say that these represent 24 computers, and that each other group of computers connected to a hub also represents 24 computers. Instead of connecting all of the computers to a single central connecting device, which might not be able to physically support all of these hosts, we have connected the groups of 24 hosts to their own hub. Then, the hubs are all daisy-chained to a *switch* at the top of the figure. The switch will most likely be a powerful (and expensive) device, in order to support all of the computers that ultimately connect to it. You can regard the individual hubs as devices that allow connectivity for single departments in a company, or perhaps for individual classrooms in a school. The master switch at the top of the hierarchical tree connects everything together. However, it also acts as a single point of failure, which we will address later in this book. As you can guess, this type of network architecture is the kind required to accomplish the goals laid out in the scenario in the beginning of the lesson.

A ***network adapter***, also known as a network interface card or NIC, is the device that enables you to send and receive data to and from your computer. This adapter might be integrated into the motherboard or act as a separate device that connects to a PCI slot, or perhaps a PC card slot or USB port. An adapter can connect to the network by cable (wired) or by air (wireless). It has its own basic CPU to process transmitted data, as well as a ROM chip to store information about itself. Network adapters also have a software component known as a driver, which defines how the card will interact with the operating system; this usually includes a properties page that can be accessed in the operating system, thereby enabling the user to configure the adapter as he or she sees fit.

 VIEW A NETWORK ADAPTER

GET READY. To view a network adapter, perform these steps:

1. Examine Figure 1-4. This shows a typical network adapter.

Figure 1-4

A typical network adapter

This particular network adapter is a PCI card, but again, network adapters come in many forms. However, notice the port on the card. This is known as an *RJ45* port (or an *8P8C*), and it is where the RJ45 plug at the end of the network cable connects. This is the most common type of network adapter port, allowing the adapter to connect to most of today's wired networks.

2. Look for the network adapter on your computer. If the computer only uses a wireless network adapter, look for an antenna on the card. Laptops have an internal antenna, but you can usually know whether you are connected wirelessly by looking at the wireless LED.

3. Examine Figure 1-5. This is a typical patch cable that connects to an RJ45 port.

Figure 1-5

A typical patch cable

This type of cable is known as twisted pair. It has an RJ45 plug on its end, which is molded so it can only connect one way to the RJ45 port. It also has a tab that locks it in place. Although the RJ45 plug looks very similar to a telephone cable's RJ11 plug, the RJ45 plug is slightly larger. Another difference is that the phone plug will *usually* have four wires, whereas the RJ45 plug will have eight.

4. Identify the cable that connects your computer to the network. Disconnect the cable (first, finish any downloads from the Internet if you have any in progress) and view the connector. If you are connected wirelessly, attempt to identify the cables that are connected to a hub, switch, or router.

5. Now, access the operating system and look at the properties of the network adapter. As an example, we will use a Windows 7 client computer with an Intel network adapter. Older versions of Windows have almost identical window and dialog box names, and the navigation to those windows is similar as well.

   a. Click **Start**.

   b. Right click **Computer**.

c. Select **Manage**. This should display the Computer Management console window.

d. Click **Device Manager**.

e. Click the plus (+) sign to expand the **Network adapters** category, as shown in Figure 1-6.

Figure 1-6

Device Manager with the Network adapters category expanded

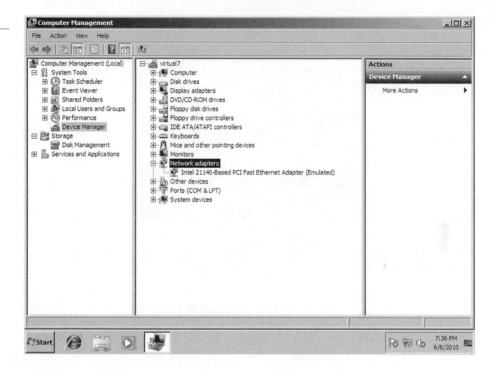

f. Right-click the network adapter and select **Properties**. This will display a window similar to Figure 1-7.

Figure 1-7

Properties window of an Intel network adapter

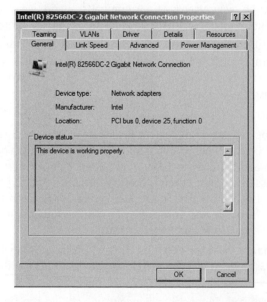

6. Next, take a look at the configured link speed for the network adapter. To do this, click on the Link Speed tab within the Properties page. This might have a slightly different name depending on the version or brand of network adapter in your computer. The resulting page should be similar to Figure 1-8.

Figure 1-8

Link speed of network adapter

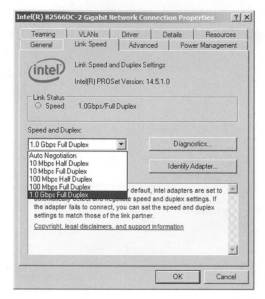

You can tell that the card in Figure 1-8 is active if the Link Status field has a green light. It also indicates that the card is connected at 1 Gbps (gigabits per second) and has negotiated a *full duplex* connection. Full duplex means that the network card can send and receive data *simultaneously*. In the Speed and Duplex drop down menu, we can select from other speeds, including 10 Mbps and 100 Mbps, and we can also select *half duplex*, which means that the network adapter will send and receive data but not at the same time. Full duplex is the superior connection, as long as your central connecting device supports it. Effectively, a full duplex connection can *transceive* (transmit and receive) twice as much information per second as a half duplex connection. So, to meet the requirements of our original scenario, we would probably want our client computers to connect at 1 Gbps as well as utilize full duplex negotiations.

7. Finally, every network adapter will have a logical name. By default, the network adapter is known as the Local Area Connection, although you can change the name if you desire. This Local Area Connection has its own properties page and status page. To view these:

   a. Click **Start**.

   b. Right click **Network** and select **Properties**. This will display the Network and Sharing Center window. If you don't have the Network option in your Start menu, you can add it from the Taskbar and Start Menu Properties dialog box, which can be accessed by right clicking the taskbar and selecting Properties. An alternate way to access the Network and Sharing Center is to go to **Start > Control Panel > Network and Internet**. Once in the Network and Internet window, select the **Network and Sharing Center** link.

   c. Click **Change adapter settings**. This will bring up the Network Connections window. (Navigation to this window will be slightly different in other versions of Windows.)

   d. In the Network Connections window, you should see the Local Area Connection icon. Right click the icon and select **Properties**. Doing this should display the Local Area Connection Properties dialog box, as shown in Figure 1-9.

Figure 1-9

Local Area Connection
Properties dialog box

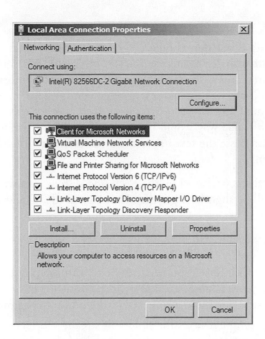

From here, you can configure Internet Protocol (IP), bind new protocols to the network adapter, and so on. We will access this dialog box frequently during the course of this book.

e. Click the **Cancel** button to close the dialog box. This should return you to the Network Connections window.

f. Now, double click the **Local Area Connection** icon. This should bring up the Local Area Connection Status dialog box, as shown in Figure 1-10. This dialog box displays the type of connectivity, speed, and how long the adapter has been connected; it also shows the total bytes sent and received. You can also get to the Properties window from here and diagnose the network adapter if necessary.

Figure 1-10

Local Area Connection Status
dialog box

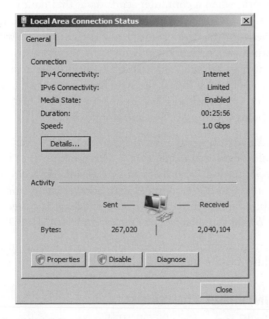

DEFINING DATA TRANSFER ON A LAN

Generally, when data is transferred on a LAN, it is sent in a serial fashion over twisted-pair cabling. *Serial data transfer* means the transfer of one bit at a time—in other words, transfer in a single-bit stream. This is the format usually used to send information from one network adapter to another. Now, let's discuss this arrangement in a little more depth. Say one user wanted to send a small text file (100 bytes in size) to another user on the network. There are many ways to do this; one way would be to map a network drive to the other user's computer and simply copy and paste the text file to the other computer's hard drive. When this occurs, a few things happen:

1. First, the text file is packaged by the operating system into what is known as a packet. The packet will be slightly larger than the original file. The packet is then sent to the network adapter.

2. Next, the network adapter takes the packet and places it inside a frame, which is slightly larger than a packet. Usually, this will be an Ethernet frame.

3. Now, the frame of information needs to be sent to the physical media—the cabling. To do this, the network adapter breaks down the frame of information into a serial data stream that is sent one bit at a time across the cables to the other computer.

4. The receiving computer takes the single-bit stream and recreates the frame of data. After analyzing the frame and verifying that it is indeed the intended recipient, the computer strips the frame information so that only the packet remains.

5. The packet is sent to the operating system, and ultimately, the text file shows up on the computer's hard drive, available to the user through Windows Explorer. This is a basic example of data transfer, and we will expand on it in Lesson 2, "Defining Networks with the OSI Model."

Usually, LANs utilize one of several Ethernet standards. *Ethernet* is a set of rules that govern the transmission of data between network adapters and various central connecting devices. All network adapters and central connecting devices must be compatible with the Ethernet in order to communicate with each other. One common type of Ethernet is known as 802.3u or Fast Ethernet, and it runs at 100 Mbps. Another common type is 802.3ab or Gigabit Ethernet.

In this type of network, when a computer sends data, that data is *broadcast* to every other host on the network by default. The problem with this method is that usually there is only one intended recipient for the data, so the rest of the computers will simply drop the data packets. This in turn wastes network bandwidth. To alleviate this problem, Ethernet switching was developed about 15 years ago, and it is still used in most networks today. Switching has many advantages, one of which is that the switch only sends unicast traffic. *Unicast* describes the situation in which information is sent to one host only. This reduces network traffic greatly, and it also helps with packet loss and duplication.

We have mentioned network speed a few times already. However, a more accurate term for network speed would be *data transfer rate*, otherwise known as bit rate. This is defined as the maximum bits per second (bps) that can be transmitted over a network. As mentioned, this value is rated in bits, and it is signified with a lowercase *b* (for example, 10 Mbps). The lowercase *b* helps differentiate this amount from data that is stored on a hard drive, which uses an upper case *B* that stands for bytes (for example 10 MB).

Of course, all this means nothing without an addressing system in place. The most common type of network address is the Internet Protocol address, or more simply, IP address.

CONFIGURING INTERNET PROTOCOL

Internet Protocol, or IP, is the part of TCP/IP that, among other things, governs IP addresses. The *IP address* is the cornerstone of networking because it defines the computer or host you are working on. Today, every computer and many other devices have such an address. An IP address allows each computer to send and receive information back and forth in an orderly and efficient manner. IP addresses are much like your home address. However, whereas your home address identifies your house number and the street you live on, an IP address identifies your computer number and the network it lives on. A typical example of an IP address would be 192.168.1.1.

Every IP address is broken down into two parts: the network portion (in this case 192.168.1), which is the network that your computer is a member of, and the host portion, which is the individual number of your computer that differentiates your computer from any others on the network. In this case, the host portion is .1. How do we know this? The subnet mask tells us.

The *subnet mask* is a group of four numbers that define what IP network the computer is a member of. All of the 255s in a subnet mask collectively refer to the network portion, whereas the 0s refer to the host portion. Table 1-1 shows a typical Class C IP address and the default corresponding subnet mask. If you were to configure the IP address of a Windows computer as 192.168.1.1, Windows would automatically default to a subnet mask of 255.255.255.0. If any other computers need to communicate with yours, they must be configured with the same network number; however, every computer on the same network needs to have a different host number, or an IP conflict might ensue. Of course, as a talented administrator, you'll learn how to avoid IP conflicts. You'll encounter some tips on how to do so in Lessons 4 and 5.

Table 1-1

An IP address and corresponding subnet mask

TYPE OF ADDRESS	FIRST OCTET	SECOND OCTET	THIRD OCTET	FOURTH OCTET
IP address	192	168	1	1
Subnet mask	255	255	255	0

IP addresses are actually 32-bit dotted-decimal numbers. If you were to convert an IP address's decimal numbers to binary, you'd have a total of 32 bits. An IP address is considered dotted because each number is separated by a dot. Altogether, each such address contains four numbers, each of which is a byte or octet. For instance, in our example, 192 is an octet, and its binary equivalent would be 11000000, which is eight bits. 168 is also an octet, its binary equivalent is 10101000, and so on. Adding all four octets together gives us 32 bits.

IP addresses are usually applied to your network adapter, but they can also be applied to other devices like switches, routers, and so on. The fact that a device or computer has an IP address is what makes it a *host*. Let's configure IP addresses on our Windows 7 host now. Remember that other Windows computers will be configured in a very similar way.

 CONFIGURE IP ADDRESSES

GET READY. To configure IP addresses, perform these steps:

1. Access the Local Area Connection Properties dialog box once again.

2. Click **Internet Protocol Version 4**, then click the **Properties** button. This displays the Internet Protocol Version 4 Properties dialog box. Write down the current settings (if there are any) so that you can return the computer to these settings at the end of the exercise.

3. By default, the dialog box options will be configured as "Obtain an IP address automatically" and "Obtain DNS server address automatically," as shown in Figure 1-11. This means that the network adapter will attempt to get all of its IP information from a DHCP server or other device like a SOHO 4-port router. However, we want to configure the adapter statically, so let's continue.

Figure 1-11

Internet Protocol Version 4
Properties dialog box

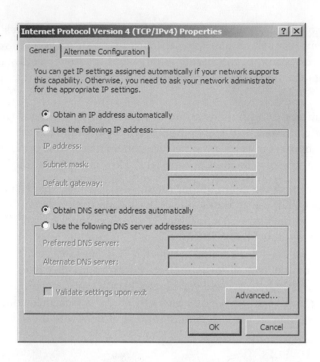

4. Click the **Use the following IP address** radio button. This enables the other fields so you can type in the desired IP information. Enter the following:

- For the IP address, enter **192.168.1.1**.
- For the Subnet mask, enter **255.255.255.0**.
- Leave the Default gateway and the Preferred DNS server fields blank.
- When you are finished, your dialog box should look like the one shown in Figure 1-12.

Figure 1-12

Internet Protocol Version 4
Properties dialog box
configured statically

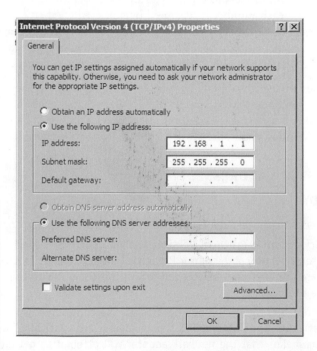

TAKE NOTE*

If you are working with others as you complete this exercise, each person should enter a different IP address. For example, the first person should enter 192.168.1.1, the second person should enter 192.168.1.2, and so on. This will avoid any possible IP conflicts.

- If you have other computers, try configuring their IP addresses as well. Remember, the host portion of the IP address should ascend once for each computer: .1, .2, .3, and so on.

5. Click **OK.** Then, in the Local Area Connection Properties dialog box, click **OK.** This will complete and bind the configuration to the network adapter.

6. Test your configuration. We will do this in two ways, first with the **ipconfig** command, and second with the **ping** command.

   a. Open a command prompt. Do this by pressing the **Windows + R** keys and typing cmd in the open field. Now, type **ipconfig**. The results should look something like Figure 1-13. Notice the IPv4 Address field in the results and the IP address that is listed. This should be the IP address you configured previously. If not, go back and check your Internet Protocol Properties dialog box.

Figure 1-13

ipconfig results

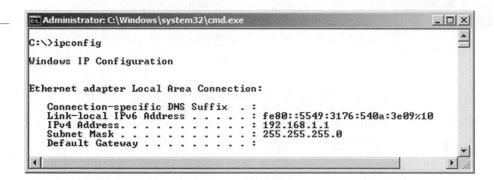

   b. Ping a computer on the same 192.168.1 network. If there are no other computers, ping your own IP address. For example, type the following command:

   ping 192.168.1.1

   This command sends requests out to the other IP address. If the other computer is running and configured properly, it should reply back. A positive ping would look similar to Figure 1-14, in which four replies are received by the pinging computer.

Figure 1-14

Ping results

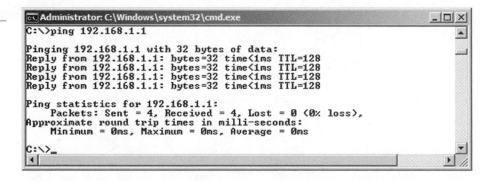

TAKE NOTE*

Always test your network configurations!

If for some reason you do not get a reply or you get another message like "request timed out," you should check the IP configuration again to make sure that the other computer you are trying to ping is configured properly. Also make sure that all involved computers are wired to the network.

You can also ping your own computer using the loopback address, also known as the local loopback. Every Windows computer automatically gets this address; it is 127.0.0.1. This address exists is in addition to the logical address that you assigned earlier. Try the command **ping loopback** and check your results. You can also try **ping localhost** and **ping 127.0.0.1**. Regardless, you should get results from 127.0.0.1. When pinging this address, no network traffic is incurred; because the network adapter is really just looping the ping back to the OS, it never places any packets on to the network. Therefore, this is a solid way to test whether TCP/IP is installed correctly to a network adapter, even if you aren't physically connected to a network.

When you are finished, return your computer back to its regular IP settings. We will explain more about IPs in Lesson 5, "Understanding Internet Protocol."

Identifying Types of LANs

There are several types of local area networks that a computer can connect to. An organization must choose whether to use wired connections, wireless connections, or a mix of the two. It is also possible to have virtual LANs.

The first and most common type of LAN is the wired LAN. Here, computers and other devices are wired together using copper-based twisted-pair cables. These cables have RJ45 plugs on each end, which make the actual connection to the RJ45 ports that reside on the computer's network adapter and on hubs, switches, or routers. (Of course, there will probably be some other cabling equipment between each of these, but we will cover that equipment in more depth in Lesson 3, "Understanding Wired and Wireless Networks.")

Figure 1-15 gives yet another diagram, but this time it depicts three LANs connected together by a router. A few new devices we haven't seen until now are shown in this figure—namely, a firewall, which protects the LAN (or LANs) from the Internet, and a super computer, which occupies its own little LAN.

Figure 1-15

Wired LAN documentation

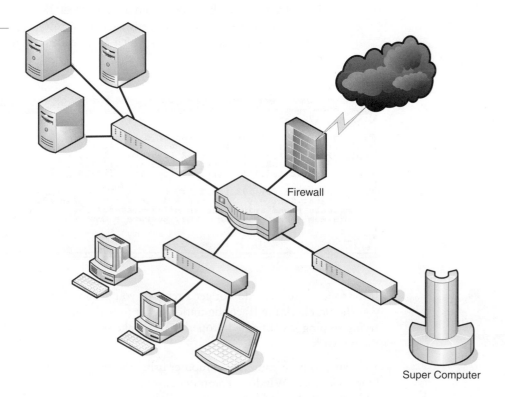

Generally, the connection from PCs to their switch will be either 100 Mbps or 1 Gbps. Whatever speed you decide to use must be supported by each port of the switch, as well as by each of the computers. In this diagram, the computers are wired to the switch. Therefore, to accomplish gigabit network speeds, the cables used would have to be Category 5e or greater (more on types of cabling in Lesson 3).

However, the connection from the server farm to the switch in the upper left of the figure, as well as from the super computer to its switch, should be faster than your average PC connection. So, if the PCs on the LAN connected at 100 Mbps, the servers might be better off connecting at 1 Gbps; similarly, if the PCs connected at 1 Gbps, the servers should connect at 10 Gbps. High-speed connections should also be made between the three switches and the router. Now we are looking at a more accurate representation of a network setup for our fictitious company. However, our network documentation is going to get much more detailed as we progress. After all, we are only in Lesson 1.

Historically, wired networks were significantly faster than wireless networks. But now, the speed difference between the two is much smaller due to the fact that wireless networking technology has progressed in giant leaps over the past decade or so. A ***wireless local area network (WLAN)*** has many advantages, the most obvious of which is the ability to roam. Here, a person with a laptop, handheld computer, PDA, or other such device can work from anywhere. However, wireless LANs pose many security problems, and because of this, some companies have opted not to use them in their main offices. Figure 1-16 illustrates some wireless devices.

Figure 1-16

Wireless LAN diagram

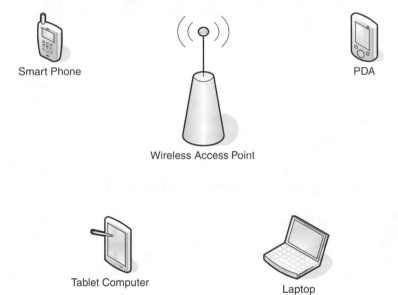

Smart Phone

Wireless Access Point

PDA

Tablet Computer

Laptop

The ***wireless access point (WAP)*** acts as the central connecting device for the network. Today, such networks can consist of many types of devices other than traditional PCs, including smart phones, PDAs, tablet computers, and micro computers. Not to mention the fact that PCs and laptops equipped with wireless network adapters can connect to these networks as well.

Wireless networks and wired networks can co-exist. In fact, in small networks, a single device can act as a wireless access point, switch, router, and firewall! However, larger networks will usually have one or more separate wireless access points that connect in a wired fashion to a network switch. Also, it's important to note that wireless access points have a limited range. Therefore, you might need to implement multiple WAPs depending on the size of the building and the area you want to cover.

There is also another type of LAN, the ***virtual LAN*** or ***VLAN***. A virtual LAN is a group of hosts with a common set of requirements that communicate as if they were connected together in a normal fashion on one switch, regardless of their physical location.

X REF

For more information about wired and wireless networks, refer to Lesson 3.

A VLAN is implemented to segment a network, reduce collisions, organize the network, boost performance, and increase security. Switches usually control the VLAN. Like subnetting, a VLAN compartmentalizes a network and can isolate traffic. But unlike subnetting, a VLAN can be set up in a physical manner; an example of this would be the port-based VLAN, as shown in Figure 1-17. In this example, each set of computers (such as "Classroom 2") has its own VLAN (which is dedicated to the 192.168.2.0 network in this case); however, computers in that VLAN can be located anywhere on the *physical* network. As another example, computers within the VLAN "Staff" could be located in several physical areas in the building, but regardless of where they are located, they are associated with the Staff VLAN because of the physical port to which they connect.

Figure 1-17

Example of a port-based VLAN

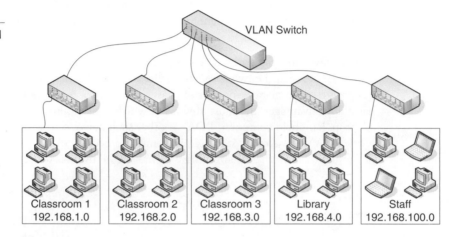

There are also logical types of VLANs, like the protocol-based VLAN and the MAC address-based VLAN, but by far the most common is the port-based VLAN. The most common standard associated with VLANs is IEEE 802.1Q, which modifies Ethernet frames by "tagging" them with the appropriate VLAN information. This VLAN information determines the VLAN to which to direct the Ethernet frame.

Getting to Know Perimeter Networks

Perimeter networks are small networks that usually consist of only a few servers that are accessible from the Internet in some way. Generally, the term "perimeter network" is synonymous with demilitarized zone (DMZ). You should be able to identify a DMZ and its purpose in an organization, as well as know how to implement a basic DMZ.

A *perimeter network* (also known as a *demilitarized zone* or DMZ) is a small network that is set up separately from a company's private LAN and the Internet. It is called a perimeter network because it is usually on the edge of the LAN, but DMZ has become a much more popular term. A DMZ allows users outside of a company LAN to access specific services located on the DMZ. However, when a DMZ is set up properly, those users are blocked from gaining access to the company LAN. Users on the LAN will quite often connect to the DMZ as well, but they can do so without having to worry about outside attackers gaining access to their private LAN. A DMZ might house a switch with servers connected to it that offer web, email, and other services. Two common configurations of DMZs include the following:

• **Back-to-back configuration:** This involves a DMZ situated between two firewall devices, which could be black box appliances or Microsoft Internet Security and Acceleration (ISA) Servers, or perhaps Microsoft Forefront devices. An illustration of this set-up is shown in Figure 1-18. In this configuration, an attacker would have to get through two firewalls in order to gain access to the LAN.

Figure 1-18

A back-to-back DMZ configuration

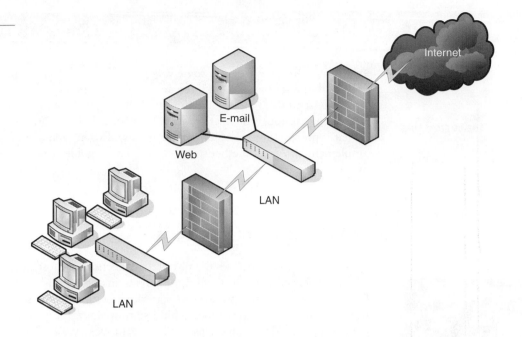

• **3-leg perimeter configuration:** In this scenario, the DMZ is usually attached to a separate connection of the company firewall. Therefore, the firewall would have three connections: one to the company LAN, one to the DMZ, and one to the Internet, as shown in Figure 1-19. Once again, this can be done with a firewall appliance or with Microsoft ISA Server. In this configuration, an attacker would only need to break through one firewall to gain access to the LAN. Although this is a disadvantage, technologies like network intrusion detection/prevention systems can help alleviate most security issues. Also, one firewall means less administration.

Figure 1-19

A 3-leg perimeter DMZ configuration

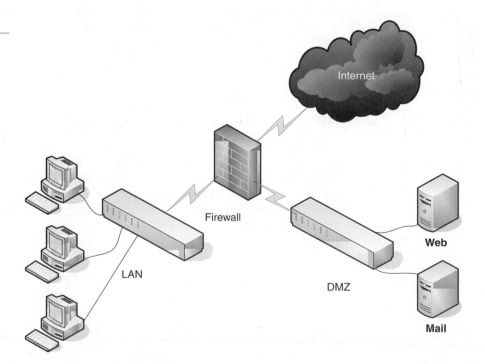

■ Identifying Network Topologies and Standards

THE BOTTOM LINE

Networks need to be situated in some way to facilitate the transfer of data. Topologies are the physical orientations of computers in a LAN. Access methods are how the computers will actually send data; the most common of these is the client/server-based Ethernet configuration, although there are others. In order to build a LAN, you must first plan out what topology (or topologies) will be used and what type of access method will be implemented. Access methods tend to be a less tangible concept, so let's begin with network topologies.

Identifying Network Topologies

CERTIFICATION READY
How do you identify network topologies and access methods?
1.5

A *network topology* defines the physical connections of hosts in a computer network. There are several types of physical topologies, including bus, ring, star, mesh, and tree. For the exam, you should know the star, ring, and mesh topologies. We throw in the tree topology, also known as the hierarchical star topology, for good measure as well, because many people consider it an extension of the star topology. We also identify logical topologies, as they are characterized differently than physical topologies.

In this exercise, we will examine the following *physical* network topologies:

- Star
- Mesh
- Ring

By far, the most common topology is the **star topology**. When a star topology is used, each computer is individually wired to a central connecting device with twisted-pair cabling. The central connecting device could be a hub, a switch, or a SOHO router. This is the type of topology usually used when implementing networks.

 IDENTIFY TOPOLOGIES

GET READY. To identify topologies, perform these steps:

1. Examine Figure 1-20. This illustrates a simple star topology. You will notice that this image is similar to Figures 1-1 and 1-2 earlier in the lesson. Indeed, those other figures also illustrate star topologies. Note that the hub in the center of the figure connects each computer by a single cable. This way, if one cable is disconnected, the rest of the network can still function. This is the standard physical topology for an Ethernet network.

Figure 1-20

Star topology

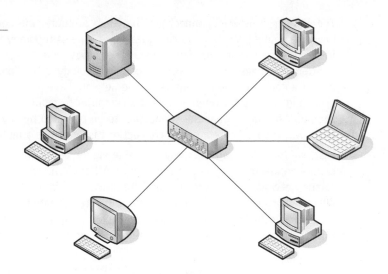

2. Examine your own computer network. Check whether it meets the characteristics of the star; namely, is each computer connected to a central connecting device? Are the computers individually cabled to that device? If you identify your network as a star topology, add that fact to your network documentation.

In the old days, networks often used what was known as the bus topology. With that topology, all computers were connected to a single bus cable; therefore, if one computer failed, the whole network went down! Despite this downfall, part of the idea behind the bus topology was passed on to the star topology. For example, two individual star networks can be connected together (by their central connecting devices) to create a star-bus topology. This is done by daisy chaining (or stacking) one or more hubs or switches, usually by a special *medium dependent interface (MDI)* port; this is where the "bus" part of a star-bus topology comes in.

The problem with the star-bus topology is that it is based on the stacking concept. This can pose organizational problems and is not the best use of bandwidth. A better solution in most scenarios is to use the hierarchical star, shown in Figure 1-3 earlier in this lesson.

3. In a *mesh topology*, every computer connects to every other computer; no central connecting device is needed. As you can guess, a true or "full" mesh requires a lot of connections, as illustrated in Figure 1-21. Examine the figure, and calculate how many connections would be needed at each computer to ensure a full mesh configuration.

We'll cover more about MDI ports in Lesson 3, "Understanding Wired and Wireless Networks."

Figure 1-21

Mesh topology

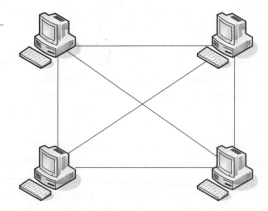

The number of network connections that each computer will need is the total number of computers minus one. As you can guess, this type of topology is rare, but it is necessary in some lab situations and fault-tolerant scenarios (where data needs to be replicated to multiple machines). A lesser version of this topology is the "partial mesh," in which only one or a couple of the computers on the network have a second network connection. (This might be useful when you need a computer to replicate a database to another computer but don't want the connection to be bothered by any other traffic.) A computer with two or more network connections is known as a multi-homed computer.

4. Last, we have the *ring topology*. Examine Figure 1-22. This illustrates how computers can be connected in a ring fashion. In a LAN environment, each computer is connected to the network using a closed loop; historically, this was done with coaxial cable. When it comes to today's LANs, this is a pretty outdated concept; however, when applied to other types of networks like Token Ring or Fiber Distributed Data Interface (FDDI), it takes on a different meaning: that of a logical topology.

Figure 1-22

Ring topology

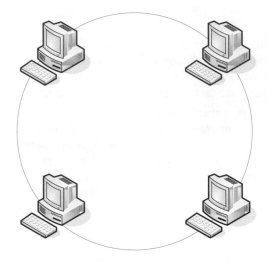

A logical topology is how data is actually sent from one computer to the next. Token Ring and FDDI utilize a token passing system. Instead of broadcasting information to all other computers on an Ethernet network that uses a star topology, Token Ring and FDDI computers wait to obtain a token. The token is passed from computer to computer, picking up data and dropping it off as needed. Most such networks have one token, but it is possible to have two in larger networks. The biggest advantage of this topology is that collisions become a nonfactor. A collision is when two computers attempt to send information simultaneously. The result is signal overlap, creating a collision of data that makes both pieces of data unrecoverable. In Ethernet networks, data collisions are common due to the whole idea of broadcasting. In token-based systems, however, there is only one item flying around the network at high speed, so it has nothing to collide with! Disadvantages of this setup include cost and maintenance. Also, Ethernet switching and other Ethernet technologies have done away with a lot of the collisions that were the banes of network engineers up until 10 or 15 years ago.

Although FDDI networks utilize ring topology logically as well as physically, Token Ring networks differ. A Token Ring network sends data logically in a ring fashion, meaning that a token goes to each computer, one at a time, and continues on in cycles. However, Token Ring computers are physically connected in a star fashion. Namely, all computers in a Token Ring network are connected to a central connecting device known as a **Multistation Access Unit (MAU** or **MSAU)**. We'll talk more about Token Rings in Lesson 2, "Defining Networks with the OSI Model."

Due: 05/05/201

Total items: 1
21/04/2015 15:29
Overdue: 0

Normal loans are nov
check due dates.

Defining Ethernet Standards

CERTIFICATION READY
How do you define
Ethernet standards?
1.5

Ethernet is far and away the most common type of LAN standard used by today's organizations. It is a scalable technology, but to get the most out of the Ethernet, devices, computers, and other hosts should be compatible. This means knowing the various Ethernet standards.

Ethernet is a group of networking technologies that define how information is sent and received between network adapters, hubs, switches, and other devices. An open standard, Ethernet is the de facto standard and has the largest share of networks in place today, with Token Ring and FDDI filling in the small gaps where Ethernet does not exist. Ethernet is standardized by the Institute of Electrical and Electronics Engineers (IEEE) as 802.3. Developed originally by Xerox, it was later championed by DEC and Intel. Today, Ethernet products are offered by hundreds of companies, including D-Link, Linksys, 3Com, HP, and so on.

Computers on Ethernet networks communicate by sending Ethernet *frames*. A frame is a group of bytes packaged by a network adapter for transmission across the network; these frames are created and reside on Layer 2 of the OSI model, which will be covered in more depth in the next lesson. By default, computers on Ethernet networks all share a single channel. Because of this, only one computer can transmit at a time. However, newer networks with more advanced switches transcend this limitation.

IEEE 802.3 defines carrier sense multiple access with collision detection or *CSMA/CD*. Because computers on a default Ethernet LAN all share the same channel, CSMA/CD governs the way that computers co-exist with limited collisions. The basic steps for CSMA/CD are as follows:

1. The network adapter builds and readies a frame for transmission across the network.
2. The network adapter checks whether the medium (e.g., twisted-pair cable) is idle. If the medium is not idle, the adapter waits for approximately 10 microseconds (10 μs). This delay is known as the interframe gap.
3. The frame is transmitted across the network.
4. The network adapter checks whether any collisions occurred. If so, it moves on to the "Collision detected" procedure.
5. The network adapter resets any retransmission counters (if necessary) and ends transmission of the frame.

If a collision was detected in step 4, another procedure called the "Collision detected procedure" is employed as follows:

1. The network adapter continues transmission until the minimum packet time is reached (known as a jam signal). This ensures that all receivers have detected the collision.
2. The network adapter increments the retransmission counter.
3. The network adapter checks whether the maximum number of transmission attempts was reached. If it was, the network adapter aborts the transmission.
4. The network adapter calculates and waits for a random backoff period based on the number of collisions detected.
5. Finally, the network adapter starts back through the original procedure at step 1.

If an organization utilizes wireless Ethernet, carrier sense multiple access with collision avoidance *(CSMA/CA)* is employed.

Devices on an Ethernet network must be compatible to a certain extent. For instance, if you are using an Ethernet switch, a computer's network adapter must also be of Ethernet origin in order to communicate with it. However, unlike some other networking technologies, different speeds can be negotiated. For example, let's say your switch has a maximum data transfer rate of 100 Mbps, but your network adapter only connects at 10 Mbps. The network adapter would still be able to communicate with the switch, but at the lesser rate. The various speeds of Ethernet and the cable medium they use are defined by the various 802.3 standards listed in Table 1-2. Although 802.3 by itself is generally thought of as 10 Mbps, it is further broken up into various subgroups, as shown in the table.

Table 1-2

802.3 Ethernet standards

802.3 Version	Data Transfer Rate	Cable Standard	Cabling Used
802.3	10 Mbps	10BASE5	Thick coaxial
802.3a	10 Mbps	10BASE2	Thin coaxial
802.3i	10 Mbps	10BASE-T	Twisted pair (TP)
802.3j	10 Mbps	10BASE-F	Fiber optic
802.3u	100 Mbps	100BASE-TX (most common)	TP using 2 pairs
		100BASE-T4	TP using 4 pairs
		100BASE-FX	Fiber optic
802.3ab	1000 Mbps or 1 Gbps	1000BASE-T	Twisted pair
802.3z	1000 Mbps or 1 Gbps	1000BASE-X	Fiber optic
802.3ae	10 Gbps	10GBASE-SR, 10GBASE-LR, 10GBASE-ER, and so on	Fiber optic
802.3an	10 Gbps	10GBASE-T	Twisted pair

All of the 10 Mbps standards listed here are a bit slow for today's network applications, but you might find them in some organizations and in other countries outside the United States. Of course, a good network administrator can make even 10 Mbps networks run quickly and efficiently. In fact, an efficient 10 Mbps network can easily outperform a poorly designed 100 Mbps network.

The 10 Gbps standards are much newer, and therefore, as of the writing of this book, they are much more expensive. Currently, 1 Gbps connections for clients and 10 Gbps connections for network backbones are common. The most common cabling standards used today are 100BASE-TX and 1000BASE-T. Keep in mind that new standards are constantly being released by the IEEE.

10 Mbps is typically referred to as Ethernet, 100 Mbps is known as Fast Ethernet, and 1 Gbps is known as Gigabit Ethernet.

Identifying the Differences Between Client/Server and Peer-to-Peer Distributed Networks

Most of today's networks are distributed. This means that CPU power and applications are not centralized, but instead, every host has a CPU, and every host has the ability to run programs that connect to other computers. The most common types of distributed networks are client-server and peer-to-peer distributed networks. It is important to know the differences between these so you can decide which technology is best for any given customer scenario.

The older type of computing was known as *centralized computing*. This was the case during the days of the mainframe, in which there was one super computer and the rest of the devices that connected to the super computer were known as terminals (or dumb terminals). Each terminal consisted solely of a keyboard and display with no processing power. Today's computing is known as *distributive computing* and is used for both client-server and peer-to-peer networks. This means that every device or workstation has its own processing power. However, in a way, the idea of centralized computing has made a comeback of sorts. Terminal services and remote sessions to computers are based off of the centralized computing model. Also, thin-client computing has been slowly gaining market share for the past decade or so. Thin-client computers do not have a hard drive and store an operating system in RAM, to be loaded up every time the device is turned on. All other applications and data are stored centrally. So, in a way, this system is a blend of some centralized computing with some distributive computing.

CERTIFICATION READY
How do you define the differences between client-server and peer-to-peer networks?
1.5

DEFINING THE CLIENT-SERVER MODEL

The *client-server* model is an architecture that distributes applications between servers such as Windows Server 2008 and client computers such as Windows 7 or Windows Vista machines. It also distributes the necessary processing power. This is extremely common in today's LANs and with most applications an average user would utilize when connecting to the Internet. For example, when a user first comes into work, he or she typically logs on to a network. Chances are this is a client-server network. The user might be using Windows 7 as the client computer to log on to a Microsoft domain that is controlled by a Windows Server. A simpler example would be a home user who is connecting to the Internet. When this person wants to go to a Web site such as Bing, he or she opens a web browser and types http://www.bing.com/ (or one of many shortcuts). The web browser is the client application. Bing's web server is obviously the "server." It serves the web pages filled with glorious HTML code. The client computer's web browser decodes the HTML and fills the user's display with Internet goodness. Another example is if you use an email program like Microsoft Outlook. Outlook is the client application; it connects to a mail server, most likely an SMTP server, perhaps run by Microsoft Exchange Server. Indeed, the examples are endless, but client-server is not the end-all when it comes to networking. Sometimes, it is more efficient not to use a server at all.

Here are some examples of uses for servers:

- *File server:* A file server stores files for computers to share. The connection to a file server could be made by browsing, by mapping a network drive, by connecting in the command line, or by connecting with an FTP client. The latter would require that special FTP server software is installed and configured on the file server. By default, Windows Server 2008, Windows Server 2003, and Windows Server 2000 can be file servers right out of the box.

- *Print server:* A print server controls printers that can be connected directly to the server or (and more commonly) are connected to the network. The print server can control the starting and stopping of document printing, as well as concepts such as spooling, printer pooling, ports, and much more. By default, Windows Server 2008, Windows Server 2003, and Windows Server 2000 can be print servers right out of the box.

- *Database server:* A database server houses a relational database made up of one or more files. SQL databases fall into this category. They require special software, such as Microsoft SQL Server. Access databases (which are just one file) do not necessarily require a database server; they are usually stored on a regular file server.

- *Network controller:* A controlling server, such as a Microsoft domain controller, is in charge of user accounts, computer accounts, network time, and the general well-being of an entire domain of computers and users. Windows Server 2008, Windows Server 2003, and Windows Server 2000 can be domain controllers, but they need to be promoted to that status. By default, a Windows Server operating system is not a controller. Network controller operating systems are also referred to as *network operating systems* or NOS.

- *Messaging server:* This category is enormous. Messaging servers include not just email servers, but also fax, instant messaging, collaborative, and other types of messaging servers. For a Windows Server to control email, special software known as Exchange Server has to be loaded in addition to the operating system.

- *Web server:* Web servers are important to share data and provide information about a company. Windows Servers can be web servers, but Internet Information Services (IIS) has to be installed and configured in order for this to work.

- *CTI-based server:* CTI is short for *Computer Telephony Integration*. This is when a company's telephone system meets its computer system. Here, special PBXs that used to control phones as a separate entity can now be controlled by servers with powerful software.

Table 1-3 shows some examples of various client and server operating systems. The table attempts to show the most compatible client operating systems next to their corresponding server operating systems. You will notice that Windows Server 2003 overlaps with Windows XP and Windows Vista.

Table 1-3

Client and server operating systems

CLIENT OPERATING SYSTEMS	SERVER OPERATING SYSTEMS
Windows 7	Windows Server 2008
Windows Vista Windows XP	Windows Server 2003
Windows 2000 Professional	Windows 2000 Server
Windows NT 4.0 Workstation Windows ME/98/95	Windows NT 4.0 Server

DEFINING THE PEER-TO-PEER MODEL

Peer-to-peer (P2P) networking first and foremost means that each computer is treated as an equal. This means each computer has an equal ability to serve data and to access data, just like any other computer on the network. Before servers became popular in PC-based computer networks, each PC had the ability to store data. Even after the client-server model became king, peer-to-peer networks still had their place, especially in smaller networks with 10 computers or less. Today, peer computers can serve data; the only difference is that they can only serve it to a small number of computers at the same time.

In organizations that use these small networks, the cost, administration, and maintenance of a server is too much for the organization to consider viable. Thus, a Microsoft peer-to-peer network might consist only of a couple Windows XP computers, a few Windows Vista computers, and some newer Windows 7 and older Windows 2000 computers. These are client operating systems, and as such are known as peers because there is no controlling server in the network. This usually works well enough for smaller organizations. The beauty of Microsoft client operating systems is that up to 10 computers (20 in Windows 7 Ultimate) can concurrently access an individual peer's shared resource. So, in these environments, one lucky peer usually acts as a sort of pseudo-server, so to speak. Still, additional resources like files, databases, printers, and so on can be added to any other computer on the network. The main disadvantage of this network model is that there is no centralized user database. Usernames and passwords are individually stored per computer. To implement a centralized user database, you need to have a Windows Server, which means that a client-server model would be employed.

Peer-to-peer has taken on a second meaning over the past decade or so. Now it refers to file sharing networks, and in this case is referred to as P2P. Examples of file sharing networks include Napster, Gnutella, and G2, but other technologies also take advantage of P2P file sharing, such as Skype, VoIP, and cloud computing. In a P2P network, hosts are added in an ad hoc manner. They can leave the network at any time without impacting the download of files. Many peers can contribute to the availability of files and resources. A person downloading information from a P2P network might get little bits of information from many different computers; afterward, the downloading computer might help share the file as well. Most file sharing peer-to-peer networks use special software to download files, such as BitTorrent. BitTorrent is a protocol as well as a program. The program (and others like it) is used to download large files from P2P networks. Instead of the files being stored on a single server, the file is distributed among multiple computers (anywhere from just a few too many). The possible benefits are availability of data and greater speed (although some torrent transfers will be slow). A computer, its BitTorrent client, and the router it is connected to can all be optimized to increase the speed of torrent downloads. In fact, it is estimated that between 20% and 35% of all data transfers on the Internet today involve torrents. Another benefit of the BitTorrent client is that you can line up a whole slew of downloads from one torrent location (or multiple locations) and just let your computer download them while you do other things. A file is seeded (stored) on one or more computers. Then, as clients (peers) download that file (or portions of the file), they are automatically set up to distribute the file (or portions of the file). This way, more and more computers are added to the "swarm," making the availability of the file much greater. Automatically, computers are set up to distribute the file; it's the default setting, but you can turn off seeding/distribution in your client. You could also block it at your firewall.

Instead of a server hosting the file, a server simply tracks and coordinates the distribution of files. The actual torrent starts with an initial small file (called a torrent file) that you download, which contains the information about the files to be downloaded. The reason the whole process is called a torrent is because it is a different type of download than a standard web or FTP server download. One of the differences is that when downloading a torrent, there is more than one TCP connection (could be quite a few) to different machines in the P2P network. Contrast this to a single file download from a web server where only one TCP connection is made. This is controlled in a pseudorandom fashion by the tracking server to ensure availability of data. Another difference is that most web servers put a cap on the amount of concurrent downloads you can do, but not so with the torrent client program. The average person uses a BitTorrent client to download movies, MP3s, and other media.

Sometimes, these are distributed with the consent of the owner; other times (and quite often) they are illegally seeded and distributed (as well as downloaded). An example of legitimate usage is with World of Warcraft. The owners of the game use the Blizzard BitTorrent to distribute just about everything involved in the game. Newer games for the PS3 and other consoles do the same type of thing. D-Link and other network equipment companies are embracing torrent technology as well.

SKILL SUMMARY

IN THIS LESSON YOU LEARNED:

- To understand local area networks (LANs), including but not limited to LAN elements, design, perimeter networks, IP addressing, and LAN types.
- To understand network topologies and access methods, including topologies such as star, mesh, and ring; Ethernet architecture; and the client-server and peer-to-peer networking models.

■ Knowledge Assessment

Multiple Choice

Circle the letter that corresponds to the best answer.

1. Which of the following regenerates a signal and broadcasts that signal to every computer connected to it?
   a. Hub
   b. Switch
   c. Router
   d. Firewall

2. Which of the following is not a central connecting device?
   a. Hub
   b. Switch
   c. SOHO router
   d. Windows 7 client

3. You need to install a network adapter to a computer so that it can be connected to a network that uses twisted-pair cabling. What type of port does the network adapter need to use?
   a. RJ11
   b. RJ45
   c. RG-58
   d. Fiber optic

4. Where can you go in Windows 7 to access the Properties of a network adapter?
   a. Device Manager
   b. Ping
   c. Advanced Firewall
   d. Task Manager

5. You need to connect a computer's network adapter to a switch. You want the connection to be able to send and receive data simultaneously. What type of connection do you need?
   a. Half duplex
   b. Full duplex
   c. Simplex
   d. 100 Mbps

6. You need to connect a computer at a rate of 100,000,000 bits per second. What speed network adapter should you install?
   a. 10 Mbps
   b. 100 MB/s
   c. 100 Mbps
   d. 1000 Mbps

7. You need to connect to a router that has the IP address 192.168.1.100 on a standard, default Class C network using the subnet mask 255.255.255.0. Which of the following is a valid IP address for your network adapter?
   a. 192.168.0.1
   b. 192.168.1.1
   c. 192.168.100.1
   d. 192.168.1.100

8. You have just installed a network adapter and configured an IP address and subnet mask. What command can you use to verify that the IP address is configured and listed properly?
   a. Ping
   b. Tracert
   c. CMD
   d. Ipconfig

9. You need to ping your own computer to see if it is alive. Which of the following would qualify as command-line syntax to do so?
   a. Ping localclient
   b. Ping 128.0.0.1
   c. Ping loopback
   d. Ping network adapter

10. You have been instructed to connect a computer to a group of hosts that have been segmented from the regular network. What kind of network is this?
    a. LAN
    b. WLAN
    c. WAN
    d. VLAN

Fill in the Blank

Fill in the correct answer in the blank space provided.

1. The manager of IT asks you to connect a perimeter network to the firewall, which will be separate from the LAN. This type of network is known as a _____

2. A _____ topology can be defined by connecting several hubs to a switch.

3. 802.3u Ethernet networks run at _____ Mbps.

4. A _____ is a program used to download files quickly from a P2P network.

5. The _____ network architecture is physically a star and logically a ring.

6. 802.3ab Ethernet networks run at _____ Mbps.

7. A _____ connection is one in which data can be both sent and received, but not at the same time.

8. A _____ topology can be defined as connecting several computers together in a circle without the use of a hub or a switch.

9. When several computers are connected in a small geographic area, it is known as a _____.

10. A _____ acts as a central connecting device and allows laptops, PDAs, and handheld computers to communicate with each other.

■ Case Scenarios

Scenario 1-1: Planning and Documenting a Basic LAN

Proseware, Inc. requires you to implement a 20-computer LAN. Fifteen of these computers will be Windows 7 clients, and five will be Windows Server 2008 computers. The company also requires a 24-port switch, router, DSL Internet connection, DMZ with web server, and a laptop for the CEO. Create a diagram of the network documentation for this in Microsoft Visio or on paper. Refer to Figures 1-1 through 1-3 for types of devices in the Visio networking stencils.

Scenario 1-2: Selecting the Right Type of Networking Model

The ABC Company requires a network that can support 50 users. Which is the correct type of networking model to use and why?

Scenario 1-3: Selecting Network Adapters for your LAN Computers

A company you are consulting for requires the installation of five new computers. Each computer's network adapter should be able to communicate at 1000 Mbps over its pre-existing twisted-pair cabling and should be able to send and receive data simultaneously. Which Ethernet standard should you select, and what technology should you utilize?

Scenario 1-4: Configure the Correct Subnet Mask

A computer is not connecting to certain network devices properly. The IP address information is as follows:

IP address: 192.168.1.210

Subnet mask: 255.254.0.0

How should the subnet mask be configured so that the computer can communicate properly with all networking devices and other hosts on the network?

✳ Workplace Ready

Utilizing Full Duplex Connections

Many network cards have the ability to run in full duplex mode, but sometimes, this ability is overlooked. Alternatively, the central connecting device in the network might not have the ability to run in full duplex, thus reducing the network capability to half duplex.

When you think about it, either situation effectively reduces your network throughput by half. You see, by using full duplex connections on the central connecting devices and all of the network adapters, 100 Mbps effectively becomes 200 Mbps because now the devices can send *and* receive at the same time.

Network devices are usually rated at their half duplex data transfer rate. So if you see a network adapter being sold as a 1 Gbps device, look a little further. See whether it is full duplex capable, and if so, you could see a maximum data transfer rate of 2 Gbps.

Remember to set this in the Properties page of the network adapter, which can be found within the Device Manager.

Go ahead and access the Internet and locate three different 1 Gbps network adapters that can operate in full duplex mode. Try manufacturers such as D-Link, Linksys, Intel, and so on. You will need to view the specifications of each device and note the link to those pages as proof of your discovery. Another great source for different equipment is www.pricewatch.com. Access this site to view networking equipment from different vendors.

Defining Networks with the OSI Model

OBJECTIVE DOMAIN MATRIX

Skills/Concepts	MTA Exam Objective	MTA Exam Objective Number
Understanding OSI Basics Defining the Communications Subnetwork Defining the Upper OSI Layers	Understand the OSI model.	3.1
Defining the Communications Subnetwork	Understand switches.	2.1

KEY TERMS

Address Resolution Protocol	**layer 3 switch**
application layer	**MAC Flood**
ARP table	**Media Access Control (MAC) address**
baseband	**network layer**
broadband	**Open Systems Interconnection (OSI)**
CAM table	**outbound ports**
communications subnetwork	**overhead**
data link layer (DLL)	**physical layer**
encapsulated	**ports**
encoded	**presentation layer**
inbound ports	**protocol stack**
Internet Assigned Numbers Authority (IANA)	**session layer**
Internet Control Message Protocol	**Transmission Control Protocol (TCP)**
Internet Engineering Task Force (IETF)	**transport layer**
Internet Protocol	**User Datagram Protocol (UDP)**
layer 2 switch	**virtual LAN (VLAN)**

The Open Systems Interconnection (OSI) reference model helps network engineers, network administrators, and systems engineers define how data networking actually works from one computer to another, regardless of where the computer is or what software it runs. This model is composed of seven layers, with each corresponding to devices, protocols, standards, and applications in the real world. Computer network specialists use the OSI model to aid them when designing, maintaining, and troubleshooting their networks. This lesson defines each of the OSI model layers through the use of hands-on labs and theory. As we discuss each layer, imagine devices and applications that you might see in a small office or home office that would be supported by that layer. Utilize the concepts from Lesson 1 and plug them into each of the layers as you work through this lesson.

Understanding OSI Basics

THE BOTTOM LINE

The ***Open Systems Interconnection (OSI)*** reference model is used to define how data communication occurs on computer networks. This model is divided into layers, each of which provides services to the layers above and below. These layers are associated with protocols and devices.

The OSI model was created and ratified by the International Organization for Standardization (ISO), and it is represented in the United States by the American National Standards Institute (ANSI). This model was created to do the following:

- Explain network communications between hosts on a LAN or WAN.
- Present a categorization system for communication protocol suites.
- Show how different protocol suites can communicate with each other.

When we say "different protocol suites," keep in mind that TCP/IP is not the only player in town, although it is by far the most common. If TCP/IP devices need to communicate with other devices using other communication protocols, the OSI model can help describe how translation between the two will take place. In addition to being described by the OSI model, TCP/IP also has its own model—the TCP model, which we will discuss toward the end of this lesson.

It is important to note that network communications existed before the OSI model was created. Accordingly this model is an abstract way of categorizing the communications that already existed. In fact, the model was created to help engineers understand what is happening with communication protocols behind the scenes. Let's go ahead and break down the OSI model into its distinct layers and functions.

Defining the Layers in the OSI Model

CERTIFICATION READY
In what way can you define the OSI model?
3.1

The OSI model was created as a set of seven layers, or levels, each of which houses different protocols within one of several protocol suites, the most common of which is TCP/IP. The OSI model categorizes how TCP/IP transactions occur, and it is invaluable when it comes to installing, configuring, maintaining, and especially troubleshooting networks.

Sometimes a protocol suite such as TCP/IP is referred to as a ***protocol stack***. The OSI model shows how a protocol stack works on different levels of transmission (that is, how it stacks up against the model). As mentioned previously, a LAN requires computers with network adapters. These must be connected together in some way to facilitate the transfer of data. It is important to define how the computers are connected together, as well as how they actually transmit data. The OSI model layers do just that. The following is a brief description of each layer:

- **Layer 1—*Physical layer:*** This is the physical and electrical medium for data transfer. It includes but is not limited to cables, jacks, patch panels, punch blocks, hubs, and MAUs. This layer is also known as the physical plant. Concepts related to the physical layer include topologies, analog versus digital/encoding, bit synchronization, baseband versus broadband, multiplexing, and serial (5-volt logic) data transfer. If you can touch a network element, it is part of the physical layer, which makes this layer one of the easiest to understand.

  The unit of measurement used on this layer is *bits*.

- **Layer 2—*Data link layer (DLL):*** This layer establishes, maintains, and decides how transfer is accomplished over the physical layer. Devices that exist on the DLL are network interface cards and bridges. This layer also ensures error-free transmission over the physical layer under LAN transmissions. It does so through physical addresses (the hexadecimal address that is burned into the ROM of the NIC), otherwise known as the MAC address (to be discussed more later in this lesson). Just about any device that makes a physical connection to a network and has the ability to move data is on the data link layer.

  The unit of measurement used on this layer is *frames*.

- **Layer 3—*Network layer:*** This layer is dedicated to routing and switching information to different networks, LANs, or internetworks. This can be on a LAN or WAN (wide area network). Devices that exist on the network layer are routers and IP switches. Here, we are getting into the logical addressing of hosts. Instead of physical addresses, the addressing system of the computer is stored in the operating system—for example, IP addresses.

  Now you can see that a typical computer will really have *two* addresses: a physical or hardware-based address such as a MAC address, and a logical or software-based address such as an IP address. Part of the trick in networking is to make sure the two addresses get along together.

  The unit of measurement used on this layer is *packets*.

- **Layer 4—*Transport layer:*** This layer ensures error-free transmission between hosts through logical addressing. Therefore, it manages the transmission of messages through layers 1 through 3. The protocols that are categorized by this layer break up messages, send them through the subnet, and ensure correct reassembly at the receiving end, making sure there are no duplicates or lost messages. This layer contains both connection-oriented and connectionless systems, which will be covered later in the book. Inbound and outbound ports are controlled by this layer. When you think "ports," think the trans*port* layer.

  The unit of measurement used on this layer is sometimes referred to as *segments* or *messages*. All layers above this one use the terms "data" and "messages."

- **Layer 5—*Session layer:*** This layer governs the establishment, termination, and synchronization of sessions within the OS over the network and between hosts—for example, when you log on and log off. This is the layer that controls the name and address database for the OS or NOS. NetBIOS (Network Basic Input Output System) works on this layer.

- **Layer 6—*Presentation layer:*** This layer translates the data format from sender to receiver in the various OSes that may be used. Concepts include code conversion, data compression, and file encryption. Redirectors work on this layer, such as mapped network drives that enable a computer to access file shares on a remote computer.

- **Layer 7—*Application layer:*** This layer is where message creation—and, therefore packet creation—begins. DB access is on this level. End-user protocols such as FTP, SMTP, Telnet, and RAS work at this layer. For example, suppose you are using Outlook Express. You type a message and click Send. This initiates SMTP (Simple Mail Transfer Protocol) and other protocols, which send the mail message down through the other layers, breaking it into packets at the network layer and so on. This layer is not the application itself, but the protocols that are initiated by this layer.

Sound like a lot of information? It is, but you need to get into the habit of picturing this model whenever you are doing data transfer and, more importantly, whenever you are troubleshooting networking issues. The more you imagine data transfer through these levels, the more you will be able to memorize and understand how the OSI model works. In addition, this model will be invaluable to you in the future when troubleshooting network problems. To help memorize the layers, some people use mnemonic devices, such as associating the first letter of each layer name with a different word—for example, *All People Seem To Need Data Processing*. That mnemonic progresses from layer 7 to layer 1. For a mnemonic that goes in the opposite direction, try *Please Do Not Throw Sausage Pizza Away*. Or, just memorize the real layer names! It's up to you.

As you look at Figure 2-1, imagine a message being created in Outlook Express. The Send button is clicked, and the message goes down the layers of the OSI model to the physical medium. It then crosses the medium (probably cables) and climbs the OSI model at the receiving machine. This happens every time two computers communicate; in fact, it happens every time a packet is sent from one computer to another. Although the OSI model is always in place, all levels may not be involved in every communication. For example, if you were to ping another computer, only layers 1 through 3 would be utilized. It all depends on the type of communication and the number of protocols being used for that specific transmission.

Figure 2-1

OSI model

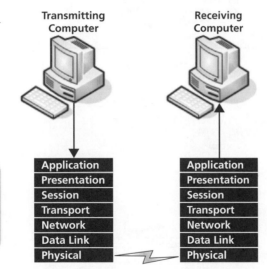

TAKE NOTE*

Use a mnemonic device such as *All People Seem To Need Data Processing* to help memorize the OSI layers.

■ Defining the Communications Subnetwork

THE BOTTOM LINE

The *communications subnetwork* is the guts of OSI model transmissions, consisting of layers 1 through 3. Regardless of what type of data transmission occurs in a computer network, the communication subnetwork will be employed.

CERTIFICATION READY
In what way can you define the communications subnetwork?
3.1

In the following exercises, you will:

- Define the physical layer by showing a data transfer.
- Define the data link layer by showing the MAC address of a network adapter.
- Define the network by using ipconfig, ping, and protocol analyzers.
- Define layer 2 and layer 3 switches.

→ DEFINE THE PHYSICAL LAYER

GET READY. Remember that the physical layer of the OSI model deals with the tangible and transmits bits of information. Let's show this by testing the "speed," or data transfer rate, of our computer's Internet connection as follows:

1. Open a web browser and access http://www.dslreports.com.
2. Click the **Tools** link.
3. Click the **Speed Tests** link.
4. Select the **Flash 8 plugin based speed test** link. (You might need to install the Flash plug-in to your browser.)
5. Locate a server in your area and click it (make sure that it has availability for testing).
6. Watch as the web application tests your download and upload speed. Shortly, you should get results similar to Figure 2-2.

Figure 2-2

Results of a DSLReports.com speed test

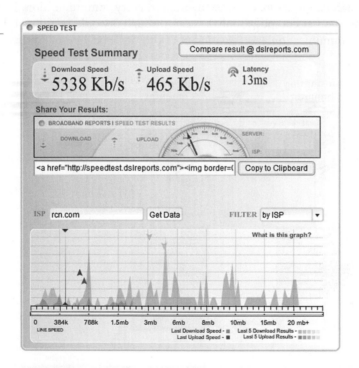

As you look at Figure 2-2, notice that the results are displayed in bits. The download data transfer rate in the figure is 5338 Kb/s, which is approximately 5.3 Mb/s. That is how many bits were delivered to the tested computer through the Internet connection. These bits are transferred on the physical layer; so, this is a test of the physical layer data transfer rate. Although there are other factors involved, such as your Internet Service Provider's speed, and so on, this exercise gives a basic example of bps (bits per second) on the physical layer.

To get a more accurate representation of your data transfer rate, run the DSLReports.com test three times, once every few minutes. Then, average your results.

Take a look at the Local Area Connection Status dialog box on a Windows computer. It should look similar to Figure 2-3. Note the LAN connection "Speed" is measured in bits as well. In the figure, the speed is 1.0 Gbps. Either Gbps or Gb/s is acceptable, but generally in this book, when bits are referred to, the value will be shown as bps.

TAKE NOTE*

Over time, DSLReports.com might change its site navigation slightly. Just remember that you are looking for the Flash speed test.

Figure 2-3

Windows Local Area
Connection Status dialog box

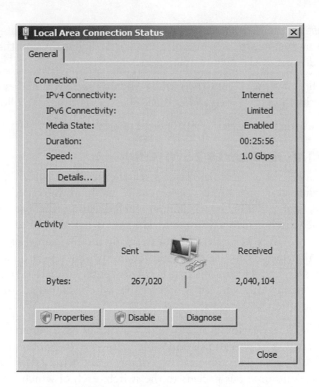

Networking standards such as 100BASE-T are based on the physical layer. The 100 in
100BASE-T stands for 100 Mbps, the BASE means *baseband*, and the T stands for twisted-
pair cabling. Baseband refers to the fact that all computers on the LAN share the same channel or frequency to transmit data, in this case 100 MHz. Conversely, *broadband* means that
there are multiple channels that can be utilized by the communications system. Although most
LANs are baseband, examples of broadband services include Cable TV and FM radio stations.

 DEFINE THE DATA LINK LAYER

GET READY. Remember that the data link layer governs devices like network adapters. All
network adapters must comply with a particular data link layer networking standard, such as
Ethernet. In an Ethernet network, every network adapter must have a unique *Media Access
Control (MAC) address*. The MAC address is a unique identifier assigned to network adapt-
ers by the manufacturer. This address is six octets in length and is written in hexadecimal.
Let's show this address in the command line by performing the following steps:

1. On a Windows computer, access the command prompt. The easiest way to do this is to
   press the **Windows + R** keys; then, in the Run prompt, type **cmd**.

2. Type the command **ipconfig/all**. The /all is necessary, otherwise the MAC address will
   not be displayed. The results should look similar to Figure 2-4. Note that the MAC
   address is actually listed as a physical address in the results. This is because it is a
   physical address—it is burned into the ROM chip of the network adapter.

Figure 2-4

MAC address in the command
prompt

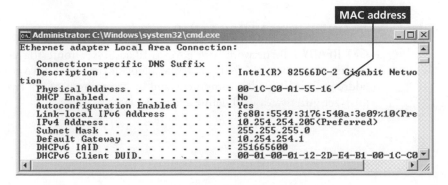

CERTIFICATION READY
How can you define and
work with switches?
2.1

3. Display the MAC addresses of other hosts that your computer has recently connected to by typing **arp –a.** This will show the IP addresses and the corresponding MAC addresses of the remote computers.

The data link layer is where networking standards such as Ethernet (802.3) and Token Ring (802.5) reside. Look up the various IEEE 802 standards at the following link:

http://standards.ieee.org/getieee802/portfolio.html

UNDERSTANDING LAYER 2 SWITCHING

The data link layer is also where layer 2 switches reside. A *layer 2 switch* is the most common type of switch used on a LAN. These switches are hardware based and use the MAC address of each host computer's network adapter when deciding where to direct frames of data; every port on the switch is mapped to the specific MAC address of the computer that physically connects to it. Layer 2 switches do not normally modify frames as they pass through the switch on their way from one computer to another. Each port on a switch is considered to be its own segment. This means that every computer connected to a layer 2 switch has its own usable bandwidth, which is whatever the switch is rated at: 10 Mbps, 100 Mbps, 1 Gbps, and so on.

Security is a concern with layer 2 switches. Switches have memory that is set aside to store the MAC address to port translation table, known as the Content Addressable Memory table or *CAM table*. This table can be compromised with a *MAC Flood* attack. Such an attack will send numerous packets to the switch, each of which has a different source MAC address, in an attempt to use up the memory on the switch. If this is successful, the switch will change state to what is known as *failopen mode*. At this point, the switch will broadcast data on all ports the way a hub does. This means two things: First, that network bandwidth will be dramatically reduced, and second, that a mischievous person could now use a protocol analyzer, running in promiscuous mode, to capture data from any other computer on the network.

Layer 2 switching can also allow for a *virtual LAN (VLAN)* to be implemented. A VLAN is implemented to segment the network, reduce collisions, organize the network, boost performance, and hopefully, increase security. It is important to place physical network jacks in secure locations when it comes to VLANs that have access to confidential data. There are also logical types of VLANs like the protocol-based VLAN and the MAC address-based VLAN, which have a whole separate set of security precautions. The most common standard associated with VLANs is IEEE 802.1Q, which modifies Ethernet frames by "tagging" them with the appropriate VLAN information, based on which VLAN the Ethernet frame should be directed to. VLANs are used to restrict access to network resources, but this can be bypassed through the use of VLAN hopping. VLAN hopping can be avoided by upgrading firmware or software, picking an unused VLAN as the default VLAN for all trunks, and redesigning the VLAN if multiple 802.1Q switches are being used.

Wireless access points, bridges, layer 2 switches, and network adapters all reside on the data link layer.

 ## DEFINE THE NETWORK LAYER

GET READY. The network layer governs IP addresses, routers/layer 3 switches, and the core communications of TCP/IP. Let's take a look at the network layer in action by analyzing IP addresses, pinging other computers, and by capturing network layer data with a protocol analyzer. Afterward, we'll define a layer 3 switch:

1. Open the command prompt.

2. Type **ipconfig**. This will display your IP address, for example, 192.168.1.1. The IP address is developed from the *Internet Protocol* (IP) that resides on layer 3 of the OSI model. Jot down your IP address and the IP address of a different computer on the network.

3. Ping the other computer's IP address by typing **ping [ip address]**, for example, **ping 192.168.1.2.** Make sure you can get replies from the other computer. Ping utilizes the *Internet Control Message Protocol* (ICMP) to send test packets to other computers; this is also a network layer protocol. Notice the size of the replies you receive; by default, they should be 32 bytes each.

4. Type **arp –a** to view the IP address to MAC address table. This table should now show the IP address you just pinged. This table is known as the Address Resolution Protocol table, or *ARP table*. The *Address Resolution Protocol* is another layer 3 protocol that resolves or translates IP addresses to MAC addresses, allowing connectivity between the layer 3 IP system and the layer 2 Ethernet system.

5. Use Wireshark to capture and analyze ICMP packets as follows:

   a. Download and install the Wireshark protocol analyzer (previously known as Ethereal) from: http://www.wireshark.org/. At the time of the writing of this book, the latest stable version is 1.2.8. Install WinPCap as part of the Wireshark installation.

   b. Go back to the command prompt and run a continuous ping to another computer, for example, **ping –t 192.168.1.2.** Verify that you get replies, and leave the command prompt open and pinging the other computer while you complete the packet capture.

   c. In the Wireshark utility, select the interface that serves as your main network adapter from the **Interface List.** This will start the capture of data from that network adapter.

   d. After a minute or so, stop the capture by clicking **Capture** on the menu bar and selecting **Stop.**

   e. View the list of captured packets in the top half of the screen. In the Protocol column, you should see many ICMP packets. Select one that says "reply" in the Info. column. When you do so, the packet's information should show up in the middle window pane, similar to Figure 2-5. The dark blue packet numbered 98 in the figure is the highlighted packet. Now, let's drill down to see the details of the packet.

Figure 2-5

Wireshark packet capture

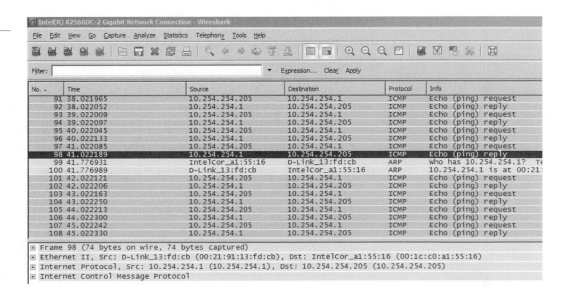

f. Click the + sign next to **Internet Control Message Protocol** to expand it and display the contents. This should display information about the ICMP packet, such as the fact that it is a reply packet, the checksum, the sequence number, and so on.

g. Click the + sign next to **Internet Protocol**. This will show you the version of IP used (IPv4), the size of the packet, and the source and destination IP addresses for the embedded ICMP packet. Both the ICMP and IP pieces of information correspond to the network layer of the OSI model.

h. Now click the + sign next to **Ethernet**. This is the network architecture used on the data link layer. This field of information tells you the source and destination MAC addresses of the computers involved in the ping transaction.

i. Now click the + sign next to **Frame** (there will be a frame number next to the word "Frame"). This tells you the size of the frame captured, as well as when it was captured. These are the frames of information that the Wireshark application actually captures directly from the network adapter.

Notice that the Ethernet frame is larger than the IP packet. That is because the IP packet is *encapsulated* into the frame. The encapsulation process started when the command prompt sent a 32-byte ping (ICMP packet). This ping was then placed inside an IP packet with a total size of 60 bytes. The additional 28 bytes are known as layer 3 *overhead*, broken down between 20 bytes for the header (includes the IP source and destination addresses) and 8 bytes for additional overhead information (for example, a trailer or checksum). Then, the IP packet was sent to the network adapter, where it was placed inside a frame. The frame added its own layer 2 overhead, an additional 14 bytes including the source and destination MAC address. This brought the grand total to 74 bytes—more than double what we started with. The frame was then sent out from the other computer's network adapter (in an effort to reply to the pinging computer) as a serial bit stream across the network medium on the physical layer. This is what happens with every single communication, and the OSI model, particularly the communications subnetwork layers 1 through 3, helps us define what is happening behind the scenes by categorizing each step with a different layer.

Routers also reside on the network layer. Routers make connections between one or more IP networks. They are known as the gateway to another IP network, and you may utilize their IP address in the Gateway address field of a computer's IP Properties window to allow the computer access to other networks. Don't confuse this definition of a gateway with the application layer gateway that will be defined later. Routers use protocols such as Routing Information Protocol (RIP) and Open Shortest Path First (OSPF) to direct packets to other routers and networks.

UNDERSTANDING LAYER 3 SWITCHING

Switches also reside on the network layer. A *layer 3 switch* differs from a layer 2 switch in that it determines paths for data using logical addressing (IP addresses) instead of physical addressing (MAC addresses). Layer 3 switches are similar to routers—it's how a network engineer implements the switch that makes it different. Layer 3 switches forward packets, whereas layer 2 switches forward frames. Layer 3 switches are usually managed switches; the network engineer can manage them utilizing the Simple Network Management Protocol (SNMP), among other tools. This allows the network engineer to analyze all of the packets that pass through the switch, which can't be done with a layer 2 switch. A layer 2 switch is more like an advanced version of a bridge, whereas a layer 3 switch is more like a router. Layer 3 switches are used in busy environments in which multiple IP networks need to be connected together.

TAKE NOTE *

There are many protocol analyzers available. Microsoft incorporates one called Network Monitor into Windows Server products.

CERTIFICATION READY

Can you define the differences between layer 2 and layer 3 switches?

2.1

■ Defining the Upper OSI Layers

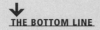

THE BOTTOM LINE

The upper OSI layers are layers 4 through 7—the transport, session, presentation, and application layers. It is this portion of the OSI model that deals with protocols such as HTTP, FTP, and mail protocols. Compression, encryption, and session creation are also classified by these layers.

CERTIFICATION READY
How do you define the upper layers of the OSI model?
3.1

In the following exercises, you will do the following:

- Define the **transport layer** by showing connections in the command prompt and describing ports.
- Define the **session layer** by logging into Web sites and other servers, as well as logging on and off of Microsoft networks and email programs.
- Define the **presentation layer** by showing encryption in Windows and within Web sites.
- Define the **application layer** by capturing web server packets and analyzing them.

Layer 4 governs the transmission of messages through the communications subnetwork. Two common TCP/IP protocols that are utilized on this layer include the *Transmission Control Protocol (TCP)*, which is a connection-oriented protocol, and the *User Datagram Protocol (UDP)*, which is connectionless. An example of an application that uses TCP is a web browser, and an example of an application that uses UDP is streaming media. When you download a web page, you don't want to lose any packets of information because graphics would appear broken, certain text wouldn't read correctly, and so on. By using TCP, we ensure that data gets to its final destination. If a packet is lost along the way, it will be resent until the destination computer acknowledges delivery or ends the session. But with streaming media, we are either watching or listening in real time. So, if a packet is lost, we don't really care, because that time frame of the video or music has already passed. Once the packet is lost, we really don't want it back. Of course, if the packet loss becomes too severe, the streaming media will become incomprehensible.

Connection-oriented (also known as CO mode) communications require that both devices or computers involved in the communication establish an end-to-end logical connection before data can be sent between the two. These connection-oriented systems are often considered reliable network services. If an individual packet is not delivered in a timely manner, it is resent; this can be done because the sending computer established the connection at the beginning of the session and knows where to resend the packet.

In connectionless communications (CL mode), no end-to-end connection is necessary before data is sent. Every packet that is sent has the destination address located in its header. This is sufficient to move independent packets, such as in the previously mentioned streaming media. But if a packet is lost, it cannot be resent, because the sending computer never established a logical connection and doesn't know which logical connection to use to send the failed packet.

Layer 4 also takes care of the ports that a computer uses for data transmission. *Ports* act as logical communications endpoints for computers. There are a total of 65,536 ports, numbering between 0 and 65,535. They are defined by the *Internet Assigned Numbers Authority* or *IANA* and divided into categories as shown in Table 2-1.

Table 2-1

IANA port categories

PORT RANGE	CATEGORY TYPE	DESCRIPTION
0–1023	Well-known ports	This range defines commonly used protocols (e.g., FTP utilizes port 21 to accept client connections).
1024–49,151	Registered ports	Ports used by vendors for proprietary applications. These must be registered with the IANA (e.g., Microsoft registered 3389 for use with the Remote Desktop Protocol).
49,152–65,535	Dynamic and private ports	These ports can be used by applications, but they cannot be registered by vendors.

Port numbers correspond to specific applications; for example, port 80 is used by web browsers via the HTTP protocol. It is important to understand the difference between inbound and outbound ports:

- *Inbound ports:* These are used when another computer wants to connect to a service or application running on your computer. Servers primarily use inbound ports so that they can accept incoming connections and serve data. IP addresses and port numbers are combined together, for example, a server's IP/port 66.249.91.104:80 is the IP address 66.249.91.104 with port number 80 open in order to accept incoming web page requests.

- *Outbound ports:* These are used when your computer wants to connect to a service or application running on another computer. Client computers primarily use outbound ports, and these are assigned dynamically by the operating system.

There are a lot of ports and corresponding protocols you should know. Although you don't need to know all 65,536 ports, Table 2-2 highlights some of the basic ones that you should memorize.

Table 2-2

Ports and associated protocols

PORT NUMBER	ASSOCIATED PROTOCOL	FULL NAME
21	FTP	File Transfer Protocol
22	SSH	Secure Shell
23	Telnet	Terminal Network
25	SMTP	Simple Mail Transfer Protocol
53	DNS	Domain Name System
80	HTTP	Hypertext Transfer Protocol
88	Kerberos	Kerberos
110	POP3	Post Office Protocol Version 3
119	NNTP	Network News Transfer Protocol
137–139	NetBIOS	NetBIOS Name, Datagram, and Session Services, respectively
143	IMAP	Internet Access Message Protocol

Table 2-2 (continued)

Port Number	Associated Protocol	Full Name
161	SNMP	Simple Network Management Protocol
389	LDAP	Lightweight Directory Access Protocol
443	HTTPS	Hypertext Transfer Protocol Secure (uses TLS or SSL)
445	SMB	Server Message Block
1701	L2TP	Layer 2 Tunneling Protocol
1723	PPTP	Point-to-Point Tunneling Protocol
3389	RDP	Remote Desktop Protocol (Microsoft Terminal Server)

DEFINE THE TRANSPORT LAYER

GET READY. Let's take a look at ports and the transport layer in action by performing the following steps:

1. Open a web browser and connect to www.google.com.

2. Open the command prompt and type the command **netstat –an**. This will display a list of all the connections to and from your computer in numeric format, as shown in Figure 2-6. Note the two Google connections. We know this is Google because the IP address for the Google Web site is 66.249.91.104. (You can test this by pinging that IP address or by entering the IP address into your web browser's address field.) The two connections were initialized by the local computer on outbound ports 49166 and 49167. Google is accepting these connections on its web server's inbound port 80. You will note that the left-hand column named "Proto" has these connections marked as TCP. So, as we mentioned earlier, HTTP connections utilize TCP on the transport layer, and they are therefore connection-oriented communications.

Figure 2-6

Netstat command

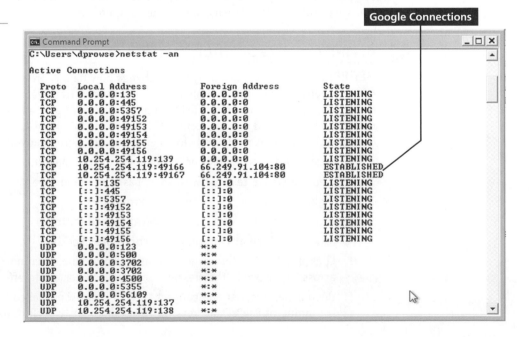

3. Now, try the following commands:

   a. **netstat** (the original command; shows basic connections)

   b. **netstat –a** (shows in depth TCP *and* UDP connections)

   c. **netstat –an** (shows TCP and UDP connections numerically)

 DEFINE THE SESSION LAYER

GET READY. Every time you connect to a Web site, a mail server, or any other computer on your network or another network, your computer is starting a session with that remote computer. Each time you log on or log off of a network, the session layer is involved. Let's explore this further by carrying out the following actions:

1. Make several connections to other computers. For example:

   a. Connect to www.microsoft.com.

   b. Connect to a mail account that you have with Gmail, Yahoo, or another such service.

   c. Connect to a network share (if available).

   d. Connect to an FTP server (if available).

2. Go back to the command prompt and run the **netstat –a** command; then, in a second command prompt, run the **netstat –an** command. Analyze the various sessions that you have created. Compare the results of both commands. See whether you can catch the names in one command prompt and their corresponding IP addresses in the other command prompt. Note the "State" of the connections or sessions: Established, Close_wait, and so on.

3. Now, log on to and off of several networks:

   a. Log off or on to your Microsoft network if you are connected to one.

   b. Log on to a Web site like Amazon or another site that you have membership with.

All of these steps are completed as part of the session layer. The session layer is also in charge of the termination of sessions. You will notice that after a certain period of no activity, web sessions change their state from Established to either Time wait, or closed, or something similar. Log off all of your sessions now, and close any connections to any Web sites or other computers you have connected to. Finally, log off the computer and log back on.

 DEFINE THE PRESENTATION LAYER

GET READY. The presentation layer will change how data is presented. This could include code conversion from one computer system to another (that both run TCP/IP), or it could be encryption or compression. This layer also comes into play when you connect to a mapped network drive (known as a redirector). Carry out the following actions to see several examples of how information is modified before being sent across the network:

1. Access Windows Explorer on a Windows client computer.

2. Create a simple text file with some basic text, and save it to a test folder.

3. Right-click the text file and select **Properties**.

4. In the Properties window, click the **Advanced** button.

5. Select the **Encrypt contents to secure data** checkbox.

6. Click **OK**. The file should now be displayed in blue. From now on, if the file is sent across the network, the presentation layer will come into effect due to the encryption.

7. Open a web browser and connect to https://www.paypal.com. Note the https at the beginning of PayPal's address, which is short for HyperText Transfer Protocol Secure.

This is a secure, encrypted connection to the PayPal Web site. Many Web sites offer this, not only when actual transactions are made, but also as a courtesy to customers, giving them peace of mind in that their entire session with the Web site is encrypted and somewhat secure. This type of encryption protocol works on port 443, and the actual transmission of encrypted data is governed by the presentation layer. One of a few protocols can be used during HTTPS transfers. The most common example as of the writing of this book is Transport Layer Security (TLS), but you might also see Secure Sockets Layer (SSL). Data that is transferred over the web is usually compressed, or **encoded**, as well. For example, many web browsers accept gzip encoding.

➤ DEFINE THE APPLICATION LAYER

GET READY. Layer 7—the application layer—is where protocols like HTTP, FTP, and POP3 reside. The application layer is not the applications themselves (Internet Explorer or Outlook), but rather the protocols that the applications initiate, such as HTTP or POP3. For example, when you open Internet Explorer, you are opening an application. If you were to type http://www.microsoft.com in the URL field and press Enter, doing so would initiate the HTTP protocol starting the transfer of data over the OSI model, beginning with the application layer. Let's capture some data as we connect to a Web site by performing the following actions:

1. Open Wireshark and begin a packet capture.

2. Connect with your browser to www.microsoft.com.

3. Stop the capture and view the information.

4. Look for the first HTTP packet in the Protocol column. This should be called GET/ HTTP/1.1 in the Info column.

5. Click the packet and drill down through the various layers in the middle pane. Not only will you see Layers 2 and 3 as we defined them in the network layer section, but you will also see the upper layers in action. Your results should be similar to Figure 2-7.

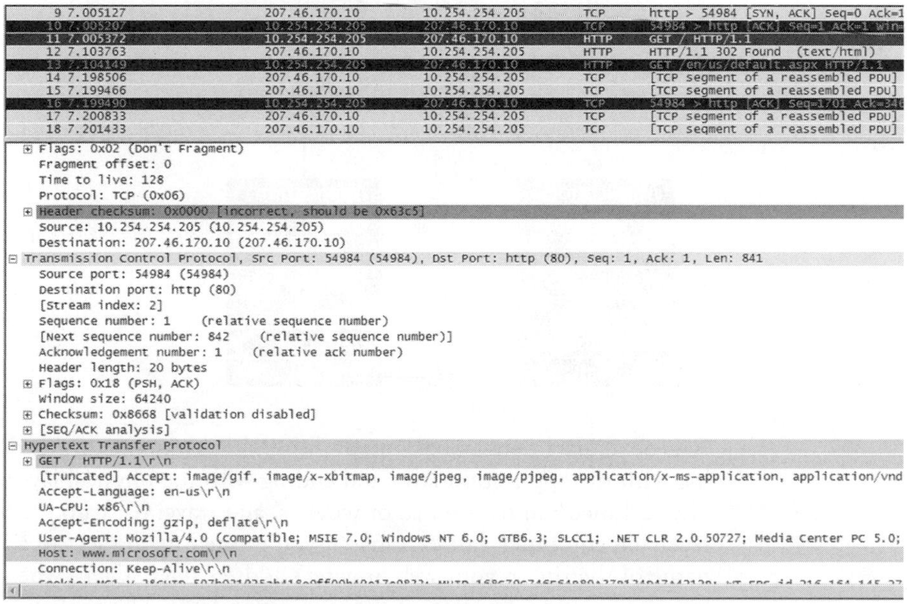

Figure 2-7

Wireshark capture of an HTTP packet

6. Click the + sign next to **Hypertext Transfer Protocol**. Here, you will see the host that you connected to: www.microsoft.com. You will also notice the gzip and deflate encoding/decoding schemes we alluded to earlier.

7. Click the + sign next to **Transmission Control Protocol**. Here, you will see the outbound port used by your computer to connect to the web server (known as a source port), as well as the inbound port (80) that the web server uses (known as a Dst or destination port).

8. Spend some time analyzing the information listed, and match it to the appropriate layer of the OSI model.

Devices known as *gateways* reside on the application layer. These are not to be confused with gateway devices (like routers) on the network layer. An application layer gateway is a computer that translates from one protocol suite to another, such as from TCP/IP to IPX/SPX. An example, albeit an out of date one, would be Client Services for NetWare when loaded on a Windows client computer.

Reviewing the OSI Layers

CERTIFICATION READY
What do you need to know to review all of the OSI layers?
3.1

The OSI model contains seven layers, each of which work collectively to define the transmission of data from one computer to another. The mnemonic device *All People Seem To Need Data Processing* can help you memorize the layer order.

Although earlier in the lesson, we defined each of the OSI layers starting at the bottom, the physical layer, and moving upward from there, quite often, you will see the layers listed from the top down, with the application layer at the top and the physical layer at the bottom, as shown in Figure 2-8. However, in Wireshark and other protocol analyzers, the physical layer will be displayed at the top. It all depends on what application or technical document you are looking at, so be ready to encounter both orientations.

Figure 2-8

OSI layers revisited

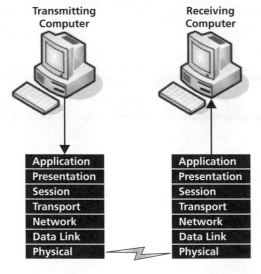

In general, data transactions start at the sending computer, travel down the OSI layers starting with the application layer and ending with the physical layer, are transmitted across the physical medium be it wired or wireless, and travel back up the layers of the OSI model at the receiving computer. For example, if you wanted to connect to a Web site, you would type the name of the site in your web browser's address field. Then, when you press Enter, the HTTP protocol would take effect at the application layer. The packets of data would be compressed (with gzip) and possibly encrypted (HTTPS by way of SSL or TLS) at the presentation layer. The web server would acknowledge the session with the client web browser at the session layer. The information would then be transmitted as TCP information on the transport layer, where ports are also selected. The TCP information would be broken up into easy-to-send packets on the network layer, and IP addressing information would be added. The packets would then be sent to the data link layer, where the network adapter would encapsulate them into frames of data. Then, at the physical layer, the network adapter would break the frames up into a serial bit stream to be sent over the cable media.

When the serial bit stream arrived at the destination client computer via the web browser, it would be reconfigured by the client's network adapter as frames of information. The header information of the frames would be checked for authenticity and stripped, leaving the packets to be sent to the operating system. The operating system would then put these packets together to form the web page that is displayed on your computer screen. Of course, this all happens 10,000 times faster than explained here, and it happens many times each second. For instance, if your computer has a 100 Mbps connection, it can take in about 12 MB maximum of data per second. Packets of information are variable in size, and they can be between approximately 60 and 1,500 bytes. Say that you are downloading a large file. This file will be broken down into the largest packet size possible, around 1,500 bytes. We can therefore calculate that an average computer can take in 8,000 packets of data per second. By the way, most client computers probably do not take advantage of this maximum data throughput, but servers and power workstations do.

Table 2-3 reviews the OSI layers and shows the corresponding devices, protocols, and network standards that apply to each layer.

Table 2-3

The OSI model layers and corresponding components

LAYER	PROTOCOL	DEVICE
7. Application	FTP, HTTP, POP3, SMTP	Gateway
6. Presentation	Compression, Encryption	N/A
5. Session	Logon/Logoff	N/A
4. Transport	TCP, UDP	N/A
3. Network	IP, ICMP, ARP, RIP	Routers
2. Data Link	802.3, 802.5	NICs, switches, bridges, WAPs
1. Physical	100BASE-T, 1000BASE-X	Hubs, patch panels, RJ45 jacks

Defining the TCP/IP Model

CERTIFICATION READY
How can you define the TCP/IP model?
3.1

The TCP/IP (or TCP) model is similar to the OSI model. It is often used by software manufacturers who are not as concerned with how information is sent over physical media, or how the data link is actually made. This model is composed of only four layers.

Although the OSI model is a reference model, the TCP/IP model (also known as the DoD model or Internet model) is more descriptive, defining principles such as "end-to-end" and "robustness," which describe strong endpoint connections and conservative transmission of data. This model is maintained by the *Internet Engineering Task Force (IETF)*. The four layers in the TCP/IP model are as follows:

- **Layer 1**: Data link layer (also simply known as the link layer)
- **Layer 2**: Network layer (also known as the Internet layer)
- **Layer 3**: Transport layer
- **Layer 4**: Application layer

The OSI physical layer is skipped altogether, and the application layer comprises the OSI application, presentation, and session layers.

Programmers utilize the TCP/IP model more often than the OSI model, whereas network administrators usually benefit to a higher degree from the OSI model. Programmers are generally interested in the interfaces made to the application and transport layers. Anything below the transport layer is taken care of by the TCP/IP stack within the operating system, which is set in stone. Programs can be made to utilize the TCP stack, but not to modify it. Again, as a networking person, you will most often refer to the OSI model, but you should know the layers of the TCP model in case you need to interface with programmers and developers, especially programmers and developers of Microsoft products.

SKILL SUMMARY

IN THIS LESSON, YOU LEARNED:

- To understand the OSI model by defining each of the layers from a theory perspective and with hands-on labs.

- To be able to separate the functions of the lower levels of the OSI, or the communications subnetwork, from the upper levels where message creation begins.

- To understand the differences between layer 2 and layer 3 switches, and to gain a basic understanding of how they operate.

- To differentiate between the OSI model and the TCP model.

■ Knowledge Assessment

Multiple Choice

Circle the letter that corresponds to the best answer.

1. How many layers are incorporated in the OSI model communications subnetwork?
   a. 2
   b. 7
   c. 3
   d. 4

2. Which of the following layers deals with the serial transfer of data?
   a. Physical
   b. Data link
   c. Network
   d. Session

3. You need to install a router on your company's network that will allow access to the Internet. What layer of the OSI does this device reside on?
   a. Physical
   b. Data link
   c. Network
   d. Transport

4. You run a **netstat –an** command in the command prompt and notice many connections being made that say TCP in the left-most column. What layer of the OSI is TCP referring to?
   a. Layer 1
   b. Layer 2
   c. Layer 3
   d. Layer 4

5. You suspect a problem with your computer's network adapter and its ability to send the correct frames of data that correspond with the network architecture used by the rest of your computers. What layer should you attempt to use as a troubleshooting starting point?
   a. Physical
   b. Data link
   c. Network
   d. Transport

6. A standard such as 100BASE-T refers to which OSI layer?
   a. Physical
   b. Data link
   c. Network
   d. Transport

7. Almost all of your users connect to Web sites with Internet Explorer. They usually type domain names such as **www.microsoft.com**. What protocol is initiated by default when they press Enter after typing the domain name?
   a. FTP
   b. HTTPS
   c. HTTP
   d. HTP

8. You need to find out the MAC address of your director's computer. He has given you permission to access his computer. You access the command prompt. What command should you type to see the computer's MAC address?
   a. ipconfig
   b. ipconfig/all
   c. arp
   d. netstat -an

9. You need to find out the MAC addresses of all the computers that a particular user's computer has connected to in the recent past. What command should you use to accomplish this?
   a. ping 127.0.0.1
   b. netstat -a
   c. arp -a
   d. arp -s

10. You have been instructed to capture and analyze packets on a server. What tool will allow you to do this? (Select the two best answers.)
    a. Protocol analyzer
    b. Command Prompt
    c. netstat -an
    d. Wireshark

Fill in the Blank

Fill in the correct answer in the blank space provided.

1. The manager of IT asks you ping his laptop to see whether your computer can find it on the network. In this scenario, the _____ protocol is being implemented.

2. A _____ switch is one that uses logical addressing to determine data paths.

3. Ports 1024–49,151 are ports used by vendors for proprietary applications. They are known as _____ ports.

4. Port _____ is used by the File Transfer Protocol.

5. Your manager wants you to allow HTTP and HTTPS connections to the company web server. In order to do this, you need to open inbound ports _____ and _____.

6. Your company hosts a DNS server that resolves domain names to IP addresses. This server must have _____ open to service those requests for name resolution.

7. You need to find out the Internet connections a particular computer has made in the recent past. You also need to see numeric information so that you know the IP address and port numbers of the destination computers. You should type the _____ command in the command prompt.

8. The IT director asks you to connect a client computer to an 802.3ab network. This network uses the _____ standard.

9. A user has connected to a Web site. The information that is sent to that user's computer is encrypted in an encoded format. This change to the data occurs at the _____ layer.

10. As you delve into a packet of data with your protocol analyzer, you notice that the frame size is bigger than the packet size. This is because the packet is _____ inside the frame.

■ Case Scenarios

Scenario 2-1: Installing the Appropriate Switch

Proseware, Inc., requires you to install a 24-port switch that directs TCP/IP traffic to logical addresses on the network. What kind of switch allows you to do this, and what kind of addresses will the traffic be directed to? Also, what layer of the OSI model are you dealing with here?

Scenario 2-2: Defining the IP Address and Ports Used by Destination Servers

A coworker's computer seems to be connecting to various computers on the Internet on its own. The computer gets pop-up advertisements and other pop-ups out of the blue. What command syntax would you use to analyze which IP addresses and ports the computer is connecting to? And what layers of the OSI model do the IP addresses and ports correspond to?

Scenario 2-3: Proving that a Newly Created Email Account's Login Is Encrypted

Your IT director wants you to create an email account to use on the company Web site. He wants the email address to be free and wants proof that when a person logs in to the email account, the password is encrypted. What services, applications, and tools can you utilize to accomplish this? And what layers of the OSI model are being used for the login?

Scenario 2-4: Creating a Permanent ARP Table Entry

Your boss's computer sleeps after 10 minutes. She wants to be able to "wake up" her desktop computer from a remote system, for example from her laptop. In order to do this, you first need to create a static entry in your boss's laptop's ARP table. Moreover, this entry needs to be re-created every time the laptop reboots. The desktop computer's IP address is 10.50.249.38, and its MAC address is 00-03-FF-A5-55-16. What command syntax should you use to do this? How will you make this command execute every time the computer boots? What layer of the OSI model are you referencing in this scenario?

✳ Workplace Ready

Analyzing an FTP Connection

The File Transfer Protocol is probably the most commonly used protocol when it comes to file transfer (quite an appropriate name). However, this protocol can be insecure. Some FTP servers use the standard port 21 for all data transfers. It is better to use port 21 for the initial connection, and then use dynamically assigned ports for subsequent data transfers. Also, some FTP implementations send the user password as clear text; this is not desirable. Passwords should be complex, and authentication should be encrypted if possible. Also, more secure FTP programs should be utilized. For example, Pure-FTPd (http://www.pureftpd.org) could be utilized on the server side, and FileZilla (http://filezilla-project.org) could be incorporated on the client side.

Research exactly what Pure-FTPd is and what it offers. Then, download and install the free FileZilla program. Next, run the Wireshark program and start a capture. Then, open FileZilla and make a connection to ftp.ipswitch.com (no username or password is necessary). Note the fact that anonymous connections can be made to this server. Look at a few of the folders in the FTP server. Stop the capture and analyze the FTP packets. See whether you can find the packets that relate to the initial connection and to the anonymous login. Document exactly what happened on the following OSI layers: application, transport, network, and data link.

3 LESSON

Understanding Wired and Wireless Networks

OBJECTIVE DOMAIN MATRIX

SKILLS/CONCEPTS	MTA EXAM OBJECTIVE	MTA EXAM OBJECTIVE NUMBER
Recognizing Wired Networks and Media Types	Understand media types.	2.3
Comprehending Wireless Networks	Understand wireless networking.	1.4

KEY TERMS

568A
568B
ad-hoc mode
Advanced Encryption Standard
attenuation
BOGB
bridge mode
category 5e
category 6
channel bonding
continuity tester
crossover cable
crosstalk
data emanation
electromagnetic interference (EMI)
far end crosstalk (FEXT)
Faraday cage
fiber optic cable
frame aggregation
IEEE 802.11
IEEE 802.1X
infrastructure mode
interference
MDI
MDI-X

multi-mode
Multiple-Input Multiple-Output (MIMO)
near end crosstalk (NEXT)
physical data rate (PHY)
plenum-rated
port-based network access control (PNAC)
punch down tool
radio frequency interference (RFI)
service set identifier (SSID)
single mode
shielded twisted pair (STP) cables
straight through cables
Temporal Key Integrity Protocol
TIA/EIA
twisted-pair cables
unshielded twisted pair (UTP) cables
Wi-Fi
Wi-Fi Protected Access
Wired Equivalent Privacy
wireless access point (WAP)
wireless bridge
wireless LAN (WLAN)
wireless network adapter
wireless repeater

Properly installed cabling and wireless networks are the keys to an efficient physical plant; physical wired and wireless connections are the core of a speedy network. In this lesson, we will refer back to our fictitious company, Proseware, Inc., and discuss all the technologies and standards that are required for Proseware to have a properly installed wired/wireless network. In order for the company to be happy, there will have to be twisted-pair cabling and fiber optic cabling, as well as shielded cabling and the latest in wireless equipment. We also have to verify that our signals are not being interfered with and are not being intercepted by undesirable parties. This requires tools, lots of cabling and additional equipment, wireless equipment, testing equipment, and plenty of know-how. As you begin this lesson, you should be prepared to learn how to cable an entire network and set up a wireless network as well.

■ Recognizing Wired Networks and Media Types

THE BOTTOM LINE

Wired networks are still the most common type of physical connection that computers make. Although wireless networks have made inroads into many organizations, the wired connection is still king. And the majority of computers use twisted-pair cabling for their physical connections.

CERTIFICATION READY
How can you identify the various media types?
2.3

Identifying and Working with Twisted-Pair Cables

Twisted-pair cable is the cable most commonly used in local area networks. It's relatively easy to work with, flexible, efficient, and fast. As a network administrator, you should know how to identify the different types of twisted-pair cabling, as well as how to install twisted-pair cabling in a permanent fashion and as a temporary solution. It's also important to know how to test twisted-pair cables in case one fails or as a way of proving that new installations work properly.

Twisted-pair cables are the most common of all copper-based cables. A single twisted-pair cable has eight wires; they are copper conductors that transmit electric signals. These eight wires are grouped into four pairs: blue, orange, green, and brown. Each pair of wires is twisted along the entire length of the cable, and all of the pairs are twisted together as well. The reason the wires are twisted is to reduce crosstalk and interference, which are described later in this lesson.

 EXAMINE TWISTED-PAIR PATCH CABLES

GET READY. In this exercise, you will examine a patch cable connected to either your computer or the central connecting device for your network.

1. Examine the back of your computer and locate the network adapter. There should be a twisted-pair patch cable that connects the network adapter to the network. If not, and if you use a wireless connection, examine the back of your central connecting device, whether it's a router, switch, or hub. Identify the patch cable that connects to that device. If you decide to disconnect the cable, keep in mind that the Internet connection will be temporarily lost and any downloads will be stopped. The cable should look something like the one in Figure 3-1, which is shown from the side of the RJ45 plug. You can see where the cable itself enters the plug and where the plastic sheath is cut, exposing the individual wires. Also notice the teeth that bite into the

Figure 3-1

Twisted-pair patch cable

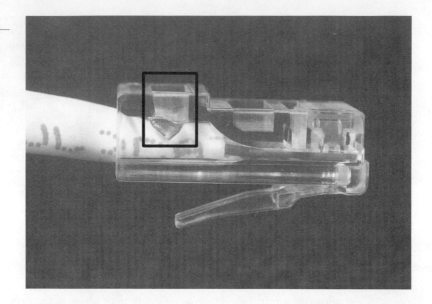

plastic jacket (they are shown in the black rectangle). Once the plug is crimped onto the cable, these teeth ensure that the cable does not slip out of the plug.

2. If you have some extra twisted-pair cable handy, cut a six-foot piece with a sharp cutting tool. Then, strip away about two inches of the plastic jacket to expose the wires. (The plastic jacket is also known as a plastic or PVC sheath.) You should see something similar to Figure 3-2, which illustrates the four twisted-pair wires. Once again, these four pairs are blue, orange, green, and brown, also known as the **BOGB** colors. Each letter represents a color: B = blue, O = orange, and so on.

Figure 3-2

Twisted-pair cable with the wires exposed

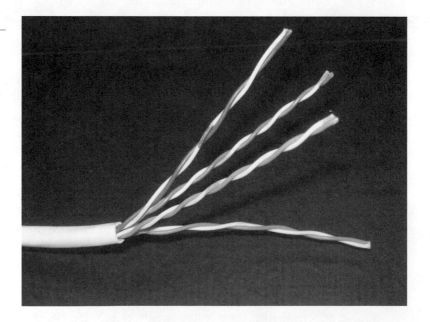

3. Untwist each of the wires so that they are all separated. The wires should now look similar to Figure 3-3. In the figure, the wires are in the proper order for most of today's twisted-pair networks. Table 3-1 summarizes the cabling standards when it comes to wire (or pin) orientation. Whereas the BOGB standard is where everything originates

Figure 3-3

Twisted-pair cable with the wires straightened

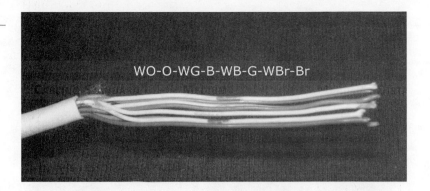

WO-O-WG-B-WB-G-WBr-Br

Table 3-1

568B, 568A, and BOGB standards

Pin #	568B	568A	BOGB
1	White/orange	White/green	White/blue
2	Orange	Green	Blue
3	White/green	White/orange	White/orange
4	Blue	Blue	Orange
5	White/blue	White/blue	White/green
6	Green	Orange	Green
7	White/brown	White/brown	White/brown
8	Brown	Brown	Brown

from, **568B** is the most common, and **568A** is an older standard. The proper name for 568B is TIA/EIA-568-B; this standard was developed by the Telecommunications Industry Association/Electronics Industries Alliance or **TIA/EIA**. When making a patch cable, the wires are placed in the RJ45 plug in order, and the plug is crimped once they are in place. If a particular wire is named white/orange, that means the bulk of the wire is white in color and it has an orange stripe. If the wire is named something like orange, it is a solid orange wire.

There are two types of networking patch cables that you might work with. The first is a **straight through cable**. This is the most common type of patch cable, and it is the type that you would use to connect a computer to a central connecting device like a switch. It's called "straight through" because the wires on each end of the cable are oriented in the same way. Generally, this is a 568B on each end. However, there is also another type of patch cable—the **crossover cable**. This type is used to connect like devices to each other, for example, a computer to another computer, or a switch to another switch. In this case, the patch cable is wired with the 568B standard on one side and the 568A standard on the other. To make a patch cable, you use a cutting tool, wire stripper, RJ45 crimper, RJ45 plugs, and a patch tester. These tools are illustrated in Figure 3-4.

Figure 3-4

Patch cable tools

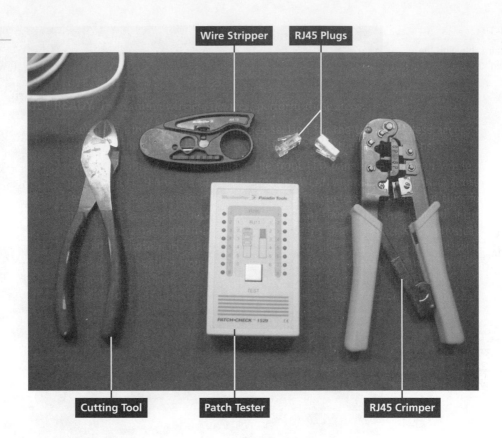

Wire Stripper   RJ45 Plugs

Cutting Tool   Patch Tester   RJ45 Crimper

Generally, Ethernet transmits data signals on the orange and green wires. This means pins one, two, three, and six. Other technologies use different pairs or possibly all four pairs of wires. Usually, twisted-pair networks are wired to the 568B standard. This means that all wiring equipment must comply with 568B, including patch panels, RJ45 jacks, patch cables, and the actual termination of wiring to each of these devices. To be more specific, the orange pair has a + and − wire, also known as tip and ring (old telco terminology). The green pair is similar. The orange pair transmits data, and the green pair receives it. If the connection is half duplex, only one of these pairs works at any given time. But if the connection is full duplex, both pairs work simultaneously.

Network adapters normally have an ***MDI*** port; this stands for medium dependent interface. However, in order for computers to communicate with other devices, the wires have to cross somewhere. In any crossed connection, pin one crosses to pin three, and pin two crosses to pin six. But instead of using crossover cables to connect computers to central connecting devices such as switches, these central connecting devices are equipped with ***MDI-X*** ports (medium dependent interface crossover), which take care of the cross. This is how straight through cables can be used to connect computers to the central connecting device, which is much easier, plus these cables are cheaper to manufacture. This is why a crossover cable is needed if you want to connect one computer to another computer directly, or a switch to another switch directly. However, some switches have a special auto MDI/MDIX port that senses whether you're trying to connect one switch to another switch with a straight through cable or a crossover cable. In other cases, the special port has a button that allows you to select whether it acts as a MDIX or a MDI port.

Patch cables are a temporary solution. They are meant to be unplugged and plugged in as necessary. Therefore, most companies also have permanent cabling solutions. For example, consider a connection between a patch panel in the server room and an RJ45 jack at a computer workstation. Figure 3-5 shows examples of both of these pieces of equipment.

Figure 3-5

Patch panel and RJ45 jack

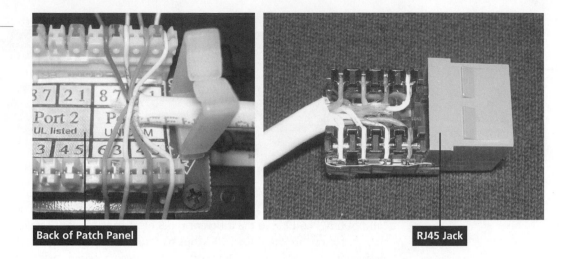

Back of Patch Panel

RJ45 Jack

The cable that connects these two pieces of equipment has the individual wires permanently punched down so that they are immovable. The front of a patch panel simply has a lot of RJ45 ports. The patch panel works great if a computer is moved to a different area of an office; the patch cable can simply be moved to the correct port on the patch panel.

The tools necessary to make the connections between patch panels and RJ45 jacks include a cutting tool, a wire stripper, a ***punch down tool***, and a testing device known as a ***continuity tester***, which tests all of the pins of a connection one by one. The tester lets you know whether any of the pins are mis-wired. It does this by testing the entire cable from end to end. The testing device is connected to one end of the run, and a terminating device connects to the other end; signals are bounced back and forth on every wire or pin. These last two tools are illustrated in Figure 3-6. Generally, twisted-pair cables can be run 100 meters before the signal degrades to such a point that it cannot be interpreted by the destination host. This is known as ***attenuation***. If a cable needs to be run farther, a signal repeater, a hub, or switch can be used. Otherwise, fiber optic cable is the solution because it can be run much farther than twisted-pair cable.

Figure 3-6

Punch down tool and continuity tester

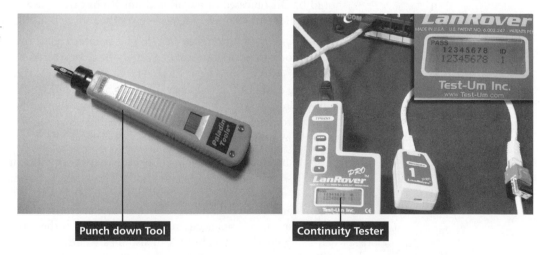

Punch down Tool

Continuity Tester

Twisted-pair cables are categorized according to the frequency at which they transmit signals and their data transfer rate or speed. Table 3-2 describes the different categories of twisted-pair cable and the types of network speed they can accommodate.

CABLE TYPE	SPEED
Category 3	10 Mbps
Category 5	100 Mbps
Category 5e	100 Mbps and Gigabit networks
Category 6	Gigabit networks

Category 5e is usually rated at 350 MHz, but the actual speed varies depending on several different networking factors. *Category 6* already has different versions that run at 250 MHz and 500 MHz. Due to the different types of category 5e and category 6, it is better to simply say that these are rated for 100 Mbps networks and gigabit networks. Take a look at one of your network cables now. Quite often, the category type is printed directly on the plastic jacket of the cable. For today's networks, category 3 (and even category 5) is not adequate; category 5e or higher is necessary for current high-bandwidth applications.

Interference can be a real problem with twisted-pair networks, or any networks for that matter. *Interference* is anything that disrupts or modifies a signal that is traveling along a wire. There are many types of interference, but there are only a few you should know for the exam, including the following:

- *Electromagnetic interference (EMI):* This is a disturbance that can affect electrical circuits, devices, and cables due to electromagnetic conduction and possibly radiation. Just about any type of electrical device causes EMI: TVs, air conditioning units, motors, unshielded electrical cables (Romex), and so on. Copper-based cables and network devices should be kept away from these electrical devices and cables if at all possible. If this is not possible, shielded cables can be used, for example *shielded twisted-pair (STP) cables*. STP cables have an aluminum shield inside the plastic jacket that surrounds the pairs of wires. Alternatively, the device that is emanating EMI can be shielded. For example, an air conditioning unit could be boxed in with aluminum shielding in an attempt to keep the EMI generated by the AC unit's motor to a minimum. In addition, electrical cables should be BX (encased in metal) and not Romex (not encased in metal); in fact, most states require this to meet industrial and office space building code.

- *Radio frequency interference (RFI):* This is interference that can come from AM/FM transmissions and cell phone towers. It is often considered part of the EMI family and is sometimes even referred to as EMI. The closer a business is to one of these towers, the greater the chance of interference. The methods mentioned in the EMI bullet can be employed to help defend against RFI. In addition, filters can be installed on the network to eliminate the signal frequency being broadcast by a radio tower, although this will usually not affect standard wired Ethernet networks.

One serious issue with data networks, especially networks with copper-based cabling is *data emanation* (also known as signal emanation). This is the electromagnetic (EM) field that is generated by a network cable or network device, which can be manipulated to eavesdrop on conversations or to steal data. Data emanation is sometimes also referred to as eavesdropping in itself, although this is not accurate. Data emanation is the most commonly seen security risk when using coaxial cable, but it can also be a security risk for other copper-based cables such as twisted pair. There are various ways to tap into these (EM) fields in order to get unauthorized access to confidential data. To alleviate the situation, you could use shielded cabling or run the cabling through metal conduits. You could also use electromagnetic shielding on devices that might be emanating an electromagnetic field. This could be done on a small scale by shielding the single device, or on a larger scale by shielding an entire room, perhaps a server room. This would be an example of a *Faraday cage*.

Another common type of interference is crosstalk. ***Crosstalk*** is when the signal that is transmitted on one copper wire or pair of wires creates an undesired effect on another wire or pair of wires. Crosstalk first occurred when telephone lines were placed in close proximity to each other. Due to the fact that the lines were so close, the signal could jump from one line to the next intermittently. If you have ever heard another conversation while talking on your home phone (and not a cell phone), then you have been the victim of crosstalk. If the signals are digital (e.g., Ethernet data transfers or voice over IP), you already have an environment that is less susceptible to crosstalk. Data can still bleed over to other wires, but it is less common. Sometimes this occurs because cables are bundled too tightly, which could also cause crimping or other damage to the cable. If this is the case, a continuity tester will let you know which cable has failed so that it can be replaced.

When it comes to twisted-pair cabling, crosstalk is broken down into two categories: ***near end crosstalk (NEXT)*** and ***far end crosstalk (FEXT)***. NEXT occurs when there is measured interference between two pairs in a single cable, measured on the cable end nearest the transmitter. FEXT occurs when there is similar interference, measured at the cable end farthest from the transmitter. If crosstalk is still a problem, even though twisted-pair cable has been employed and digital data transmissions have been implemented, shielded twisted pair (STP) could be used. Normally, companies opt for regular twisted-pair cabling, which is ***unshielded twisted pair*** (also known as ***UTP***), but sometimes, there is too much interference in the environment to send data effectively, and STP must be utilized.

Cables that are installed inside walls or above drop ceilings where they cannot be accessed by sprinkler systems in the case of a fire should be ***plenum-rated*** or low-smoke rated. Plenum-rated cables have a Teflon coating that makes them more impervious to fire. They are used in these situations because standard twisted-pair cables have a PVC jacket, which when burned can emit deadly gas into the air that ultimately gets breathed in as hydrochloric acid.

Finally, the physical plant should be grounded. Quite often, server rooms or wiring closets are the central connecting point for all the cabling. All of the cables are punched down to patch panels, which are screwed into data racks. These racks should be bolted to the ground and connected with 10 gauge or thicker grounding wire (usually with a green jacket) to a proper earth bonding point, such as an I-beam in the ceiling. This protects all of the cabling (and the devices it connects to) from surges, spikes, lightning strikes, and so on.

Phew! That was a lot of information about twisted-pair cabling. We could go on and on, but that should suffice for now. Be sure to look over all of the key terms listed in the beginning of this lesson for review.

Identifying and Working with Fiber Optic Cable

Fiber optic cable is employed when longer distance runs and even higher data transfer rates are needed. Fiber optic cables are used as part of the backbone of the fastest networks. However, they are far more difficult to install and to maintain, as well as to troubleshoot.

Fiber optic cable transmits light (photons) instead of electricity, and this light is transmitted over glass or plastic. Glass is known as the media for fiber optics, just like copper is known as the media for twisted-pair cabling. The glass or plastic strands in fiber optic cabling are extremely small; in fact, they are measured in microns.

 EXAMINE FIBER OPTIC CABLE

GET READY. Because fiber optic cable is rarer than twisted-pair cable in networks, and because it is expensive, we will search the Internet for the various types of cables and connectors.

If you happen to have fiber optic cables, connectors, and devices available, attempt to identify those after you have completed the following steps:

1. Execute a Bing search in the Images section for "optical fiber."
2. Run Bing searches for the following connector images:
   - FC connector
   - LC connector
   - MT-RJ connector
   - SC connector
   - ST connector
   - TOSLINK
3. Execute a Bing image search for the following devices:
   - Fiber optic network adapter
   - Fiber optic switch
   - Fiber optic router
4. If you do have any fiber optic equipment handy, go ahead and identify it now, based on what you have seen on the Internet.

Fiber optic cable can be either single mode or multi-mode:

- ***Single-mode*** (**SM**) optic is a cable with an optical fiber that is meant to carry a single ray of light—one ray of light, one mode. This type of cable is normally used for longer distance runs, generally 10 km and up to 80 km.
- ***Multi-mode*** (**MM**) optic is a cable with a larger fiber core, capable of carrying multiple rays of light. This type of cable is used for shorter distance runs, up to 600 meters. Though much shorter than single mode fiber runs, this is still six times the distance of twisted-pair cable runs.

Usually, fiber optic cable is used for high-speed connections, backbone connections, storage area networks (SANs), and direct connections between servers. 1 Gbps and 10 Gbps speeds are common, although you will still see 100 Mbps connections. Table 3-3 defines some of the 100 Mbps, 1 Gbps, and 10 Gbps versions of fiber optics, as well as their medium type and typical maximum distance.

Table 3-3

Types of fiber optic cable

CABLING STANDARD	MEDIUM	MAXIMUM DISTANCE
100BASE-FX	Mutli-mode fiber Single-mode fiber	Half duplex: 400 meters; full duplex: 2 km Full duplex: 10 km
100BASE-SX	Multi-mode fiber	550 meters
100BASE-BX	Single-mode fiber	40 km
100BASE-LX10	Single-mode fiber	10 km
1000BASE-SX	Multi-mode fiber	550 meters
1000BASE-LX	Multi-mode fiber	550 meters
1000BASE-LX	Single-mode fiber	5 km
1000BASE-LX10	Single-mode fiber	10 km
1000BASE-ZX	Single-mode fiber	Up to 70 km

Table 3-3 (continued)

Cabling Standard	Medium	Maximum Distance
1000BASE-BX10	Single-mode fiber	10 km
10GBASE-SR	Multi-mode fiber	26–82 meters
10GBASE-LR	Single-mode fiber	10–25 km
10GBASE-LRM	Multi-mode fiber	220 meters
10GBASE-ER	Single-mode fiber	40 km

When it comes to interference, a cable itself can be its worst enemy. Generally, fiber optic cables are not affected by EMI, because they are inherently light based, not electricity based. Although a fiber optic cable will still produce a type of electromagnetic radiation, the cable is not traditionally affected by EMI in the same way copper-based cables are. However, if a fiber run is installed improperly, it can give strange results when it comes to the data signal. Exact installation rules must be followed including proper termination, specific radii for turns, avoiding bunching, and so on. Improper installation results in the signal becoming "bent," which causes data loss. Chromatic dispersion is also a factor, as opposed to attenuation on twisted-pair cables. If the light is refracted too often, again, the signal will degrade. Fiber optic cable in general is the most secure cable, allows for the longest runs, and offers data transfer rates that are equal to or greater than twisted-pair cable. However, due to the complexity of installation, cost, and so on, fiber optic cable is not usually a first choice for all of the individual client computer runs. Instead, it is used for backbone connections; switch connections at the top of hierarchical star topologies, and other high-bandwidth or long-distance applications.

Comprehending Wireless Networks

THE BOTTOM LINE

Wireless networks are everywhere. There are wireless networks for computers, handheld devices, wide-area connections, and more. Chances are you have used a wireless network in the past. In order to install and troubleshoot wireless networks, you must understand the basics of wireless communications and have knowledge of the devices, standards, frequencies, and security methods.

Identifying Wireless Devices

CERTIFICATION READY
How do you identify wireless devices?
1.4

Wireless devices might allow for central connectivity of client computers and handheld devices. Or, they might offer an extension of connectivity to a pre-existing wireless network and could be used to connect entire local area networks to the Internet. In addition, some wireless devices can be connected directly to each other in a point-to-point fashion.

By far the most well-known wireless device is the ***wireless access point (WAP)***. This device quite often also acts as a router, firewall, and IP proxy. It allows for the connectivity of various wireless devices such as laptops, PDAs, handheld computers, and so on. It does so by making connections via radio waves on specific frequencies. Client computers and handheld devices must use the same frequency in order to connect to the WAP. In the following exercise, we will identify wireless access points, wireless network adapters, and wireless bridges and repeaters.

EXAMINE WIRELESS DEVICES

GET READY. To examine wireless devices, perform these steps:

1. Execute a Bing search in the images section for the term "wireless access point." Take a look at some of the various types of WAPs and their connections.

2. Examine Figure 3-7. This displays the front LED panel of a common wireless access point. Notice there is a green LED for the WLAN connection. WLAN is short for wireless local area network; the LED tells us that wireless is enabled on this device. This particular device also acts as a 4-port switch; these ports are labeled "Ethernet," and two of them have green-lit LEDs, which means that computers are physically connected to those ports and are active. Finally, the "Internet" LED is lit, which is the physical connection from the WAP to the Internet. Although a WAP by itself is just a wireless transmitter, usually with a single port to connect to the LAN, multifunction network devices like these are very common in small networks and home offices.

Figure 3-7

Wireless access point

3. Execute a Bing search in the images section for the term "wireless network adapter." Examine the results. *Wireless network adapters* allow for connectivity between a desktop computer or laptop and the wireless access point. They come in many shapes and sizes, including USB, PC Card, ExpressCard, and, of course, as an internal PCI or PCI Express adapter card for a personal computer. Most laptops today have built-in wireless network adapters, which are basically a chip on a circuit board with an antenna attached.

4. Access the Internet and execute searches on various wireless manufacturers' Web sites to find out about the latest wireless access points and network adapters they offer. Write down your results for each of the following manufacturers' fastest access points and network adapters:
   - www.d-link.com
   - http://home.cisco.com/en-US/wireless/
   - http://www.netgear.com/
   - http://www.belkin.com/

5. Execute a Bing search in the images section for the term "wireless repeater." Examine the results. A *wireless repeater* is used to extend the coverage of a wireless network. Due to the fact that most WLANs only have a range of about 100 feet or so (depending on the standard), wireless repeaters are often needed to extend that signal further. They can be wired to the access point, but more often than not, they are placed on the perimeter of the existing wireless network area.

6. Execute a Bing search in the images section for the term "wireless bridge." Examine the results. A *wireless bridge* is similar to a wireless repeater, but the bridge can connect different 802.11 standards together; this is known as *bridge mode*.

7. Access a wireless access point simulator. We use the D-link DIR-655 emulator later in this lesson. Take a look at the following link now, and login to the **DIR-655 Device UI** emulator to become acquainted with its interface. There is no password:

   http://support.dlink.com/emulators/dir655/

Identifying Wireless Networking Standards

CERTIFICATION READY
How do you identify wireless networking standards?
1.4

> In order to set up a functional wireless LAN, a network administrator has to know several wireless standards, as well as ways to secure the wireless network transmissions.

A *wireless LAN (WLAN)* is a network composed of at least one WAP and at least one computer or handheld device that can connect to the WAP. Usually these networks are Ethernet based, but they can be based off other networking architectures. In order to ensure compatibility, the WAP and other wireless devices must all use the same *IEEE 802.11* WLAN standard. These standards are collectively referred to as 802.11x (not to be confused with 802.1X), and they are defined by the data link layer of the OSI model. The term "WLAN" is often used interchangeably with Wi-Fi. However, *Wi-Fi* refers to a trademark created by the Wi-Fi Alliance. Wi-Fi products and technologies are based on the WLAN standards. These WLAN standards dictate the frequency (or frequencies) used, speed, and so on. Table 3-4 shows the most common standards and their maximum data transfer rate and frequency.

Table 3-4

IEEE 802.11 WLAN standards

IEEE 802.11 STANDARD	DATA TRANSFER RATE (MAX.)	FREQUENCY
802.11a	54 Mbps	5 GHz
802.11b	11 Mbps	2.4 GHz
802.11g	54 Mbps	2.4 GHz
802.11n	600 Mbps (300 Mbps typical)	5 GHz and/or 2.4 GHz

In the United States, 802.11b and g have 11 usable channels, starting with channel 1 centered at 2.412 GHz and ending with channel 11 centered at 2.462 GHz. This is a smaller range than some other countries use.

Many of the channels in a WLAN overlap. To avoid this, organizations may put, for example, three separate WAPs on channels 1, 6, and 11, respectively. This keeps them from overlapping and interfering with each other. If two WAPs on channels 4 and 5 are in close proximity to each other, there will be a decent amount of interference. It's also wise to keep WLAN WAPs away from Bluetooth devices and Bluetooth access points, because Bluetooth also uses the 2.4 GHz frequency range.

It should go without saying that compatibility is key. However, many WAPs are backward compatible. For example, an 802.11g WAP might also allow 802.11b connections. Perhaps it even allows 802.11a connections, which would be an example of wireless bridging. But generally, companies are looking for the fastest compatible speed possible from all of their wireless networking equipment—and today, that means 802.11n. 802.11n is superior to older WLAN standards in the following ways:

- *Multiple-Input Multiple-Output (MIMO):* This means that wireless devices can have more antennas, up to four maximum.

- *Frame aggregation:* This is the sending of two or more frames of data in a single transmission. By aggregating frames, the amount of data transferred on the data link layer can be doubled in the 802.11n standard.

- *Channel bonding:* Here, two channels that do not overlap are used together in an effort to double the *physical data rate (PHY)*. Channel bandwidth therefore becomes 40 MHz instead of the previously used 20 MHz.

Of course, all this great technology can be easily manipulated if it is not protected. To mitigate risk, encryption should be used. There are several types of encryption available for wireless networks, but the most secure is WPA2 when used with AES, as shown in Table 3-5. Without the proper encryption turned on at the client, and without knowledge of the correct key or pass phrase, a client computer will not be able to connect to the WAP.

Table 3-5

Wireless encryption options

WIRELESS ENCRYPTION PROTOCOL	DESCRIPTION	ENCRYPTION LEVEL (KEY SIZE)
WEP	Wired Equivalent Privacy	64-bit
WPA2	Wi-Fi Protected Access	256-bit
TKIP	Temporal Key Integrity Protocol	128-bit
AES	Advanced Encryption Standard	128-, 192-, and 256-bit

WEP also has 128-bit and 256-bit versions, but these versions are not commonly found in wireless network hardware. WEP in general is an out of date protocol, and it is not recommended. However, if there are no other options available to you, WEP is far superior to *no* encryption!

Another way to secure a wireless connection is to use 802.1X. *IEEE 802.1X* is *port-based network access control (PNAC)*. This provides strong authentication to devices that need to connect to the WLAN; it can also be used for regular wired LANs. There are three components to an 802.1X set-up. The first is the supplicant, or the computer that is attempting to connect to the WLAN. The second is the authenticator, or the wireless access point. The third is the authentication server; often this will be a RADIUS server, which enables advanced authentication techniques. RADIUS servers can be setup within Windows Server 2003 products by installing the Internet Authentication Service (IAS). Windows Server 2008 includes RADIUS within the Network Policy Server (NPS).

There several different ways to connect to a wireless network—primarily *infrastructure mode* and *ad-hoc mode*:

- **Infrastructure** mode is more common. It occurs when wireless clients connect to and are authenticated by a wireless access point, which can be expanded by creating a wireless distribution system—a group of WAPs interconnected wirelessly. When utilizing infrastructure mode, the base unit (normally a WAP) will be configured with a *service set identifier (SSID)*. This then becomes the name of the wireless network, and it is broadcast over the airwaves. Thus, when clients want to connect to the WAP, they can identify it by the SSID.

- **Ad-hoc** mode is less common, and it is used more often in a handheld computer environment. Ad-hoc (also referred to as peer-to-peer or P2P) networks occur when all of the clients communicate directly with each other. There is no "base" so to speak, meaning a wireless access point. Generally, this type of network is configured so that two individual wireless devices can connect to each other and communicate, perhaps privately.

EXAMINE WIRELESS NETWORKING SETTINGS

GET READY. In the following exercise, we will access the D-Link DIR-655 emulator and show some standard wireless configurations. To do so, perform these steps:

1. Log in to the DIR-655 emulator and view basic settings:

   a. Connect to a router. The username cannot be changed, and the password is blank, meaning there is no password. This displays the main **Device Information** page. Examine this page. Note the LAN IP address of the device. It should be 192.168.0.1, the default for D-Link WAPs. If a client wants to connect to this device, it has to be configured via DHCP or statically, but it will need to be on the 192.168.0 network.

   b. Scroll down and examine the wireless settings. Wireless should be enabled by default. Note the mode, channel width, channel used, and so on.

2. Modify the SSID:

   a. Click the **Setup** link on the top banner.

   b. Click the **Wireless Settings** link on the left side.

   c. Click the **Manual Wireless Network Setup** button. This should display the **Wireless** page.

   d. Look for the Wireless Network Name. This is the SSID. The default for D-Link devices is none other than **dlink**. It is highly recommended that you modify the default SSID on any WAP. Change it now to something a bit more complex.

3. Modify the wireless configuration:

   a. Examine the **802.11 Mode** drop-down menu. Note the variety of settings. Modify this so that it says 802.11n only.

   b. Deselect the **Enable Auto Channel Scan** checkbox. This should enable the **Wireless Channel** drop-down menu. Select channel 11, which is centered at 2.462 GHz. Subsequent WAPs should be set to channel 6 and channel 1 in order to avoid channel overlapping.

   c. Modify the **Channel Width** setting to 40 MHz. This will incorporate channel bonding.

4. Enable encryption:

   a. At the **Security Mode** drop-down menu, select **WPA-Personal.** This should display additional WPA information. You would only select **WPA-Enterprise** if you had the aforementioned RADIUS server available.

   b. Scroll down, and in the **WPA Mode** drop-down menu, select **WPA2 Only.**

   c. In the **Cipher Type** drop-down menu, select **AES.**

   d. Finally, type in a complex Pre-Shared Key. This is the pass-phrase that clients need to enter in order to connect to the WLAN.

   This is the highest level of security this device offers (aside from WPA-Enterprise). Your configuration should look similar to Figure 3-8.

5. Disable the SSID:

   a. When all clients are connected to the WAP, the SSID should be disabled. This will not allow new connections to the WAP unless the person knows the SSID name, but computers that have already connected may continue to do so.

   b. To do this, click the **Invisible** radio button in the **Visibility Status** field.

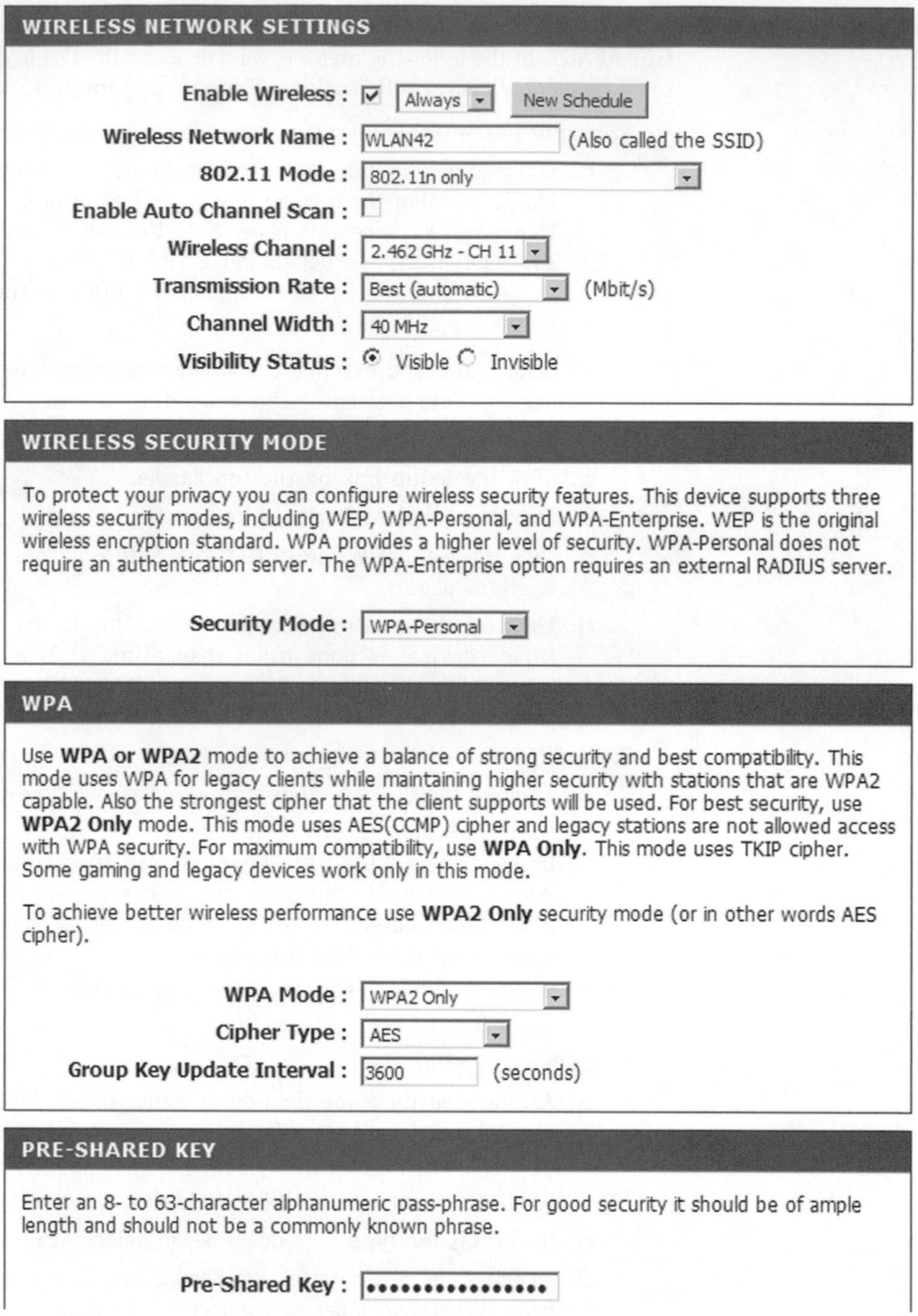

Figure 3-8

D-Link DIR-655 wireless
configuration

WIRELESS NETWORK SETTINGS

Enable Wireless : ☑ [Always ▾] [New Schedule]

Wireless Network Name : [WLAN42_____] (Also called the SSID)

802.11 Mode : [802.11n only _____▾]

Enable Auto Channel Scan : ☐

Wireless Channel : [2.462 GHz - CH 11 ▾]

Transmission Rate : [Best (automatic) ▾] (Mbit/s)

Channel Width : [40 MHz ▾]

Visibility Status : ⦿ Visible ○ Invisible

WIRELESS SECURITY MODE

To protect your privacy you can configure wireless security features. This device supports three wireless security modes, including WEP, WPA-Personal, and WPA-Enterprise. WEP is the original wireless encryption standard. WPA provides a higher level of security. WPA-Personal does not require an authentication server. The WPA-Enterprise option requires an external RADIUS server.

Security Mode : [WPA-Personal ▾]

WPA

Use **WPA or WPA2** mode to achieve a balance of strong security and best compatibility. This mode uses WPA for legacy clients while maintaining higher security with stations that are WPA2 capable. Also the strongest cipher that the client supports will be used. For best security, use **WPA2 Only** mode. This mode uses AES(CCMP) cipher and legacy stations are not allowed access with WPA security. For maximum compatibility, use **WPA Only**. This mode uses TKIP cipher. Some gaming and legacy devices work only in this mode.

To achieve better wireless performance use **WPA2 Only** security mode (or in other words AES cipher).

WPA Mode : [WPA2 Only ▾]

Cipher Type : [AES ▾]

Group Key Update Interval : [3600____] (seconds)

PRE-SHARED KEY

Enter an 8- to 63-character alphanumeric pass-phrase. For good security it should be of ample length and should not be a commonly known phrase.

Pre-Shared Key : [●●●●●●●●●●●●●●●●]

6. Save the settings:

   a. At this point, you should save the settings. The emulator doesn't allow anything to be saved. It reverts back to defaults when you log out or disconnect from the Web site, so clicking **Save Settings** won't do anything. But on an actual DIR-655, the settings would save and a reboot would be necessary.

   b. It's also important to back up the configuration. This can be done by clicking **Tools** on the top banner, then **System** on the left side and selecting **Save Configuration**; this is a real time saver in case you have to reset the unit. It is also wise to update the device to the latest firmware. Save your settings before doing so because they will be lost when the upgrade is complete; if saved, they can later be loaded back in.

SKILL SUMMARY

IN THIS LESSON, YOU LEARNED:

- To recognize wired networks and media types. This includes identifying twisted-pair cable, cabling tools, and testers. You also learned what can interfere with twisted-pair cabling and how to avoid it, and you read about a slew of wiring standards you should know for the real world. You also learned some of the basics about fiber optic cabling and some of the standards attached to these extremely quick cables.

- To comprehend wireless networks. This included wireless devices, wireless settings and configurations, wireless standards, and encryption protocols.

■ Knowledge Assessment

Multiple Choice

Circle the letter that corresponds to the best answer.

1. You are in charge of installing 200 twisted-pair cable drops. What wiring standard should you most likely use?
   a. 568A
   b. BOGB
   c. 568B
   d. 586B

2. Your boss wants you to connect two of his laptops directly to each other using their network adapters. What kind of cable should you use?
   a. Rolled cable
   b. Crossover cable
   c. Straight through cable
   d. Patch cable

3. You are making a specialized wired connection for a server that will operate on an Ethernet network. Which two wiring colors should you use?
   a. Orange and green
   b. Orange and blue
   c. Orange and brown
   d. White and blue

4. One of the network connections to a programmer's computer has failed. You suspect it involves a problem with the twisted-pair cable. What tool should you use to test for any problems in the cable?
   a. Patch tester
   b. Wireshark
   c. Continuity tester
   d. Fox and hound

5. The IT director has asked you to connect three new super computers to the backbone of a network that runs at 1 Gbps. The pressure is on! What type of cable will be sufficient for this task?
   a. Category 3
   b. Category 5
   c. Category 5e
   d. Category 10a

6. Your network contains many fiber optic connections. Which one of the following does not belong in your fiber network?
   a. FC connector
   b. ST connector
   c. TOSLINK
   d. 8P8C

7. You need to connect 802.11a, 802.11b, and 802.11n wireless networks together. What wireless tool will guarantee you connectivity between these networks?
   a. Wireless network adapter
   b. Wireless hub
   c. Wireless router
   d. Wireless bridge

8. Your boss has asked you to connect three new laptops to the wireless network "WLAN42." It runs at a speed of 54 Mbps only and a frequency of 2.4 GHz only. What IEEE 802.11 standard should you implement when connecting the laptops to the WAP?
   a. 802.11a
   b. 802.11b
   c. 802.11g
   d. 802.11n

9. You need to connect a desktop computer to a WLAN using the strongest encryption type possible. Of the following choices, which is the strongest?
   a. WEP
   b. RADIUS
   c. WPA2
   d. WPA

10. You have connected thirteen PCs and laptops to a wireless network. To make your WLAN more secure, what should you do to disallow additional client access to the WAP?
    a. Enable channel bonding
    b. Enable frame aggregation
    c. Disable SSID broadcasting
    d. Disable WPA2

Fill in the Blank

Fill in the correct answer in the blank space provided.

1. The manager of IT asks you to connect a computer to an RJ45 jack. You should use a _____ cable to do so.

2. A twisted-pair cable was run 140 meters without any repeaters. Now, the signal cannot be picked up by the destination host. This cable is the victim of _____.

3. Your network uses category 3 cabling, but it needs to be upgraded so that it can support faster 100 Mbps applications. In this situation, _____ would be the minimum cable needed to accomplish this.

4. The type of cable known as _____ cable will protect the copper wires inside the cable from EMI.

5. Your boss complains about hearing a background conversation when he is talking on the phone. This is an example of _____.

6. You need to connect LANs in two buildings in a campus area network. The buildings are several kilometers apart. You would need _____ fiber optic cable to accomplish this.

7. Your boss doesn't know exactly how to do it, but he knows that he wants port-based authentication for his network. He is searching for a _____ implementation.

8. In order to connect to WLANs that are faster than 54 Gbps, you would need to utilize the IEEE _____ standard.

9. The _____ wireless encryption mode can be as strong as 256-bit.

10. A _____ is when two or more wireless clients communicate directly with each other, without the need for a WAP.

■ Case Scenarios

Scenario 3-1: Selecting Channels for a WLAN

Proseware, Inc. requires you to implement an infrastructure mode WLAN that will have three WAPs. How should these WAPs be configured so that there is no signal overlap between the three?

Scenario 3-2: Running Cable Drops Properly

The ABC Company requires you to run several cabling drops between patch panels and RJ45 jacks. What tools will you need to accomplish this task?

Scenario 3-3: Selecting Network Adapters for Your WLAN Computers

A company you are consulting for needs five new computers installed with wireless connections. Each of the wireless network adapters in the computers should be able to communicate at 300 Mbps. Which wireless Ethernet standard should you select, and what layer of the OSI model does this deal with?

Scenario 3-4: Secure the WLAN

Proseware, Inc. is keeping you busy. The company needs you to secure its wireless LAN. Name three things you can do to make the wireless LAN more secure.

✳ Workplace Ready

The 802.11n Explosion

The IEEE 802.11n standard took several years to be finalized, and it has been causing quite a stir since it was first ratified as a draft version. Aside from enabling speeds that approach gigabit wired connections, which are between six and twelve times the speed of earlier wireless standards, this standard is more secure and more efficient. Accordingly, many companies have jumped on the 802.11n bandwagon.

Access the Internet and look up the following wireless devices:

-**Cisco Aironet:** https://www.cisco.com/en/US/products/ps8382/index.html

-**HP ProCurve:**

http://www.procurve.com/products/wireless/420_series/overview.htm

-**bluesocket:** http://www.bluesocket.com/products

-**D-Link:** http://www.dlink.com/products/?pid=396

Compare these products and determine which would be the best for a network with 275 wireless users that need speed and a high level of security.

In your analysis, consider the total number of wireless connections allowed, IEEE 802.11 standards, encryption types, and ease of administration.

LESSON 4

Understanding Internet Protocol

OBJECTIVE DOMAIN MATRIX

SKILLS/CONCEPTS	MTA EXAM OBJECTIVE	MTA EXAM OBJECTIVE NUMBER
Working with IPv4	Understand IPv4.	3.2
Working with IPv6	Understand IPv6.	3.3

KEY TERMS

anycast address

Automatic Private IP Addressing (APIPA)

broadcast address

classful network architecture

classless inter-domain routing (CIDR)

default gateway

DNS server address

dual IP stack

dynamic IP address

global routing prefix

interface ID

IP conflict

IPv4

IPv4-mapped addresses

IPv6

IPv6 subnet

IPv6 tunneling

logical IP address

loopback IP address

masked

multicast address

multicasting

network address translation (NAT)

node

port address translation (PAT)

private IP addresses

public IP addresses

static IP address

subnetting

TCP/IP

truncated

unicast address

unmasked

variable-length subnet masking (VLSM)

As a network administrator, you will use the Transmission Control Protocol/Internet Protocol (*TCP/IP*) communications protocol suite most often. Most techs refer to this simply as Internet Protocol or IP. Although the newer IPv6 has many advantages over its predecessor, IPv4 is still used in the majority of local area networks. In this lesson, we will cover both. To truly be a master of IP networks, a network administrator must know how the different versions of IP work and how to configure, analyze, and test them in the GUI and in the command line. By utilizing knowledge about IP classes and reserved ranges, a well planned network can be implemented. And by taking advantage of technologies like network address translation and subnetting, a more efficient and secure network can be developed. Finally, by incorporating IPv6 whenever possible, you are opening the door to the future of data communications and enabling easier administration, bigger and more powerful data transmissions, and a more secure IP network.

To return to our ongoing example, say that Proseware, Inc., expects its network administrators to be able to set up a fully functional IPv4/IPv6 network. In this lesson, we will discuss how to enable computers on the LAN or the Internet to communicate through layer 3 IP addressing. By the end of the lesson, you will be able to configure advanced IP network connections on LANs, WANs, and the Internet.

■ Working with IPv4

THE BOTTOM LINE

Internet Protocol version 4 or *IPv4* is the most frequently used communications protocol. IP resides on the network layer of the OSI model, and IP addresses consist of four numbers, each between 0 and 255. The protocol suite is built into most operating systems and used by most Internet connections in the United States and many other countries. As mentioned in Lesson 1, it is composed of a network portion and a host portion, which are defined by the subnet mask. In order for an IP address to function, there must be a properly configured IP address and compatible subnet mask. To connect to the Internet, you will also need a gateway address and DNS server address. Advanced examples of IP configurations include subnetting, network address translation (NAT), and classless inter-domain routing (CIDR).

Categorizing IPv4 Addresses

CERTIFICATION READY
How do you categorize IPv4?
3.2

IPv4 addresses have been categorized into five IP classes. Some have been reserved for private use, whereas the rest are utilized by public connections. This classification system helps define what networks can be used on a LAN and what IP addresses can be used on the Internet.

The IPv4 classification system is known as the *classful network architecture* and is broken down into five sections, three of which are commonly used by hosts on networks—Classes A, B, and C. All five sections are displayed in Table 4-1. The first octet of the IP address defines which class the address is a member of.

Table 4-1

IPv4 classful network architecture

Class	IP Range (1st octet)	Default Subnet Mask	Network/Node Portions	Total Number of Networks	Total Number of Usable Addresses
A	0–127	255.0.0.0	Net.Node.Node.Node	2^7 or 128	$2^{24} - 2$ or 16,777,214
B	128–191	255.255.0.0	Net.Net.Node.Node	2^{14} or 16,384	$2^{16} - 2$ or 65,534
C	192–223	255.255.255.0	Net.Net.Net.Node	2^{21} or 2,097,151	$2^8 - 2$ or 254
D	224–239	N/A	N/A	N/A	N/A
E	240–255	N/A	N/A	N/A	N/A

Class A network addresses are used by the government, ISPs, big corporations, and large universities. Class B network addresses are used by mid-sized companies and smaller ISPs. Class C network addresses are used by small offices and home offices.

In the table, the term *node* is synonymous with "host." If an IP address is Class A, the first octet is considered to be the "network" portion. The other three octets are then the node or host portion of the address. So, a computer might be on the 11 network and have an individual host ID of 38.250.1, making the entire IP address 11.38.250.1. In looking at the table, you might also have noticed a pattern. In particular, Class B addresses use two octets as the network portion (e.g., 128.1). The other two octets are the host portion. Meanwhile, Class C addresses use the first three octets as the network portion (e.g., 192.168.1). Here, the last octet is the host portion.

There are several other notations we need to make to this table.

First, as shown, the range for Class A is 0–127. However, the 127 network number isn't used by hosts as a *logical IP address*. Instead, this network is used for *loopback IP addresses*, which allow for testing. For example, every computer that runs IPv4 is assigned a logical IP address such as 192.168.1.1. However, every computer is also automatically assigned the address 127.0.0.1, and any address on the 127 network (for example, 127.200.16.1) redirects to the local loopback. Therefore, this network number cannot be used when designing your logical IP network, but it can definitely be used to aid in testing.

Second, as you look at Table 4-1, note the default subnet masks for each class. Notice how they ascend in a corresponding fashion to the network/node portions. Memorize the default subnet masks for Class A, B, and C.

Third, be aware that the total number of usable addresses is always going to be two less than the mathematical amount. For example, in a Class C network such as 192.168.50.0, there are 256 mathematical values: the numbers including and between 0 and 255. However, the first and last addresses can't be used. The number 0 and the number 255 cannot be used as logical IP addresses for hosts because they are already utilized automatically. The 0 in the last octet of 192.168.50.0 defines a network number, not a single IP address, it is the entire network. And 192.168.50.255 is known as the *broadcast address*, which is used to communicate with all hosts on the network. So, because you can never use the first and last addresses, you are left with two fewer addresses—in this case, 254 usable IP addresses. This applies to bigger networks as well. For instance, a Class A network can use 16,777,214 addresses instead of 16,777,216. If we examine this more carefully, we will see that the number zero in binary equals 00000000 and the number 255 in binary is 11111111. Thus, we can't use the "all zeros" octet and the "all ones" octet. This rule applies to total hosts, but not to total networks within a particular class. We build on this concept in the subnetting section later in this lesson. One other related notion is the network 0, which generally isn't used but is listed in the table because it is technically considered part of Class A.

Next, Class D and Class E are not used by regular hosts. Therefore, they are not given a network/node classification, and as a result of that, they are not given a specific number of networks or total hosts they can utilize. Instead, Class D is used for what is known as *multicasting*—transmitting data to multiple computers (or routers). Class E was reserved for future use, but this has given way to IPv6 instead.

Finally, try to get into the habit of converting IP octets into their binary form. For example, the binary range of the first octet in Class A (0–127) is 00000000–01111111. For Class B, it is 10000000–10111111, and for Class C, it is 11000000–11011111. To practice doing this, you can use one of many decimal-to-binary conversion methods (such as the one shown in Table 4-2), or for now, you can use the scientific calculator in Windows by navigating to the **Run** prompt and typing **calc.exe**. Then click **View** on the calculator's menu bar and select **Scientific**. This will help you when it comes to more complex IP networks and when you attempt to create subnetworks. Keep in mind that computer certification exams might not allow use of a calculator.

Table 4-2

Decimal-to-binary conversion

CONVERSION AREA								DECIMAL EQUIVALENT
128	64	32	16	8	4	2	1	
1	1	1	0	0	0	0	0	224
1	0	1	0	1	0	1	0	170
0	1	0	1	0	1	0	1	85

Table 4-2 offers a simple method of converting from decimal to binary, or vice versa, with three examples. Try this on paper as well. Make a table that begins with a 1 in the upper right corner. Then, double the one, moving to the left each time as you do so, until you have eight place-holders that will act as column headers. These headers should be 1, 2, 4, 8, 16, 32, 64, and 128.

To convert a decimal number to binary, place the decimal number to the right or left of the table. For example, if the number is 224, check whether the placeholders can fit inside that number, starting with the placeholder on the left. Because 128 fits into 224, we place a binary 1 under the 128 column. Then, move to the right one step at a time. If we add 128 to 64, this equals 192, which also fits inside 224, so we place a binary 1 in that column as well. Next, we add 192 + 64 + 32, which equals 224. This fits (exactly) with the number we are trying to convert, so we place a binary 1 in the 32 column and leave the rest of the columns as zeroes. As a second example, the number 170, we see that 128 fits inside it, so we place a 1 in the first column. However, 128 + 64 = 192, which is larger than 170, so we place a zero in the second column. But we carry the 128 over, so next is 128 + 32, which equals 160. This fits inside 170, so we place a 1 in the third column, and so on. Keep going through the octet until the binary number is equal to the decimal number.

To convert a binary number to decimal, just place the binary octet from left to right under the placeholders. In the third example, using the number 85, we placed 01010101 under the placeholders. To convert, we just multiply down and add across. Or you could think of it as adding together all the placeholders that have ones in the column to get the final result. In the third example, ones inhabit the 64, 16, 4, and 1 columns; so, 64 + 16 + 4 + 1 = 85.

Again, this is an important skill for network administrators, and it is especially vital for networking certification exams. Try a few more of these conversions in both directions. Then, use the scientific calculator to check your work. By default, the calculator works in decimal, but you can simply type a number such as 5 and click the **Bin** radio button to make the conversion. The F8 key also activates this button. You will notice that leading zeroes (any on the left side) are omitted from final results. By the way, F6 will activate the **Dec** radio button.

 CONFIGURE CLASS A ADDRESSES

GET READY. In this exercise, you will configure two computers with Class A IP addresses, then verify the configuration through the use of ipconfig and ping. Pay close attention to the exact IP addresses you type and their corresponding subnet masks:

1. Access the Local Area Connection Properties dialog box.
2. Click **Internet Protocol Version 4**, then click the **Properties button**. This displays the Internet Protocol Version 4 Properties dialog box. Write down the current settings so that you can return the computer to these settings at the end of the exercise.
3. Click the **Use the following IP address** radio button. This enables the other fields so you can type in the IP information. Enter the following:
   - For the IP address of the first computer, enter **10.0.0.1**.
   - For the IP address of the second computer, enter **10.0.0.2**.
   - If necessary, configure the router to act as a host on this network (for example, using 10.0.0.3). Do this for subsequent exercises also, but only if the router gets in the way of the computers trying to ping each other.
   - For the Subnet mask of both computers, enter **255.0.0.0**.
   - Leave the Default gateway and the Preferred DNS server fields blank.
   - When you are finished, the first computer's configuration should look like Figure 4-1.
   - If you have other computers, try configuring their IP addresses as well; the host portion of the IP should ascend once for each computer: .3, .4, .5, and so on.

Figure 4-1

IPv4 properties using a Class A IP address

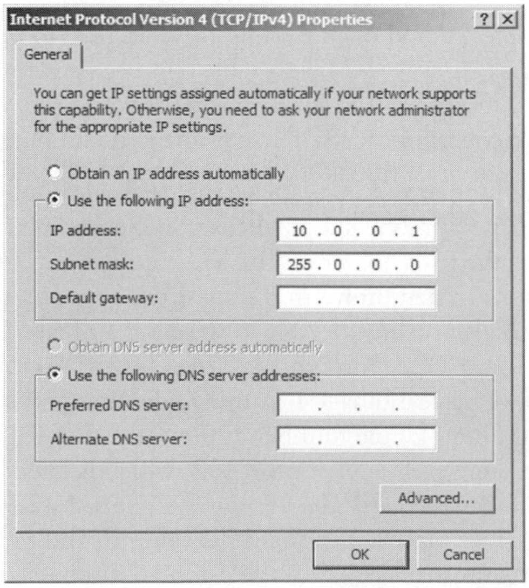

4. Click **OK**. Then, in the Local Area Connection Properties dialog box, click **OK**. This will complete and bind the configuration to the network adapter.
5. Now it's time to test your configuration. We will do this in two ways, first with the **ipconfig** command, and second with the **ping** command within the command prompt:
   a. Type ipconfig. Verify that the IP configuration is accurate and corresponds to what you typed in the IP Properties window. If not, go back and check your Internet Protocol Properties dialog box.

b. Ping the other computer. Also try to ping any other computers that were configured as part of this Class A network (for example, **ping 10.0.0.2**). Make sure you get replies. If you do not, check the IP configurations of both computers. Also make sure the computers are physically connected to the same network. In addition, as mentioned in previous exercises, verify that firewalls are disabled if necessary. Furthermore, it is important to avoid an *IP conflict*. IP conflicts occur when two computers are configured with the same IP address. If this happens, a small pop-up window at the lower right of your screen will alert you, as shown in Figure 4-2. When configuring computers statically as we are in this exercise, it is all too easy to become confused as to which computers have which IP addresses. Consider labeling every computer you work on with a different number; computer1, computer2, and so on. Use that number as the last octet of the computer's IP address in each exercise. This will help reduce your chances of an IP conflict.

Figure 4-2

IP conflict pop-up window

 CONFIGURE CLASS B ADDRESSES

GET READY. In this exercise, you will configure two computers with Class B IP addresses, then verify the configuration through the use of ipconfig and ping:

1. Access the Local Area Connection Properties dialog box.

2. Click **Internet Protocol Version 4**, then click the **Properties** button. This displays the Internet Protocol Version 4 Properties dialog box. Write down the current settings so that you can return the computer to these settings at the end of the exercise.

3. Click the **Use the following IP address** radio button. This enables the other fields so you can type in the IP information. Enter the following:

   • For the IP address of the first computer, enter **172.16.0.1**.

   • For the IP address of the second computer, enter **172.16.0.2**.

   • For the Subnet mask of both computers, enter **255.255.0.0**.

   • Leave the Default gateway and the Preferred DNS server fields blank.

   • When you are finished, the first computer's configuration should look like Figure 4-3.

   • If you have other computers, try configuring their IP addresses as well; the host portion of the IP should ascend once for each computer: .3, .4, .5, and so on.

Figure 4-3

IPv4 Properties dialog box using a Class B IP address

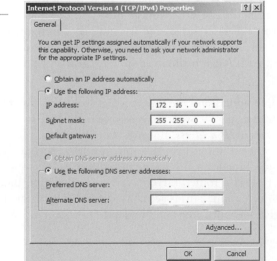

4. Click **OK**. Then, in the Local Area Connection Properties dialog box, click **OK**. This will complete and bind the configuration to the network adapter.

5. Now it's time to test your configuration. We will do this in two ways, first with the **ipconfig** command, and second with the **ping** command:

   a. Type **ipconfig**. Verify that the IP configuration is accurate and corresponds to what you typed in the IP Properties window. If not, go back and check your Internet Protocol Properties dialog box.

   b. Ping the other computer. Also try to ping any other computers that were configured as part of this Class B network (for example **ping 172.16.0.2**). Make sure you get replies. If you do not, check the IP configurations of both computers. Also make sure the computers are physically connected to the same network.

IPv4 addresses are further classified as either public or private. *Public IP addresses* are ones that are exposed to the Internet; any other computers on the Internet can potentially communicate with them. *Private IP addresses* are hidden from the Internet and any other networks. They are usually behind an IP proxy or firewall device. There are several ranges of private IP addresses that have been reserved by the IANA, as shown in Table 4-3. The majority of the other IPv4 addresses are considered public.

Table 4-3

Private IPv4 addresses as assigned by IANA

CLASS	START OF RANGE	END OF RANGE
A	10.0.0.0	10.255.255.255
B	172.16.0.0	172.31.255.255
C	192.168.0.0	192.168.255.255

The only private Class A network is 10. However, there are multiple Class B and C private networks. 172.16, 172.17, and so on through 172.31 are all valid private Class B networks. And 192.168.0, 192.168.1, 192.168.2, and so on all the way through 192.168.255 are all valid private Class C networks. Remember that for an address to be Class C, the first three octets must be part of the network portion; for Class B, the first and second octets; and for Class A, only the first octet.

Another type of private range was developed by Microsoft for use on small peer-to-peer Windows networks. It is called *APIPA*, which is an acronym for *Automatic Private IP Addressing*. It uses a single Class B network number: 169.254.0.0. If a Windows client cannot get an IP address from a DHCP server and has not been configured statically, it will auto-assign a number on this network. If, for some reason, APIPA assigns addresses even though a DHCP server exists, APIPA can be disabled in the registry. See the Microsoft Support site for details.

Although most people understand the difference, it would be wise to revisit the topic of static versus dynamic IP addresses. All of the exercises we have done in this lesson have been examples of setting up a *static IP address*. But most commonly, computers are set up to obtain an IP address (and other IP information) automatically. In this example of a *dynamic IP address*, the computer broadcasts out to the network in an attempt to find a DHCP server, whether it's a 4-port SOHO router, DHCP server, or other appliance. The server then replies with the required information. This is actually accomplished through a four-step process known as DORA that we will cover in more depth in Lesson 6, "Working with Networking Services."

CONFIGURE CLASS C PRIVATE ADDRESSES

GET READY. In this exercise you will configure two computers with Class C private IP addresses, then verify the configuration through the use of ipconfig and ping:

1. Access the Local Area Connection Properties dialog box.

2. Click **Internet Protocol Version 4**, then click the **Properties** button. This displays the Internet Protocol Version 4 Properties dialog box. Write down the current settings so that you can return the computer to these settings at the end of the exercise.

3. Click the **Use the following IP address** radio button. This enables the other fields so you can type in the IP information. Enter the following:

   • For the IP address of the first computer, enter **192.168.50.1**.

   • For the IP address of the second computer, enter **192.168.50.2**.

   • For the Subnet mask of both computers, enter **255.255.255.0**.

   • Leave the Default gateway and the Preferred DNS server fields blank.

   • When you are finished, the first computer's configuration should look like Figure 4-4.

   • If you have other computers, try configuring their IP addresses as well; the host portion of the IP should ascend once for each computer: .3, .4, .5, and so on.

4. Click **OK**. Then, in the Local Area Connection Properties dialog box, click **OK**. This will complete and bind the configuration to the network adapter.

5. Test your configuration. We will do this in two ways, first with the **ipconfig** command, and second with the **ping** command.

   a. Open the command prompt. Type ipconfig. Verify that the IP configuration is accurate and corresponds to what you typed in the IP Properties window. If not, go back and check your Internet Protocol Properties dialog box.

   b. Ping the other computer. Also try to ping any other computers that were configured as part of this Class C network (for example, **ping 192.168.50.2**). Make sure you get replies. If you do not, check the IP configurations of both computers. Also make sure both computers are physically connected to the same network.

Figure 4-4

IPv4 Properties dialog box using a Class C private IP address

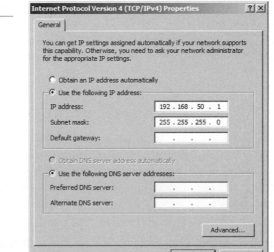

CERTIFICATION READY
How do you define gateways and DNS servers?
3.2

Default Gateways and DNS Servers

To complete our IP configuration, we need a default gateway address and a DNS server address. This will help our client computers access the Internet.

Up until now, we have only configured the IP address and Subnet mask fields of our IP Properties dialog box. To have a fully functional computer, however, we also need to configure two more fields.

The first such field is the *default gateway* field. The default gateway is the first IP address of the device that a client computer will look for when attempting to gain access outside the local network. This device could be a router, server, or other similar device; it is the device that grants access to the Internet or other networks. This device's address is on the same network number as the client. So, for example, if the client is 192.168.50.1, the gateway might be 192.168.50.100. Many gateway devices come preconfigured with their own LAN IP, but this is almost always configurable. For example, the D-Link DIR-655 we accessed in the previous lesson was configured as 192.168.0.1, but we could change that if we wanted to. Without a default gateway address configured within our local computer's IP Properties dialog box, we cannot gain access to any other networks. It is possible to have more than one gateway address in case the default gateway device fails. This can be done in Windows 7 by navigating to the Network Connections window, right clicking the network adapter in question (for example, Local Area Connection), selecting **Properties**, selecting **Internet Protocol Version 4**, and selecting the **Properties** button. In the Internet Protocol Version 4 Properties dialog box, click the **Advanced** button. Additional gateway addresses can be added to the Default gateways field.

The second field we need to configure is the *DNS server address*. The DNS server address is the IP address of the device or server that resolves DNS addresses to IP addresses. This could be a Windows Server or an all-in-one multifunction network device—it depends on the network environment. Also, it could be on the LAN (common in large networks) or located on the Internet (common in smaller networks). One example of a name resolution would be the domain name www.google.com, which currently resolves to the IP address 66.249.91.104. To demonstrate this, try typing this command in the command prompt: **ping www.google. com**. You should get results similar to "Reply from 66.249.91.104…". Google can change its IP address at any time, but the results should be similar. By the way, this is an example of a public IP address. The whole concept here is that computers ultimately communicate by IP address. However, it is easier for people to remember www.google.com than it is for them to remember an IP address. The DNS server resolves domain names like www.proseware.com, host names like server1.proseware.com, and so on. Without this DNS server address, a client computer will not be able to connect by name to any resource on the Internet. DNS servers are also necessary in Microsoft domain environments. If your computer is a member of such an environment and the DNS server address is not configured properly, domain resources will most likely be inaccessible.

 CONFIGURE CLASS C ADDRESSES, SUBNET MASKS, GATEWAY ADDRESS, AND DNS SERVER ADDRESS

GET READY. In this exercise, you will configure two computers with Class C private IP addresses, subnet masks, default gateways, and DNS server addresses. Then you will verify the configuration through the use of ipconfig and ping. Additional documentation will be required for steps 7 through 9:

1. Access the Local Area Connection Properties dialog box.
2. Click **Internet Protocol Version 4**, then click the **Properties** button. This displays the Internet Protocol Version 4 Properties dialog box. Write down the current settings so that you can return the computer to these settings at the end of the exercise.
3. Click the **Use the following IP address** radio button. This enables the other fields so you can type in the IP information. Enter the following:
   - For the IP address of the first computer, enter **192.168.50.1**.
   - For the IP address of the second computer, enter **192.168.50.2**.

- For the Subnet mask of both computers, enter **255.255.255.0**.
- For the Gateway address of both computers, enter **192.168.50.100**.
- Then, in the next field, enter a Preferred DNS server address of **192.168.50.201**. Do this for both computers as well.
- When you are finished, the first computer's configuration should look like Figure 4-5.
- If you have other computers, try configuring their IP addresses as well; the host portion of the IP should ascend once for each computer: .3, .4, .5, and so on.

Figure 4-5

IPv4 Properties dialog box using a Class C private IP address, subnet mask, default gateway, and DNS server address

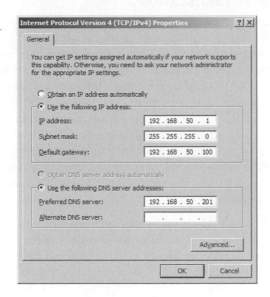

4. Click **OK**. Then, in the Local Area Connection Properties dialog box, click **OK**. This will complete and bind the configuration to the network adapter.

5. Now test your configuration. We will do this in two ways, first with the **ipconfig** command, and second with the **ping** command.

   a. Type **ipconfig**. Verify that the IP configuration is accurate and corresponds to what you typed in the IP Properties window. If not, go back and check your Internet Protocol Properties dialog box.

   b. Ping the other computer. Also try to ping any other computers that were configured as part of this Class C network (for example, ping **192.168.50.2**). Make sure you get replies. If you do not, check the IP configurations of both computers. Also make sure the computers are physically connected to the same network.

6. Now attempt to connect to the Internet. You should not be able to! This is the case because we used fictitious gateway and DNS server addresses. (I can't possibly know exactly what addresses you use on your network!) So . . . move on to step 7.

7. Get the following from your instructor or from other documentation:
   - At least two static IP addresses that you can use for your client computers that will be allowed access to the gateway.
   - The proper subnet mask, default gateway, and DNS server address that correspond with the static IPs.

8. Configure the computers with the new information and save the config.

9. Test the LAN connection with ping, and test the Internet connections by using a web browser to connect to a Web site. If either fails, check each address individually for any typos, IP conflicts, or other configuration mistakes.

Defining Advanced IPv4 Concepts

Methods such as network address translation, subnetting, and classless inter-domain routing (CIDR) can make networks faster, more efficient, and more secure. These advanced IP configurations are found in most networks today. Therefore, to be a proficient network engineer, you must master these concepts.

NETWORK ADDRESS TRANSLATION

Network address translation (NAT) is the process of modifying an IP address while it is in transit across a router, computer, or similar device. This is usually so one larger address space (private) can be re-mapped to another address space, or perhaps re-mapped to a single public IP address. This process is also known as IP masquerading, and it was originally implemented due to the problem of IPv4 address exhaustion. Today, NAT hides a person's private internal IP address, making it more secure. Some routers only allow for basic NAT, which carries out IP address translation only. However, more advanced routers allow for *port address translation (PAT)*, a subset of NAT, which translates both IP addresses and port numbers. A NAT implementation on a firewall hides an entire private network of IP addresses (e.g., the 192.168.50.0 network) behind a single publicly displayed IP address. Many SOHO routers, servers, and similar devices offer this technology to protect a company's computers on a LAN from outside intrusion.

Figure 4-6 illustrates how NAT might be implemented with some fictitious IP addresses. Here, the router has two network connections. One goes to the LAN—192.168.50.254—and is a private IP address. This is also known as an Ethernet address and is sometimes referred to as E^0 or the first Ethernet address. The other connection goes to the Internet or WAN—64.51.216.27—and is a public IP address. Sometimes, this will be referred to as S^0, which denotes a serial address (common to vendors such as Cisco). So, the router is employing NAT to protect all of the organization's computers (and switches) on the LAN from possible attacks initiated by mischievous persons on the Internet or in other locations outside the LAN.

Figure 4-6

NAT implementation

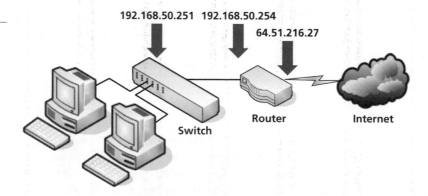

An example of a D-Link DIR-655 multifunction network device that implements NAT is shown in Figure 4-7. This screen capture displays the main Device Information page. Notice in the WAN section that there is a public IP address of 216.164.145.27. This is the WAN address, and this particular testing device obtains that address (and the subsequent WAN information) from an ISP's DHCP server. You will also note the LAN IP address of 10.254.254.1. That is the private IP address on the local side of the router. Accordingly, this device is translating for all computers on the 10.254.254.0 network and allowing them to communicate with the Internet, but it is only displaying one IP address to the Internet: 216.164.145.27.

Figure 4-7

NAT on a DIR-655 router

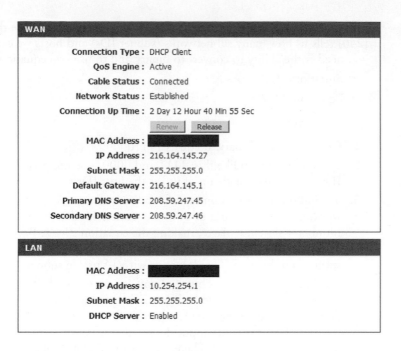

SUBNETTING

Subnetting could be considered one of the most difficult concepts in networking—but it can be simplified with some easy equations and a well-planned implementation process. Until now, we have used default subnet masks. However, one reason for having a subnet mask is to gain the ability to create subnetworks logically by IP. We must ask, what is a subnet? It is a subdivision of your logical IP network; by default, all computers are on one subnet or network with no divisions involved. And . . . what is a mask? It is any binary number that is a 1. If the binary digit is a 1, then it is ***masked***. If the binary digit is a 0, then it is ***unmasked***. Let's review the standard default subnet masks, as shown in Table 4-4.

Table 4-4

Standard subnet mask review

TYPE	DECIMAL	BINARY
Class A	255.0.0.0	11111111.00000000.00000000.00000000
Class B	255.255.0.0	11111111.11111111.00000000.00000000
Class C	255.255.255.0	11111111.11111111.11111111.00000000

Note the binary numbers that are 1s and the binary numbers that are 0s in the table. ***Subnetting*** is the act of dividing a network into smaller logical subnetworks. It is accomplished by transforming the default subnet mask into something else by borrowing bits. One or more of the 0s in the subnet masks in Table 4-4 will become masked, thus changing the amount of subnets and hosts per subnet. Network administrators implement subnetting in an effort to organize and compartmentalize networks, reduce broadcast traffic, and increase network security. By default, computers in one subnet cannot communicate with computers on another subnet, even if they are part of the same total IP network.

For the upcoming exercise, we will use a Class C network and show how we can subdivide it into smaller subnetworks. We will use 192.168.50.0 for our network number. By default, the subnet mask would be 255.255.255.0. But what if we wanted to divide the network into four distinct IP subnetworks?

There are a lot of different subnetting options, but as one example, we could use 255.255.255.*240*. This would also be known as 192.168.1.0 /28 because the binary equivalent of the subnet mask has 28 masked bits and 4 unmasked bits.

The first three 255s are the same, and we can pretty much ignore them, but the fourth octet (240) tells us how many subnetworks (subnet IDs) and hosts we can have per subnetwork. All you need is the ability to convert to binary and to use two equations:

- Equation #1: $2^n = x$
- Equation #2: $2^n - 2 = x$

Here's how you do it:

1. Convert 240 to binary. It equals 11110000.
2. Break the octet up like this: 1111 and 0000. Use the part made up of 1s for the subnet IDs and the part made up of 0s for the host IDs.
3. To find out the total number of subdivisions (or subnet IDs) you can have in your network, input the amount of 1s into equation #1. There are four 1s in 11110000, so the number 4 should replace n, making the equation $2^4 = x$. Because $2^4 = 16$, this means the maximum number of subnets is 16. However, it is recommended that the first and last subnets not be used. That leaves us with 14 usable subnets.
4. But (and there's always a but . . .) you can never use the first and the last IP address for a host ID. "All Ones" and "All Zeros" cannot be used as they are for identifying the subnetwork and for doing broadcasting. To find out the total number of hosts *per subnet* you can use in your network input the number of 0s into equation #2. There just happen to be four 0s in 11110000. Therefore, the number 4 should replace n, making the equation $2^4 - 2 = x$. Because $2^4 - 2 = 14$, the maximum number of hosts per subnet is 14.

So we now have 14 possible subnets and 14 possible hosts per subnet. That gives us a total of 196 usable hosts on our entire network. Although you lose out on total hosts when you subnet, it should work fine for our original plan of having four subnetworks. Table 4-5 shows all of the subnets and hosts that are possible for this particular scenario.

Table 4-5

Possible subnets and hosts in the 192.168.50.0/28 subnetworking scenario

Subnet ID#	Subnet ID Binary Equivalent	Host IP Range in Binary	Host IP in Decimal
0	0000	0000–1111	0–15 (not recommended)
1	0001	0000–1111	16–31
2	0010	0000–1111	32–47
3	0011	0000–1111	48–63
4	0100	0000–1111	64–79
5	0101	0000–1111	80–95
6	0110	0000–1111	96–111
7	0111	0000–1111	112–127
8	1000	0000–1111	128–143
9	1001	0000–1111	144–159
10	1010	0000–1111	160–175
11	1011	0000–1111	176–191
12	1100	0000–1111	192–207
13	1101	0000–1111	208–223
14	1110	0000–1111	224–239
15	1111	0000–1111	240–255 (not recommended)

As you can see, there are 16 values in each subnet host range, but you can't use the first and last because they are all 0s and all 1s, respectively. So for example, in Subnet ID #1, the 16 and the 31 are unavailable; 16 is the actual subnet ID, and 31 is the broadcast address for that subnet. The usable IP addresses in that subnet are 17–30. In subnet ID #2, 32 and 47 are unavailable; therefore, the usable range is 33–46. Keep in mind that computers in different subnets cannot communicate with each other by default. So, the IP address 192.168.50.17 cannot communicate with 192.168.50.3,3 and vice versa. Another item of note is that most operating systems (including Windows) either discourage, or flat out don't allow, use of the first and last subnet IDs. This is to avoid confusion with the main network number (prior to subnetting) and the broadcasting segment.

That was a lot of information. So, the best way to really explain the subnetting process is to do it.

 SUBNET A NETWORK

GET READY. Let's create a working subnet. Use the following information to create your working subnetwork:

- Network: 192.168.50.0
- Subnet mask: 255.255.255.240
- Subnet ID to be used: ID 7

1. Go to the first computer (we will call this computer1).
2. Disable any secondary network adapters. Make sure only one adapter is enabled; this is the one you will use for the exercise.
3. Access the IP Properties window of computer1 and change the IP settings to reflect the supplied subnet information. If you look back at Table 4-5, you will notice that subnet ID 7 dictates that you can use IP addresses between 192.168.50.112 and 192.168.50.127. However, remember the "golden rule": You cannot use the first and last addresses. This means you are left with just 113–126. You can use any of these IPs as long as no two computers get the *same* IP address. For the purposes of simplicity, we chose the first valid IP for computer1, as shown in Figure 4-8. No gateway address or subnet mask is necessary.

Figure 4-8

IP properties of computer1

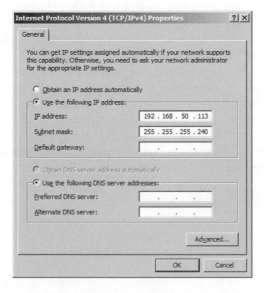

4. Click **OK** for both windows.
5. Go to a second computer; we will call this computer2.

6. Disable any secondary network adapters. Make sure only one adapter is enabled; this is the one you will use for the exercise.

7. Access the IP Properties window of computer2 and change the IP settings to reflect the supplied subnet information. This time select 192.168.50.114. Again, no gateway address or subnet mask is necessary.

8. Click **OK** for both windows.

9. Return to computer1 and open the command prompt.

10. Type **ipconfig/all** and verify that your settings are as they should be.

11. Now type **ping 192.168.50.114**. You should get replies! If not, recheck your configuration on both computers.

12. Now try pinging a host that is not within your network, such as 192.168.1.1. Type **ping 192.168.1.1**. It should not reply, and you should get either a transmit failed error or a message similar to "Destination host unreachable," depending on the OS used. Either way, the connection will fail because it is on a different network number. Even if a device does exist on that network number, it will not reply to you.

13. Now try pinging a host that is not within your subnet, such as 192.168.50.17. Type **ping 192.168.50.17**. It should not reply, and you should get a similar error message as in step 12. This is shown in Figure 4-9. This ping attempt failed because the host is on a different *subnet* and, by default, cannot communicate with computers on your subnet.

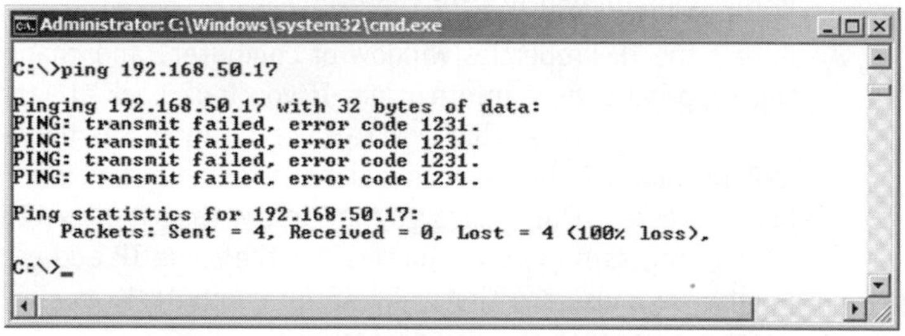

Figure 4-9

Failed ping from a computer on a subnet

```
Administrator: C:\Windows\system32\cmd.exe                        _ □ ×

C:\>ping 192.168.50.17

Pinging 192.168.50.17 with 32 bytes of data:
PING: transmit failed, error code 1231.
PING: transmit failed, error code 1231.
PING: transmit failed, error code 1231.
PING: transmit failed, error code 1231.

Ping statistics for 192.168.50.17:
    Packets: Sent = 4, Received = 0, Lost = 4 (100% loss),

C:\>_
```

You now have a working subnet that compartmentalizes the two computers from the other subnets on the network. Network engineers create subnets to compartmentalize networks. This could be to decrease broadcasts, increase data throughput, add security, limit access, and use IP addresses more wisely. There are many other examples of subnetting, and there are other kinds of subnet masks you can use beyond subnet mask 255.255.255.240. For example, 255.255.255.224 gives you the ability to have eight subnets (recommended six usable) and thirty usable IP addresses per subnet. You can also create subnets within Class A networks and Class B networks as well. Tables 4-6 through 4-8 show all of the possibilities when it comes to subnetting within any of the three IP classes. These tables take into account the fact that most OS and IOS (internetwork operating system) manufacturers will recommend not using the first or last subnet for any given subnetting scheme.

Table 4-6

Class A subnetting matrix

NetID	SubnetID	HostID	Mask		# of Usable Subnets	# of Hosts per
8	0	24	255.0.0.0	/8	N/A	16,777,14
8	1	23	255.128.0.0	/9	N/A	N/A
8	2	22	255.192.0.0	/10	2	4,194,302
8	3	21	255.224.0.0	/11	6	2,097,150
8	4	20	255.240.0.0	/12	14	1,048,574
8	5	19	255.248.0.0	/13	30	524,286
8	6	18	255.252.0.0	/14	62	262,142
8	7	17	255.254.0.0	/15	126	131,070
8	8	16	255.255.0.0	/16	254	65,534
8	9	15	255.255.128.0	/17	510	32,766
8	10	14	255.255.192.0	/18	1,022	16,382
8	11	13	255.255.224.0	/19	2,046	8,190
8	12	12	255.255.240.0	/20	4,094	4,094
8	13	11	255.255.248.0	/21	8,190	2,046
8	14	10	255.255.252.0	/22	16,382	1,022
8	15	9	255.255.254.0	/23	32,766	510
8	16	8	255.255.255.0	/24	65,534	254
8	17	7	255.255.255.128	/25	131,070	126
8	18	6	255.255.255.192	/26	262,142	62
8	19	5	255.255.255.224	/27	524,286	30
8	20	4	255.255.255.240	/28	1,048,574	14
8	21	3	255.255.255.248	/29	2,097,150	6
8	22	2	255.255.255.252	/30	4,194,302	2
8	23	1	255.255.255.254	/31	N/A	N/A
8	24	0	255.255.255.255	/32	N/A	N/A

Table 4-7

Class B subnetting matrix

NetID	SubnetID	HostID	Mask		# of Usable Subnets	# of Hosts per
16	0	16	255.255.0.0	/16	N/A	65,534
16	1	15	255.255.128.0	/17	N/A	N/A
16	2	14	255.255.192.0	/18	2	16,382
16	3	13	255.255.224.0	/19	6	8,190
16	4	12	255.255.240.0	/20	14	4,094
16	5	11	255.255.248.0	/21	30	2,046
16	6	10	255.255.252.0	/22	62	1,022
16	7	9	255.255.254.0	/23	126	510
16	8	8	255.255.255.0	/24	254	254
16	9	7	255.255.255.128	/25	510	126
16	10	6	255.255.255.192	/26	1,022	62
16	11	5	255.255.255.224	/27	2,046	30
16	12	4	255.255.255.240	/28	4,094	14
16	13	3	255.255.255.248	/29	8,190	6
16	14	2	255.255.255.252	/30	16,382	2
16	15	1	255.255.255.254	/31	N/A	N/A
16	16	0	255.255.255.255	/32	N/A	N/A

Table 4-8

Class C subnetting matrix

NetID	SubnetID	HostID	Mask		# of Usable Subnets	# of Hosts per
24	0	8	255.255.255.0	/24	N/A	254
24	1	7	255.255.255.128	/25	N/A	N/A
24	2	6	255.255.255.192	/26	2	62
24	3	5	255.255.255.224	/27	6	30
24	4	4	255.255.255.240	/28	14	14
24	5	3	255.255.255.248	/29	30	6
24	6	2	255.255.255.252	/30	62	2
24	7	1	255.255.255.254	/31	N/A	N/A
24	8	0	255.255.255.255	/32	N/A	N/A

Defining Classless Inter-Domain Routing (CIDR)

Classless inter-domain routing (CIDR) is a way of allocating IP addresses and routing Internet Protocol packets. It was intended to replace the prior classful IP addressing architecture in an attempt to slow the exhaustion of IPv4 addresses. Classless inter-domain routing is based on *variable-length subnet masking (VLSM)*, which allows a network to be divided into different-sized subnets to make one IP network that would have previously been considered a class (such as Class A) look like Class B or Class C. This can help network administrators efficiently use subnets without wasting IP addresses.

One example of CIDR would be the IP network number 192.168.0.0/16. The /16 means that the subnet mask has 16 masked bits (or 1s) making 255.255.0.0. Usually, that would be a default Class B subnet mask, but because we are using it in conjunction with what used to be a Class C network number, the whole kit and caboodle becomes classless.

 CONFIGURE A CIDR-BASED IP NETWORK

GET READY. In this exercise, you will configure two computers with classless private IP addresses, then verify the configuration through the use of ipconfig and ping. In this particular exercise, the IP network (10.254.254.0), which would have previously appeared to be a Class A network, will use a Class C subnet mask. This effectively makes it classless:

1. Access the Local Area Connection Properties dialog box.

2. Click **Internet Protocol Version 4**, then click the **Properties** button. This displays the Internet Protocol Version 4 Properties dialog box. Write down the current settings so that you can return the computer to these settings at the end of the exercise.

3. Click the **Use the following IP address** radio button. This enables the other fields so you can type in the IP information. Enter the following:

   • For the IP address of the first computer, enter **10.254.254.115**.

   • For the IP address of the second computer, enter **10.254.254.116**.

   • For the Subnet mask of both computers, enter **255.255.255.0**. This would be written out as 10.254.254.0/24, signifying that we are creating a classless 10.254.254.0 network with a subnet mask that has 24 masked bits.

   • Leave the Default gateway and the Preferred DNS server fields blank.

   • When you are finished, the first computer's configuration should look like Figure 4-10.

Figure 4-10

IPv4 Properties dialog box configured with a classless IP address

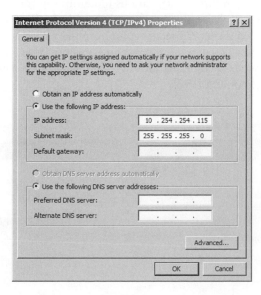

4. Click **OK**. Then, in the Local Area Connection Properties dialog box, click **OK**. This will complete and bind the configuration to the network adapter.

5. Now test your configuration. We will do this in two ways, first with the **ipconfig** command, and second with the **ping** command.

   a. Type **ipconfig**. Verify that the IP configuration is accurate and corresponds to what you typed in the IP Properties window. If not, go back and check your Internet Protocol Properties dialog box.

   b. Ping the other computer. Also try to ping any other computers that were configured as part of this classless network (for example, **ping 10.254.254.116**). Make sure you get replies. If you do not, check the IP configurations of both computers, watch for IP conflicts, and make sure the computers are physically connected to the same network.

■ Working with IPv6

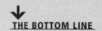

THE BOTTOM LINE

IPv6 is the new generation of IP addressing for the Internet, but it can also be used in small office networks and home networks. It was designed to overcome the limitations of IPv4, including address space and security.

Understanding IPv6

CERTIFICATION READY
How do you define IPv6?
3.3

Before you can configure IPv6, you first need to understand a few concepts, some of which are similar to IPv4, but others of which are quite different. In this section, we will categorize the types of IPv6 addresses and specifically explain why IPv6 is to be the *successor* to IPv4. (Remember, IPv4 is still the dominant IP protocol in today's world.)

IPv6 has been defined for over a decade, and it has slowly been gaining acceptance in the networking world, although it is still considered in its infancy. The number-one reason to use IPv6 is address space. IPv6 is a 128-bit system, whereas its still-dominant predecessor IPv4 is only a 32-bit system. What does this mean? Well, whereas IPv4 can have approximately 4 billion IP addresses in the whole system, IPv6 can have 340 undecillion addresses. That's 340 with 36 zeroes after it! Of course, various limitations in the system will reduce that number, but the final result is still far greater than with the IPv4 system. Yet another reason to use IPv6 is advanced integrated security; for example, IPSec is a fundamental component of IPv6 (we will discuss IPSec in more depth in Lesson 6). IPv6 also has many advancements and simplifications when it comes to address assignment. Table 4-9 summarizes some of the differences between IPv4 and IPv6.

Table 4-9

IPv4 versus IPv6

IPv4		IPv6	
32-bit	4 billion addresses	128-bit	340 undecillion addresses
Less security in general		More security, IPsec is mandatory	
n/a		Simplification of address assignment	

IPv6 also supports jumbograms. These are much larger packets than IPv4 can handle. IPv4 packets are normally around 1,500 bytes in size, but they can go as large as 65,535 bytes. In comparison, IPv6 packets can optionally be as big as approximately 4 billion bytes.

We mentioned already that IPv6 addresses are 128-bit numbers. They are also hexadecimal in format and divided into eight groups of four numbers each, with each group separated by a colon. These colon separators contrast with IPv4's dot-decimal notation. In Windows, IPv6 addresses are automatically assigned and auto-configured, and they are known as link local addresses. There are three main types of IPv6 addresses:

- *Unicast address:* This is a single address on a single interface. There are two types of unicast addresses. The first, global unicast addresses, are routable and displayed directly to the Internet. These addresses start at the 2000 range. The other type is the aforementioned link local address. These are further broken down into two subtypes, the Windows auto-configured address, which starts at either FE80, FE90, FEA0 and FEB0, and the loopback address, which is known as ::1, where ::1 is the equivalent of IPv4's 127.0.0.1.

- *Anycast address:* These are addresses assigned to a group of interfaces, most likely on separate hosts. Packets that are sent to these addresses are delivered to only one of the interfaces—generally, the first one, or closest, available. These addresses are used in failover systems.

- *Multicast address:* These addresses are also assigned to a group of interfaces and are also most likely on separate hosts, but packets sent to such an address are delivered to all of the interfaces in the group. This is similar to IPv4 broadcast addresses (such as 192.168.1.255). Multicast addresses do not suffer from broadcast storms the way their IPv4 counterparts do.

Table 4-10 summarizes these three types of addresses.

Table 4-10

IPv6 address types

IPv6 Type	Address Range	Purpose
Unicast	Global Unicast starts at 2000 Link-local ::1 and FE80::/10	Address assigned to one interface of one host. ::/10 means that addresses starting with FE80, FE90, FEA0, and FEB0 are part of the range. These are assigned by the IANA, and this range has many more addresses than the entire IPv4 system.
Anycast	Structured like unicast addresses	Address assigned to a group of interfaces on multiple nodes. Packets are delivered to the "first" or "closest" interface only.
Multicast	FF00::/8	Address assigned to a group of interfaces on multiple nodes. Packets are delivered to all interfaces.

Here is an example of a global unicast address that used to be one of Google's public IPv6 addresses: **2001:4860:0000:2001:0000:0000:0000:0068**. This address once corresponded to the Google Web site: ipv6.google.com. However, as of the writing of this book, Google is using a new address (that we will ping later), and that address could easily change again in the future.

IPv6 addresses are broken down into three parts:

- *Global routing prefix:* This is the first three groups of numbers, and it defines the "network" of the address.

- **IPv6 subnet:** This defines the individual subnet of the network that the address is located on.
- **Interface ID:** This is the individual host IP portion. It can be assigned to one interface or more than one interface, depending on the type of IPv6 address.

Table 4-11 breaks down an example of an IPv6 address.

Table 4-11

Global unicast address break-down

GLOBAL ROUTING PREFIX	SUBNET	INTERFACE ID
2001:4860:0000	2001	0000:0000:0000:0068

An IPv6 address can be abbreviated or *truncated* by removing unnecessary and/or leading 0s. For example, the address in Table 4-11 can be truncated in the following manner:

- **Original IP:**   2001:4860:0000:2001:0000:0000:0000:0068
- **Truncated IP:**   2001:4860:0:2001::68

Notice that the first group of 0s has been changed from **0000** to just **0**. In hexadecimal (just like in any other numbering system), 0 is 0. So, the leading 0s can be removed, and this can be done within an individual group of four 0s as many times as necessary in one IPv6 address. Also, multiple groups of consecutive 0s can be abbreviated to a double colon. So, **0000:0000:0000:0068** is abbreviated to **::68**. However, this can only be done once in an IPv6 address.

Here is an example of an abbreviated link-local unicast address that was auto-assigned by Windows: **fe80::260:8ff:fec0:98d%4**. Notice that it starts with FE80, defining it as a link-local address. The % sign specifies interface index of the interface that traffic is sent from. Sometimes, this is a tunneling interface that corresponds to an IPv4 address.

Packet structure works pretty much the same way in IPv6 as it does in IPv4. An IPv6 packet is broken down into three parts:

- **Header:** This is also known as a fixed header. This is 40 bytes and contains the source and destination addresses plus other forwarding information. Because IPv6 addresses have more characters (and are therefore bigger) than IPv4 addresses, a larger fixed header is necessary. However, due to the maximum size available for an IPv6 packet (jumbograms), the percentage of total overhead can actually be less in an IPv6 packet. Even without jumbograms, the increase in header size is negligible.
- **Optional extension header:** This incorporates options for special treatment of the packet, such as routing and security.
- **Payload:** By default, this is 64 KB maximum, just like IPV4 packets. But again, this can be increased much further if jumbograms are used.

Now, let's run through some IPv6 exercises.

Configuring IPv6

CERTIFICATION READY
How do you configure IPv6?
3.3

Configuring IPv6 is in some ways easier than configuring IPv4 and in other ways more difficult. For example, installation of the IPv6 protocol is quite painless, but configuration of a static IPv6 address can be trickier given the length and complexity of an IPv6 address. In general, though, IPv6 is designed to be easier to work with once you learn the basics.

 INSTALL, CONFIGURE, AND TEST IPv6

GET READY. In the following exercises, we will install IPv6, work with auto-configured addresses, add static addresses, and test our connections. This lab will function better if

Windows 7 or Vista client computers are used. Different Windows operating systems may require slightly different navigation to the various dialog boxes described below:

1. Install TCP/IPv6. This might be installed on your computer already. Otherwise, you can install it by accessing the Local Area Connections Properties dialog box. If it is already installed, uninstall it by highlighting it and selecting the **Uninstall** button. Then select **Install** and **Protocol**. Select the IPv6 protocol. You can also download IPv6 from the Internet, if an older Windows operating system does not support it out-of-the-box. Once IPv6 is installed, your screen should look similar to Figure 4-11.

Figure 4-11

TCP/IPv6 on a Windows computer

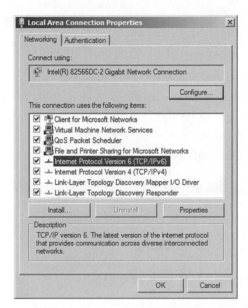

2. Modify the main network adapter's name. Find your main network adapter; it will probably be called **Local Area Connection**. Rename it **LAN**. This will simplify the syntax we will be using later and make it easier to find the network adapter when running ipconfig/all commands, especially if you have more than one adapter.

3. View the auto-assigned address. Windows automatically assigns an IPv6 address, similar to how APIPA works. This address starts with FE80 (usually). Let's take a look at the new address by opening the command prompt and typing **ipconfig/all**. The results should be similar to Figure 4-12's Link-local IPv6 Address entry. Be sure to locate your primary network adapter.

Figure 4-12

TCP/IPv6 address with ipconfig/all

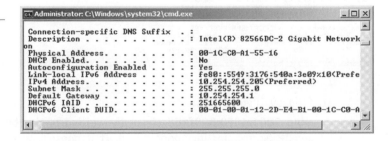

4. Ping the local loopback address. This can be done by typing **ping::1**. The results should look similar to Figure 4-13. If you do not get replies, verify that IPv6 is installed. You can also try **ping −6::1** if it appears that IPv4 results are getting in the way.

Figure 4-13

Testing the IPv6 loopback address with ping

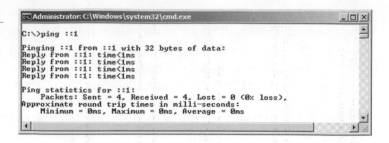

5. Ping another computer on the network that is also running IPv6. Do so by pinging its IPv6 link-local address. For example:

   a. Ping by IPv6 address:

      Example: **Ping fe80::5549:3176:540a:3e09%10**

      The exact IP address will be different depending on what computer you ping. Your results should look similar to Figure 4-14.

   b. Ping by host name:

      Example: **ping computer1**

Figure 4-14

Testing another computer's IPv6 link-local address with ping

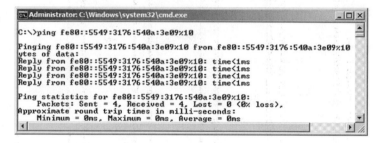

6. Attempt to ping an IPv6 host on the Internet. Results will vary depending on your network configuration and other factors:

   a. Ping by domain name:
      ping −6 ipv6.google.com. Your results should look similar to Figure 4-15.

Figure 4-15

Pinging ipv6.google.com

   b. Ping by IPv6 address:

      ping 2001:4860:800f::68. As of the writing of this book, this is the corresponding IP address for ipv6.google.com. If it doesn't work, simply look at your results from step 6a. The correct IPv6 address should be listed on the first line. Notice the extent to which this address is truncated. Your results should look similar to Figure 4-16.

Figure 4-16

Pinging ipv6.google.com using an IPv6 address

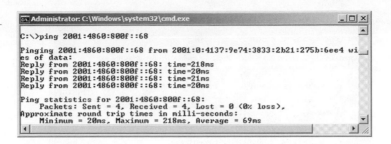

7. Configure a global unicast address in the GUI:

a. This can be done in the Internet Protocol Version 6 Properties dialog box. Just click **Internet Protocol Version 6** and select **Properties** in the Local Area Connection Properties dialog box (which should now be the **lan** Properties dialog box).

b. Click the **Use the following IPv6 address:** radio button. This will enable the IPv6 configuration fields.

c. Enter an address such as:

2001:ab1:442e:1323::1

The address can be on any network of your choosing. If the number is not valid, Windows will inform you when you attempt to go to the next field.

d. Enter an address that is one higher for the second computer, for example:

2001:ab1:442e:1323::2

e. Ascend from there for each additional computer.

f. For the subnet prefix length, either tab through or enter **64**. That is the default length; if you tab through, it will be entered automatically.

g. For the default gateway on all computers, enter:

2001:ab1:442e:1323::9

This is just an example. If you are using a different network, just make sure your gateway address is on the same network but uses a different host number (in this case, the last octet). If you have specific network documentation with a real IPv6 gateway address, utilize it!

h. For the preferred DNS server on all computers, enter:

2001:ab1:442e:1323::8

This is just an example. If you have specific network documentation with a real IPv6 gateway address, utilize it! The DNS server could even be on a different network—it all depends on the network configuration.

Your configuration should look similar to Figure 4-17.

8. Click **OK** for the IPv6 Properties dialog box.

9. Click **Close** for the lan Properties dialog box. That should bind the information to the network adapter.

10. Verify the configuration in the command prompt with **ipconfig/all**. Your results should be similar to Figure 4-18. The address you just added should show up in the **IPv6 Address** field. This is usually just above the **Link-local IPv6 Address** field. Also check for the IPv6 gateway and DNS server addresses.

Figure 4-17

IPv6 GUI configuration

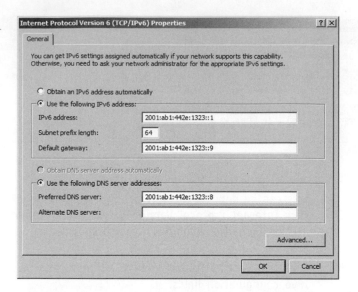

Figure 4-18

Ipconfig/all results of added IPv6 address

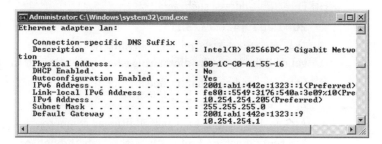

11. Verify connectivity to another IPv6 host. For example, this can be done by typing the following command in the command prompt:

    ping –6 2001:ab1:442e:1323::2

    You should get replies. If not, check the configuration of both computers.

12. Configure a global unicast address in the command prompt. For this exercise, we will use the Net Shell command, which is **netsh**. Netsh is a tool that administrators can use to configure and monitor Windows computers from the command prompt. This is a complex command with lots of variables. It is commonly used to configure TCP/IP and other networking functions. Add the following example:

    netsh interface ipv6 add address interface=lan address=2001:ab1:442e:1323::7

    You should get a simple OK as a result. If there are other computers you would like to configure with the netsh command, make sure they all get separate host IDs.

13. Check that the new address has been added with **ipconfig/all**.

14. Verify connectivity to other computers with ping.

15. Delete the address you just added with the netsh command. Use the following syntax:

    **netsh interface ipv6 delete address interface=lan address=2001:
    ab1:442e:1323::7**

    If you have any issues deleting the address, try using a nontruncated number. The equivalent for this address would be:

    2001:0ab1:442e:1323:0000:0000:0000:0007

16. Reset the GUI IPv6 Properties dialog box by selecting **Obtain an IPv6 address automatically**. If you wish, run an ipconfig to find out your auto-assigned address and another computer's address. Try pinging those addresses as well.

Lots more information about configuring IPv6 can be found at the Microsoft TechNet.

DEFINING THE DUAL IP STACK

A *dual IP stack* exists when there are two Internet Protocol software implementations in an operating system, one for IPv4 and another for IPv6. Dual stack IP hosts can run IPv4 and IPv6 independently, or they can use a hybrid implementation, which is the most commonly used method for modern operating systems.

Dual stack TCP/IP implementations enable programmers to write networking code that works transparently on IPv4 or IPv6. The software can use hybrid sockets designed to accept both IPv4 and IPv6 packets. When used in IPv4 communications, hybrid stacks use IPv6 methodologies but represent IPv4 addresses in a special IPv6 address format known as the IPv4-mapped address.

IPv4-mapped addresses have the first 80 bits set to 0 (note the double colon), the next 16 set to 1 (shown as ffff), and the last 32 bits populated by the IPv4 address. These addresses look like IPv6 addresses, other than the last 32 bits, which are written in the customary dot-decimal notation. Here is an example:

::ffff:10.254.254.1

This is an IPv4-mapped IPv6 address for the IPv4 address **10.254.254.1**.

DEFINING IPv4 TO IPv6 TUNNELING

IPv6 packets can be encapsulated inside IPv4 datagrams. This is known as *IPv6 tunneling*, or IP 6 to 4. In Microsoft operating systems, this is generally done with the Teredo adapter, which is a virtual adapter or "pseudo-interface," not a physical network adapter. This allows connectivity for IPv6 hosts that are behind an IPv4 device or IPv6 unaware device. It ensures backward compatibility. An example of one of these addresses would be:

Fe80::5efe:10.0.0.2%2

Notice that this is a link-local address and that the IPv4 address (10.0.0.2) is actually part of the whole IPv6 address. IPv6 tunneling requires little router configuration and no client computer configuration whatsoever, so it is fairly easy to implement, enabling IPv6 clients to interact with IPv6 servers on the Internet, even though the router is not IPv6 aware.

SKILL SUMMARY

IN THIS LESSON, YOU LEARNED:

- How to categorize IPv4 addresses using classifications such as Class A, B, and C.
- What the default gateway and DNS server are and how to configure them within a network adapter's TCP/IP properties dialog box.
- How to define advanced TCP/IP concepts, such as NAT and subnetting, and how to create a subnetted network.
- How to define CIDR.
- The basics of IPv6 and how to configure IPv6 in the command line.
- How to define IPv6 dual stack and tunneling technologies.

Knowledge Assessment

Multiple Choice

Circle the letter that corresponds to the best answer.

1. Your client requires that you install 284 computers on a single IP network. Which of the following IP classes would be your best option?
   a. Class A
   b. Class B
   c. Class C
   d. Class D

2. Your boss wants you to set up three computers on a classful network with a default sub-net mask of 255.0.0.0. What class does he want the computers to be set up on?
   a. Class A
   b. Class B
   c. Class C
   d. Class D

3. Proseware, Inc., needs you to set up 100 computers on a private Class A network. Which of the following IP network numbers meet all of the criteria for a private Class A net-work?
   a. 100.10.1.0
   b. 192.168.1.0
   c. 172.16.0.0
   d. 10.0.0.0

4. You need to subnet a 192.168.1.0 network. You decide to use the 255.255.255.240 sub-net mask. What is 240 equal to in binary?
   a. 11100000
   b. 11000000
   c. 11110000
   d. 10000000

5. The IT director has asked you to set up 14 separate IP networks that can each have up to 400 computers. What IANA private IP range should you select?
   a. 10.0.0.0–10.255.255.255
   b. 172.16.0.0–172.31.255.255
   c. 192.168.0.0–192.168.255.255
   d. 169.254.0.0–169.254.255.255

6. You are troubleshooting a computer that cannot obtain the proper IP address from a DHCP server. When you run an ipconfig/all, you see that the computer has obtained the address 169.254.67.110 automatically. What has occurred? (Select the best answer.)
   a. The DHCP server has auto-assigned an IP address to the computer.
   b. APIPA has auto-assigned an IP address to the computer.
   c. A SOHO router has auto-assigned an IP address to the computer.
   d. The ISP has auto-assigned an IP address to the computer.

7. You need to connect 802.11a, 802.11b, and 802.11n wireless networks together. What wireless tool will guarantee connectivity between these networks?
   a. Wireless network adapter
   b. Wireless hub
   c. Wireless router
   d. Wireless bridge

8. Your boss's computer cannot connect to the Internet. Examine the following ipconfig results and select the best answer explaining why this has occurred.

IPv4 Address .... : 10.254.254.1

Subnet Mask.. : 255.255.255.0

Default Gateway.. : 10.254.254.255

   a. The subnet mask is incorrect.
   b. The IP address is incorrect.
   c. The default gateway is incorrect.
   d. The subnet mask and the IP address are incorrect.

9. A user cannot connect to any Web sites. Review the ipconfig results that follow and select the best answer explaining why this has occurred.

Windows IP Configuration

     Host Name .... : Computer1

     Primary Dns Suffix.................................. :

     Node Type... : Hybrid

     IP Routing Enabled............................... : No

     WINS Proxy Enabled.............................. : No

Ethernet adapter lan:

     Connection-specific DNS Suffix.:

     Description.. : Intel(R)
       82566DC-2 Gigabit Network Connection

     Physical Address .... : 00-1C-C0-A1-55-16

     DHCP Enabled .... : No

     Autoconfiguration Enabled .... : Yes

     IPv4 Address .... : 10.254.254.105(Preferred)

     Subnet Mask... : 255.255.255.0

     Default Gateway................................... : 10.254.254.1

     DNS Servers... : 10.255.254.1

   a. The MAC address is incorrect.
   b. The DNS server address is incorrect.
   c. The default gateway address is incorrect.
   d. The computer has no IP address.

10. You have installed a device that has two IP addresses. One address, 64.51.216.27, is displayed to the Internet. The other address, 192.168.50.254, communicates with the LAN. What type of technology have you implemented?
   a. Subnetting
   b. IPv6
   c. Network address translation
   d. Class A public IP address

Fill in the Blank

Fill in the correct answer in the blank space provided.

1. The manager of IT asks you to subnet a group of computers on the 192.168.50.0/28 network. This will provide you with _____ number of subnets.

2. You have configured IP network 192.168.1.0 with the subnet mask 255.255.255.240. Two computers have the IP addresses 192.168.1.113 and 192.168.1.114. Another

computer cannot communicate with them. That computer is using the IP address 192.168.1.145. Here, the third computer cannot communicate with the others because it is on Subnet ID _____.

3. Your network uses the subnetted IP network 192.168.100.0/26. Its subnet mask is _____.

4. You are troubleshooting an IP network with the following number: 10.254.254.0/24. This type of IP network number is known as _____.

5. Your boss worries about how many IPv4 addresses are left and inquires about installing IPv6. Whereas IPv4 is a 32-bit system, IPv6 is a _____ -bit system.

6. A client wants you to set up a group of IPv6 network interfaces in such a way that each of them will have all packets delivered to them. Here, you should implement a _____ address.

7. You are troubleshooting a server that needs to connect directly to the Internet. After you run an ipconfig/all, you see that the server has been auto-assigned the IPv6 address fe80::260:8ff:fec0:98d%4. The server won't connect to the Internet due to the fact that this is a _____ address.

8. To save time when working with IPv6 addresses in the command line, you like to truncate them. The truncated version of 2001:4860:0000:2001:0000:0000:0000:0068 would be _____.

9. You see an IPv6 address displayed as fe80::5efe:10.0.0.2%2. This is an example of _____.

10. You are troubleshooting a client's network. The client is using the following IP network scheme:

   IP network: 192.168.50.0

   Subnet mask: 255.255.255.240

   The client has 196 computers that are functioning properly, but another 30 computers will not connect to the network. This is because _____.

■ Case Scenarios

Scenario 4-1: Defining a Private Class C IP Network

Proseware, Inc., requires that you implement a private Class C network for its 200 computers. What is the range of IP *networks* that you can select from?

Scenario 4-2: Specifying the Correct Device

The ABC Company wants to protect its LAN computers. The company would like a device that displays one public IP address to the Internet, yet allows all of the local clients with private IPs on the LAN to communicate out to the Internet. What kind of device does the company require, and what network technology should be implemented on that device?

Scenario 4-3: Implementing the Correct Class Network

A client wants you to design a single IP network that can support 84,576 computers. Complete Table 4-12 and state which IP class is the correct one to use.

Table 4-12

IPv4 class analysis

CLASS	IP RANGE (1ST OCTET)	DEFAULT SUBNET MASK	NETWORK/NODE PORTIONS	TOTAL NUMBER OF NETWORKS	TOTAL NUMBER OF USABLE ADDRESSES
A					
B					
C					
D	224–239	N/A	N/A	N/A	N/A
E	240–255	N/A	N/A	N/A	N/A

Scenario 4-4: Implementing the Correct Subnet Mask

Proseware, Inc., wants you to set up a Class C subnetting scheme that will allow for six sub-nets and thirty hosts per subnet. Complete Table 4-13 and state which subnet mask is the correct one to use and why.

Table 4-13

Class C subnetting analysis

SUBNET MASK	SUBNETS (RECOMMENDED USABLE)	HOSTS PER SUBNET	TOTAL HOSTS
255.255.255.192			
255.255.255.224			
255.255.255.240			
255.255.255.248			

✴ **Workplace Ready**

IPv6—Here, Yet Still Waiting

IPv6 has been defined since 1998, but it has yet to become the powerhouse that analysts predicted. Even though IPv6 involves advancements in packet structure, packet size, security, and of course, the number of addresses it can support, this technology is still in its "infancy."

Search the Internet and make a list of organizations, companies, and governmental bodies that already use IPv6. Now, describe how they use it. Is it internal only? Do they have servers that support IPv6 directly to the Internet, or do they have a sort of hybrid IPv4/Ipv6 network?

Next, search the Internet (and your local library if you have the time) for articles about IPv6. See what analysts have to say about it. Pool your knowledge, analyze it, and imagine a time frame for when IPv6 will become the dominant IP technology in use. Pick an approximate year when you think this will become a reality, and state your case to support your theory.

Implementing TCP/IP in the Command Line

OBJECTIVE DOMAIN MATRIX

SKILLS/CONCEPTS	MTA EXAM OBJECTIVE	MTA EXAM OBJECTIVE NUMBER
Using Basic TCP/IP Commands	Understand TCP/IP.	3.6
Working with Advanced TCP/IP Commands	Understand TCP/IP.	3.6

KEY TERMS

command prompt

elevated mode

FTP

ipconfig

nbtstat

net command

netsh

netstat

nslookup

open shortest path first (OSPF)

pathping

ping

route

Routing information protocol (RIP)

Telnet

tracert

universal naming convention

Proseware, Inc., doesn't tolerate delays. If there is an issue on the network, the network administrator needs to straighten it out as soon as possible. One way to work quickly and efficiently is to use the command-line interface (CLI) whenever necessary. It might seem counterintuitive, but typing commands in an effort to run network tests can be quicker than using the GUI. TCP/IP commands in particular, if used properly, can increase your speed and accuracy when analyzing network issues and troubleshooting. This lesson defines what you need to know in order to use basic and advanced TCP/IP commands in the Windows command prompt. This develops the important skills you will need as a network administrator.

■ Using Basic TCP/IP Commands

 THE BOTTOM LINE Ipconfig and ping are some of a network administrator's best friends. These basic TCP/IP commands can help you analyze and troubleshoot various networking issues that might occur. They also offer a certain amount of configurative ability, as well as the ability to create performance baselines. These commands are used in the Windows command prompt, a tool with which every network administrator should feel confident.

Working with the Command Prompt

In order to better understand how to work with TCP/IP in the command line, it is first necessary to discuss how to access the command prompt as an administrator. It is also important to explore some ways to make the command prompt work for you, as well as how to view help files.

The Windows *command prompt* is Microsoft's version of a command-line interface or CLI. Just about anything you can accomplish in the GUI can also be done in the command prompt— and when it comes to TCP/IP commands, command prompt can be more effective. Today's command prompt is the executable file cmd.exe. This is located in C:\Windows\system32. The older command.com is not recommended when working with TCP/IP commands.

Some of the commands you will be using in the lesson require administrative privileges. Some operating systems use User Account Control (UAC) to check that you are an administrator. Be sure to log in as an administrator of the computer in question before going through the exercises. If you are using a system with UAC enabled, open the command prompt as an administrator in one of the following ways:

- Click **Start > All Programs > Accessories;** then right click **Command Prompt** and select **Run as Administrator**.
- Click **Start** and type **cmd** in the search field, but instead of pressing Enter, press **Ctrl+Shift+Enter**.

Running the command prompt as an Administrator is also known as running it in *elevated mode*. Of course, you could turn off UAC, but that is not recommended.

Once opened, the command prompt should look similar to Figure 5-1. Notice in the title bar that the directory path is preceded by the word "Administrator." This is how you will know that the command prompt has been opened in elevated mode.

Figure 5-1

Windows command prompt

Open the command prompt now, and configure it as you wish, including size, colors, and so on.

→ **UNDERSTAND COMMAND PROMPT BASICS**

GET READY. You might be familiar with the command prompt or you might not. If you aren't, the command line in general can be daunting. But there are some tips and tricks to make the transition to the command line a bit easier. Let's explore some quick pointers about how to get around quickly using the command prompt:

1. Type the command **cd**.

   This should change the prompt to C:\>, without any additional folders. This can help when you are dealing with long lines of code, because the prompt will take up less space.

2. Type the command **cls**.

   This clears the command prompt screen and any history buffer. However, you can still bring up older commands that you previously typed by pressing the up (and down) arrow keys or by using F3, F5, or F7. The arrow keys can cycle back and forth though the history of commands. F3 only goes back one command, and F7 allows you to see a table of previously typed commands from which to select.

3. Try using the arrow keys and function keys to bring up previous commands.

4. Type the command **cls /?**.

   This displays the help file for the cls command, telling you that cls clears the screen. This is a basic help file; more complex commands will have more in-depth help files.

5. Type the command **dir /?**.

   This shows the help file for the directory command, as shown in Figure 5-2, which has much more content than the previous help file we displayed.

Figure 5-2

Dir help file

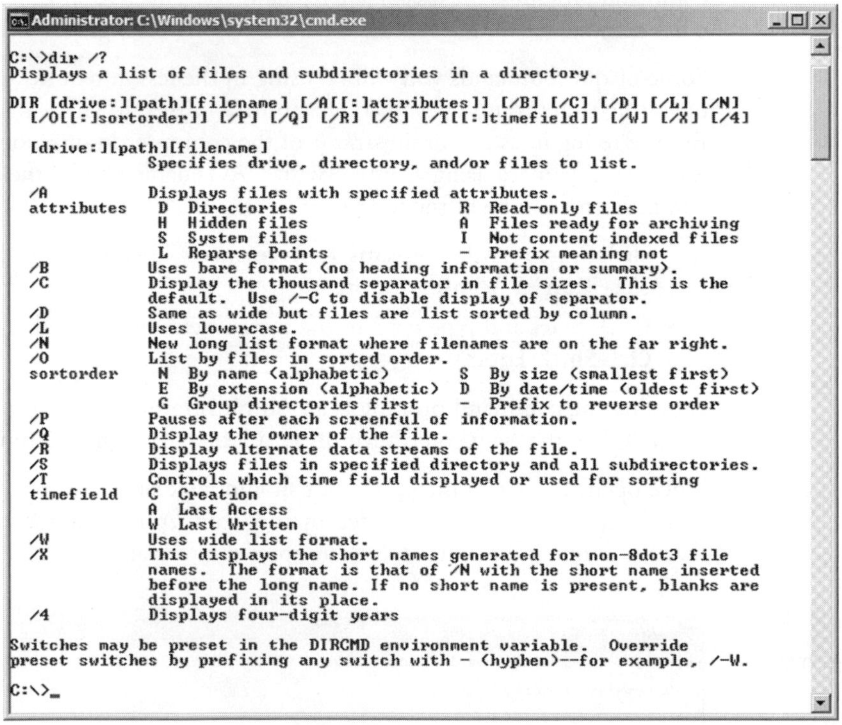

On the Microsoft Web site, you can find an entire command-line reference from A to Z with in-depth explanations of most commands. The Help command also gives a list of shell commands but does not include TCP/IP commands.

Use the **/?** option when you need more information about a TCP/IP command. In some cases, you will have to type the command followed by **-?** instead.

Sometimes, a help file or the results of a command are too large to fit in one screen. In some cases, you might be able to press a key to see more. In other cases, you will need to add the **| more** option to the end of your syntax (pronounced "pipe more"). The | or pipe sign shares the backslash key. Use this when faced with extremely long results. For example, go to the root of C by typing **cd**. Then change to the System 32 directory by typing **cd\windows\ system32**. This should bring you directly to the System32 directory. Now type **dir**. This will flash hundreds of line items across the screen. To see these one page at a time, type the command **dir | more**. You will see that doing so displays the information one page at a time showing "more" at the bottom of each screen of information. Press the space bar to show the next screen of information. Or, to show one line at a time, press the Enter key.

Working with Ipconfig and Ping

Ipconfig and ping can be used to analyze, test, troubleshoot, and configure IPv4 and IPv6 connections. Before moving to more advanced TCP/IP commands, it is important to master these commands by learning what each of the commands and their options do, as well as why you would use those options in a real-world scenario.

The ipconfig and ping commands are probably the two most commonly used commands when analyzing and troubleshooting networking issues. Although ipconfig displays information, it can also be used to make basic configuration changes and reset certain facets of DHCP and DNS. Ping is used to test connectivity to other hosts; here, command-line results tell you whether a remote host is "alive" on the network.

→ ANALYZE AND CONFIGURE WITH IPCONFIG AND PING

In this exercise, you will learn more about *ipconfig* and ping, their switches, and how to use them effectively when troubleshooting.

1. Type the command **ipconfig**.

   This should display results similar to Figure 5-3. The **ipconfig** command displays information pertaining to your network adapter, namely TCP/IP configurations.

Figure 5-3

Ipconfig command

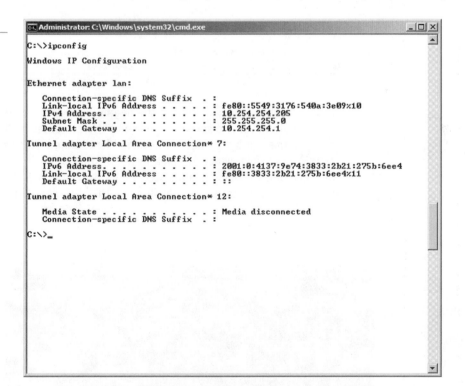

TAKE NOTE*

Disable any firewalls (hardware or software) that might interfere with the following exercises and tests.

Your IP address and other actual configurations might be different. Regardless, this is where you can find out the IP address, subnet mask, and default gateway of your network adapter. IPv4 and possibly IPv6 information will be listed depending on your configuration.

Note that this is not all the information ipconfig can display. If you wanted to know the MAC address of the network adapter, for instance, you could use one of several options of ipconfig.

2. Type the command **ipconfig /all**.

The results that appear should have much more information, including the MAC address as shown in Figure 5-4 (the field is named "Physical Address"). The space after the word ipconfig is not necessary in this case; however, some commands will not function properly without a space.

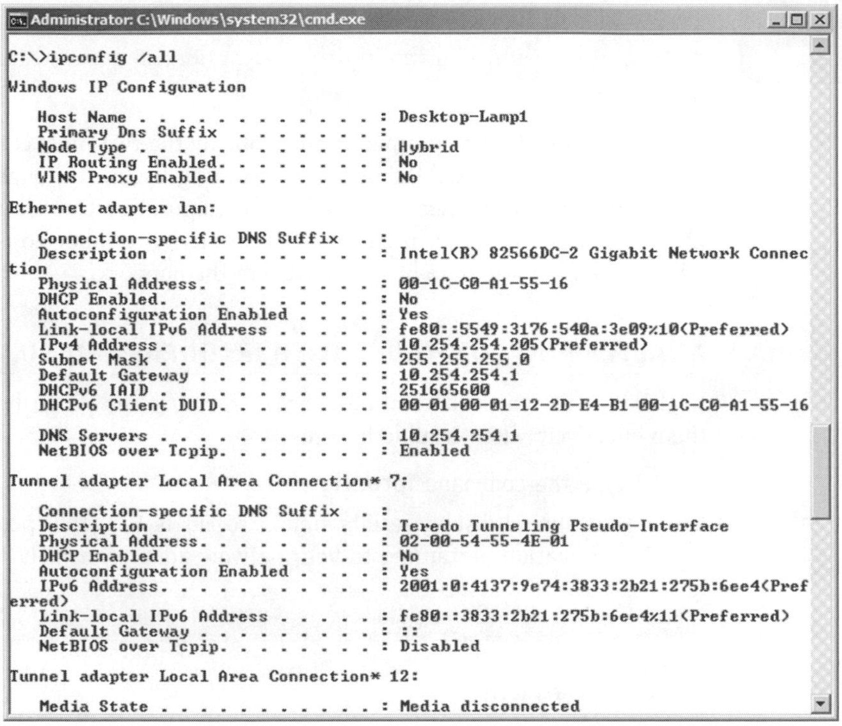

```
Administrator: C:\Windows\system32\cmd.exe
C:\>ipconfig /all

Windows IP Configuration

   Host Name . . . . . . . . . . . . : Desktop-Lamp1
   Primary Dns Suffix  . . . . . . . :
   Node Type . . . . . . . . . . . . : Hybrid
   IP Routing Enabled. . . . . . . . : No
   WINS Proxy Enabled. . . . . . . . : No

Ethernet adapter lan:

   Connection-specific DNS Suffix  . :
   Description . . . . . . . . . . . : Intel(R) 82566DC-2 Gigabit Network Connec
tion
   Physical Address. . . . . . . . . : 00-1C-C0-A1-55-16
   DHCP Enabled. . . . . . . . . . . : No
   Autoconfiguration Enabled . . . . : Yes
   Link-local IPv6 Address . . . . . : fe80::5549:3176:540a:3e09%10(Preferred)
   IPv4 Address. . . . . . . . . . . : 10.254.254.205(Preferred)
   Subnet Mask . . . . . . . . . . . : 255.255.255.0
   Default Gateway . . . . . . . . . : 10.254.254.1
   DHCPv6 IAID . . . . . . . . . . . : 251665600
   DHCPv6 Client DUID. . . . . . . . : 00-01-00-01-12-2D-E4-B1-00-1C-C0-A1-55-16

   DNS Servers . . . . . . . . . . . : 10.254.254.1
   NetBIOS over Tcpip. . . . . . . . : Enabled

Tunnel adapter Local Area Connection* 7:

   Connection-specific DNS Suffix  . :
   Description . . . . . . . . . . . : Teredo Tunneling Pseudo-Interface
   Physical Address. . . . . . . . . : 02-00-54-55-4E-01
   DHCP Enabled. . . . . . . . . . . : No
   Autoconfiguration Enabled . . . . : Yes
   IPv6 Address. . . . . . . . . . . : 2001:0:4137:9e74:3833:2b21:275b:6ee4(Pref
erred)
   Link-local IPv6 Address . . . . . : fe80::3833:2b21:275b:6ee4%11(Preferred)
   Default Gateway . . . . . . . . . : ::
   NetBIOS over Tcpip. . . . . . . . : Disabled

Tunnel adapter Local Area Connection* 12:

   Media State . . . . . . . . . . . : Media disconnected
```

Figure 5-4

Ipconfig /all command

Notice that there is a section at the beginning of the results called "Windows IP Configuration." This displays the name of the computer or "host name." (You can also find information by typing the command **hostname**.) This section additionally shows a DNS suffix field, which is blank in this instance, but if the computer was a member of a domain, it would be populated similar to Figure 5-5. In the figure, the DNS suffix is dpro2.com, which is the domain name that this computer belongs to. If the computer does belong to a domain, an additional field called "DNS Suffix Search List" will be added.

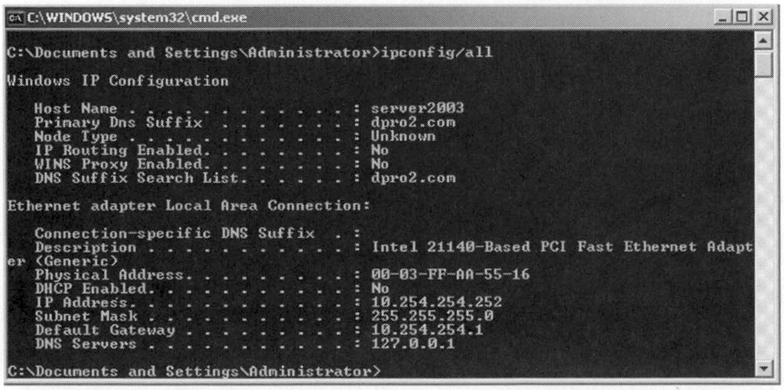

```
C:\WINDOWS\system32\cmd.exe
C:\Documents and Settings\Administrator>ipconfig/all

Windows IP Configuration

   Host Name . . . . . . . . . . . . : server2003
   Primary Dns Suffix  . . . . . . . : dpro2.com
   Node Type . . . . . . . . . . . . : Unknown
   IP Routing Enabled. . . . . . . . : No
   WINS Proxy Enabled. . . . . . . . : No
   DNS Suffix Search List. . . . . . : dpro2.com

Ethernet adapter Local Area Connection:

   Connection-specific DNS Suffix  . :
   Description . . . . . . . . . . . : Intel 21140-Based PCI Fast Ethernet Adapt
er (Generic)
   Physical Address. . . . . . . . . : 00-03-FF-AA-55-16
   DHCP Enabled. . . . . . . . . . . : No
   IP Address. . . . . . . . . . . . : 10.254.254.252
   Subnet Mask . . . . . . . . . . . : 255.255.255.0
   Default Gateway . . . . . . . . . : 10.254.254.1
   DNS Servers . . . . . . . . . . . : 127.0.0.1

C:\Documents and Settings\Administrator>
```

Figure 5-5

Ipconfig /all command on a second host

The ipconfig/all command also defines whether IP routing or WINS proxy is enabled. We will cover these services in Lesson 6.

Up until now, these steps should be review. However, there are more options for the command ipconfig. You may hear professionals refer to "options" as "switches" or "parameters" as well.

3. Type the command **ipconfig /?**.

This displays the help file for ipconfig, which is rather extensive. It describes what ipconfig is and what it does, and it shows the various options you can use with the command, as well as some examples. The results of this command are shown in Figure 5-6.

Figure 5-6

Ipconfig /? command

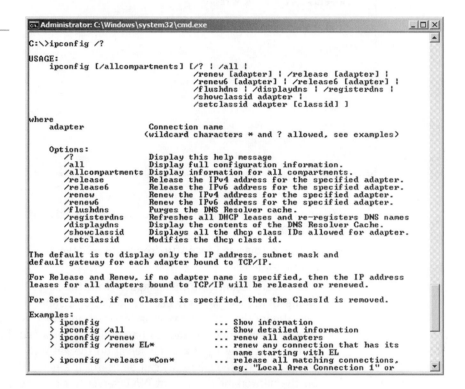

4. Type the command **ipconfig /allcompartments**.

Network adapters can be compartmentalized so that traffic from one doesn't leak to the other (e.g., VPN traffic on one adapter and private LAN traffic on another). This command shows the adapters in their compartmentalized format. You can also use the **ipconfig /allcompartments /all** command to see extended information about each compartment (similar to ipconfig /all).

5. Work with a dynamically assigned address:

a. On a computer that obtains its IP information automatically, type the command **ipconfig /release**.

The ipconfig /release command releases any IP configurations received from a DHCP server. Figure 5-7 shows an example of a released IP address.

Figure 5-7

A released IP configuration

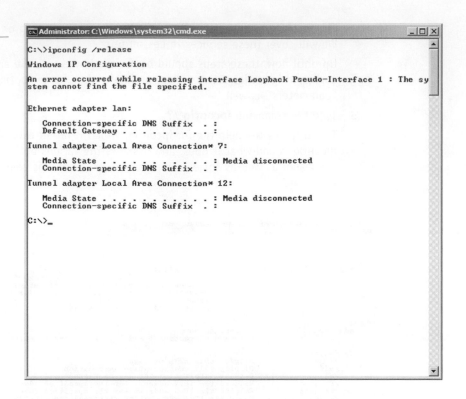

There is actually no address assigned to the computer at this time. It is known as the IP 0.0.0.0.

b. Type the command **ipconfig /renew** to retrieve an IP address and other IP configurations.

This should reconfigure the computer with the same IP address it used before. If the IP address has only been released for a short time, the /renew option will reconfigure the address based on information stored in the registry. If no information is available or the address has expired after a certain amount of time, the computer will seek out a DHCP server on the network from which to obtain an IP address. These commands can be useful if a new DHCP server has been placed on the network or the current DHCP server has been reconfigured. The commands are also helpful if an error has occurred in the network adapter's IP configuration, or if APIPA has gotten in the way and has self-assigned a 169.254.0.0 address to the client. The commands issued in step 5a and 5b pertain to IPv4; however, to release and renew IPv6 addresses, simply add a 6 to the option—for example **ipconfig /release6**. More information about this process and DHCP is provided in Lesson 6.

6. Display, flush, and register DNS information:

a. Type the command **ipconfig /displaydns**.

This displays Domain Name System records for the client computer, including localhost connections.

b. Type the command **ipconfig /flushdns**.

This empties the DNS cache.

c. Type the command **ipconfig /registerdns**.

This registers the computer with the nearest DNS server. The last two commands can be useful if there is an error with the DNS configuration on the client, or if a new DNS server or newly configured DNS server becomes live on the network.

As you can see, the ipconfig command has many uses. It can be used to analyze and troubleshoot basic networking connections, as well as to troubleshoot DHCP and DNS issues.

Let's move on to the ping command. **Ping** is used to test the existence of other hosts on the network. However, there are many permutations of ping.

7. Type the command **ping /?**.

This displays the help file for the command. Note the various options available to you.

8. Ping the local host computer and other computers on the network:

a. Type the command **ping localhost**.

b. Type the command **ping loopback**.

c. Type the command **ping 127.0.0.1**.

The first two commands are basically the same. However, when you ping 127.0.0.1, the results do not include any hostname resolution information. This is the best way to ping the localhost when testing IPv4. When pinging 127.0.0.1, no traffic is placed on the network segment; rather, all traffic is kept inside the computer or local loopback.

Now select another computer to ping; it could be a partner's computer, a secondary computer, or a router. Make note of its IP address. For this example, we will use the address 10.254.254.252.

d. Type the command **ping [IP address]**. For example **ping 10.254.254.252**.

This tests whether another host on the network is live. You can also ping another computer on the network by host name. To find out the host name of a computer, type either the command **hostname** or the command **ipconfig**. Examples of pinging an IP address and pinging the corresponding host name are shown in Figure 5-8. Notice the IP address in the first ping (10.254.254.252), as well as the host name (server2003) and resolved IP address (10.254.254.252) in the second ping.

TAKE NOTE*

Disable IPv6 in the Local Area Connection Properties window before continuing with this portion of the exercise. If you get replies that include::1 in the address, then IPv6 is still functioning.

Figure 5-8

Pinging by IP address and host name

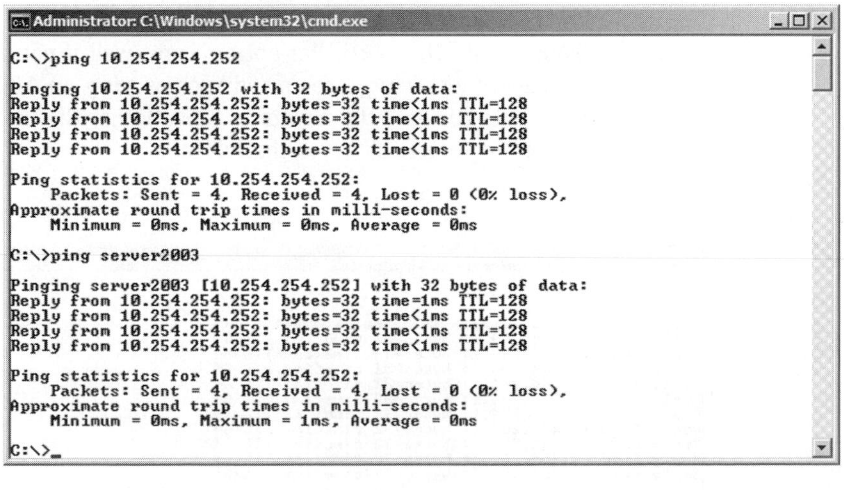

```
Administrator: C:\Windows\system32\cmd.exe

C:\>ping 10.254.254.252

Pinging 10.254.254.252 with 32 bytes of data:
Reply from 10.254.254.252: bytes=32 time<1ms TTL=128
Reply from 10.254.254.252: bytes=32 time<1ms TTL=128
Reply from 10.254.254.252: bytes=32 time<1ms TTL=128
Reply from 10.254.254.252: bytes=32 time<1ms TTL=128

Ping statistics for 10.254.254.252:
    Packets: Sent = 4, Received = 4, Lost = 0 (0% loss),
Approximate round trip times in milli-seconds:
    Minimum = 0ms, Maximum = 0ms, Average = 0ms

C:\>ping server2003

Pinging server2003 [10.254.254.252] with 32 bytes of data:
Reply from 10.254.254.252: bytes=32 time=1ms TTL=128
Reply from 10.254.254.252: bytes=32 time<1ms TTL=128
Reply from 10.254.254.252: bytes=32 time<1ms TTL=128
Reply from 10.254.254.252: bytes=32 time<1ms TTL=128

Ping statistics for 10.254.254.252:
    Packets: Sent = 4, Received = 4, Lost = 0 (0% loss),
Approximate round trip times in milli-seconds:
    Minimum = 0ms, Maximum = 1ms, Average = 0ms

C:\>
```

If the computer you pinged is alive, the pinging computer will get replies. However, if the computer is not live or is not available, you will get one of several error messages (e.g., "Request timed out," "Destination host unreachable," or a similar error).

When troubleshooting network connectivity issues, start with the local computer and then branch out. For example, start with a ping of 127.0.0.1, then try pinging other hosts on the same network, ultimately ending up with the router. Next, try pinging hosts on other networks.

9. Ping a computer with a larger packet size:

   a. Select another computer to ping; it could be a partner's computer, a secondary computer, or a router. Make note of its IP address. For this example, we will use the address 10.254.254.1.

   b. Type the command **ping –1 1500 [IP address]**. For example, **ping –1 1500 10.254.254.1**.

   The results should be similar to Figure 5-9. Notice that each of the replies equals 1,500 bytes instead of the standard 32 bytes. The –1 option allows you to modify the packet size of the ICMP echoes that are sent. The most bytes that you can send in this fashion is 65,500; however, this will create fragmented packets. This ping option can help simulate network traffic to a particular host.

Figure 5-9

Ping –l

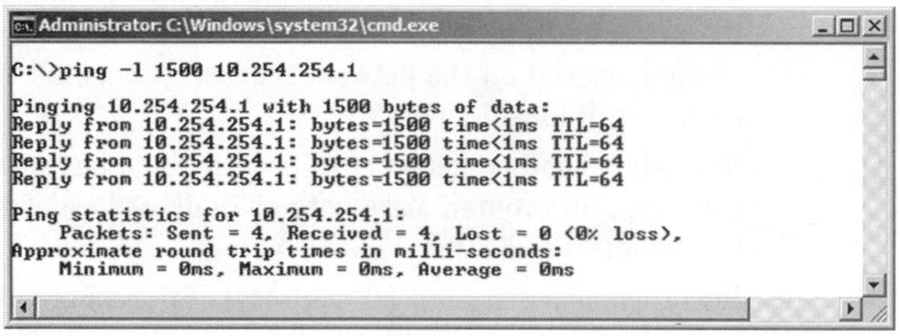

```
Administrator: C:\Windows\system32\cmd.exe                      _ □ ×

C:\>ping -l 1500 10.254.254.1

Pinging 10.254.254.1 with 1500 bytes of data:
Reply from 10.254.254.1: bytes=1500 time<1ms TTL=64
Reply from 10.254.254.1: bytes=1500 time<1ms TTL=64
Reply from 10.254.254.1: bytes=1500 time<1ms TTL=64
Reply from 10.254.254.1: bytes=1500 time<1ms TTL=64

Ping statistics for 10.254.254.1:
    Packets: Sent = 4, Received = 4, Lost = 0 (0% loss),
Approximate round trip times in milli-seconds:
    Minimum = 0ms, Maximum = 0ms, Average = 0ms
```

10. Ping a computer *X* amount of times:

   a. Use the same computer you pinged in step 9.

   b. Type the command **ping –n 10 [IP address]**. For example, **ping –n 10 10.254.254.1**.

   The results should be similar to Figure 5-10. Notice that there were a total of 10 ICMP echo replies. The –n option allows you to ping with as many ICMP packets as you wish. This particular option works well if you are creating a performance baseline. By running a command such as **ping –n 1000 10.254.254.1** every day, you could compare the results to see whether the destination computer is performing better or worse than usual.

Figure 5-10

Ping –n

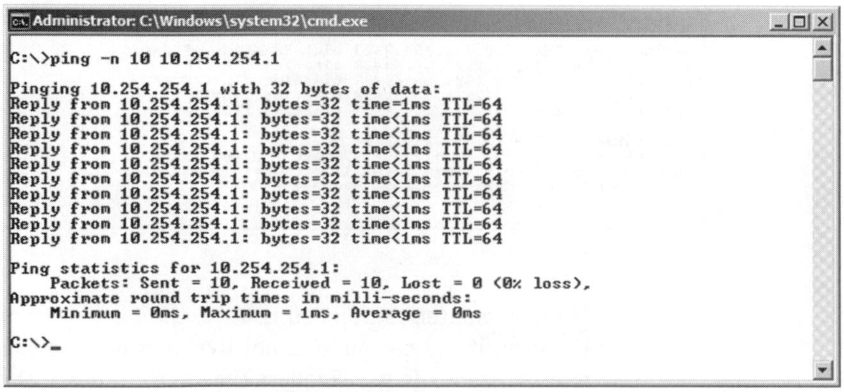

```
Administrator: C:\Windows\system32\cmd.exe                      _ □ ×

C:\>ping -n 10 10.254.254.1

Pinging 10.254.254.1 with 32 bytes of data:
Reply from 10.254.254.1: bytes=32 time=1ms TTL=64
Reply from 10.254.254.1: bytes=32 time<1ms TTL=64
Reply from 10.254.254.1: bytes=32 time<1ms TTL=64
Reply from 10.254.254.1: bytes=32 time<1ms TTL=64
Reply from 10.254.254.1: bytes=32 time<1ms TTL=64
Reply from 10.254.254.1: bytes=32 time<1ms TTL=64
Reply from 10.254.254.1: bytes=32 time<1ms TTL=64
Reply from 10.254.254.1: bytes=32 time<1ms TTL=64
Reply from 10.254.254.1: bytes=32 time<1ms TTL=64
Reply from 10.254.254.1: bytes=32 time<1ms TTL=64

Ping statistics for 10.254.254.1:
    Packets: Sent = 10, Received = 10, Lost = 0 (0% loss),
Approximate round trip times in milli-seconds:
    Minimum = 0ms, Maximum = 1ms, Average = 0ms

C:\>_
```

11. Ping a computer continuously:

    a. Use the same computer you pinged in steps 9 and 10.

    b. Type the command **ping –t [IP address]**. For example, **ping –t 10.254.254.1**.

    This command option sends pings endlessly to a destination IP address. This can only be stopped by pressing **Ctrl + C** on the keyboard or by closing the command prompt altogether. This option works well if you need to test whether a network connection is being made. For example, if you aren't sure which patch cable to use or which RJ45 port to connect to, you could run this command, then test one connection at a time, checking the results on the screen each time until you get replies.

By the way, most of the time, an option can be typed after an IP address as well. However, it is a good habit to place options directly after the command they are modifying.

These are just a few of the ping options, but they are some of the more commonly used ones. Do your best to memorize the various switches we employed during this exercise.

■ Working with Advanced TCP/IP Commands

THE BOTTOM LINE

Advanced TCP/IP commands like netstat, nbtstat, and tracert allow you to analyze more facets of a TCP/IP connection than ipconfig and ping can. Also, FTP, Telnet, netsh, and route allow you to do more than just analyze a system—they can help you configure the system.

CERTIFICATION READY
How do you configure
TCP/IP commands with
TCP/IP?
3.6

In the following exercises, we will be showing results from two computers. One is a server computer; its command prompt windows will be displayed with a black background. The other is a client computer; its command prompt windows will be displayed with a white background. The results work basically the same way on both types of computers; however, a server computer will often have more results because it generally has more networking connections.

 ANALYZE THE TCP/IP CONFIGURATION WITH NETSTAT AND NBTSTAT

GET READY. In this exercise, we will analyze our system with the *netstat* and *nbtstat* commands. Both show statistics of the network connection, but netstat centers on the local computer, whereas nbtstat can also show statistics for remote machines:

1. Type the command **netstat** and view the results. They may take up to a minute to appear, depending on your network configuration and number of current network connections. Your results should be similar to Figure 5-11, although you may have fewer line items of information.

The netstat command is used to display active TCP (or UDP) connections, as well as a host of other statistics that we will cover later in the exercise. Note that there are four columns. The Proto column shows the transport layer protocol being used for the connection. The netstat command by itself only shows TCP connections in this column. The Local Address column displays the local computer by name (server2003), followed by the outbound port number. The Foreign Address column shows the remote computer that is being connected to; in some cases, this can be the same computer. The State column shows what the status of the connection is (for example,

Figure 5-11

Netstat

Established, Close_Wait, Closed, Listen, and so on). These are pretty self-explanatory, but let's look at another example of an established session.

2. Open Internet Explorer and connect to www.google.com. Move to step 3 right away.

3. Type the **netstat** command again. Now you should see additional entries, as shown in Figure 5-12.

Figure 5-12

Netstat with additional entries

In the figure, notice the two extra entries in the Foreign Address column that start with the letters "lga." This is part of the domain name called 1e100.net, which is controlled by four name servers at google.com. These two connections were made when the computer browsed to www.google.com; they are established connections.

The host names are followed by the inbound port called http, which is the equivalent of port 80. The local computer is making connections to Google on outbound ports 2472 and 2473. Note that the ports used by your computer will be different because they are dynamically assigned. This command and the following two commands can be helpful when tracking applications and the network connections they make.

4. Type the command **netstat –a**. This displays TCP and UDP connections.

5. Type the command **netstat –an**. This displays TCP and UDP connections in numeric format. For many administrators, being able to view IP addresses and port numbers is easier than going by name. Netstat –n produces numerical results but for TCP connections only.

6. Type the command **netstat –e**. This displays Ethernet statistics such as the number of packets and bytes sent and received, as shown in Figure 5-13.

Figure 5-13

Netstat –e

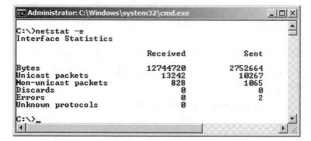

7. Type the command **netstat –r**. This displays the route table, which is the same result you would get if you were to type the **route print** command that we describe later.

8. Type the command **netstat –s**. This displays statistics per protocol, such as TCP, UDP, ICMP, IP, and so on.

   Check out the rest of the options for netstat. You will note that you can fine tune the results of the netstat command in several ways.

   Now, let's move on to nbtstat.

9. Type the command **nbtstat**. This displays the help file for the command. Nbtstat will display NetBIOS over TCP/IP statistics for local and remote computers. NetBIOS was developed in the 1980s to allow applications to communicate over a network via the session layer of the OSI model. NetBIOS over TCP/IP sends the NetBIOS protocol within TCP and UDP sessions.

10. Type the command **nbtstat –a [local computername]**; for example: **nbtstat –a desktop-lamp1**, as shown in Figure 5-14. The same results can also be achieved by typing **nbtstat –n**.

Figure 5-14

Nbtstat –a

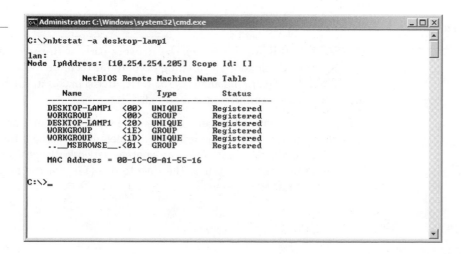

11. Type the command **nbtstat –a [remotename]**. Use the name of a computer on your network that you can connect to with ping.

The results of the nbtstat command will display the major services that are running on that machine. For example, <00> is the workstation service, used to allow connections to remote computers. <20> is the server service, used to allow other computers to connect to the local computer. If you see <03>, this is the messenger service. Many organizations have policies stating that this should be turned off. This command works well to discern the services running on a local or remote machine and can help when troubleshooting why a computer cannot make particular network connections. You can also connect by IP address.

12. Type the command **nbtstat –A [IPAddress]**; for example, **nbtstat –A 10.254.254.205**. This produces the same information but allows you to connect via IP address. So, the lowercase "a" option is used for names and the uppercase "A" is used for IP addresses. Let's attempt to stop a service and view the results with nbtstat:

   a. Stop the workstation service on a remote computer. This can be done in the Computer Management console window or by typing the command **net stop workstation**.

   b. Next, run the **nbtstat –A** command to that remote computer's IP address. You should see that the <00> service is no longer listed.

   c. Restart the service on the remote computer within Computer Management.

   d. Run the **nbtstat –A** command again to verify that it is listed. A restart of the remote computer might be necessary.

13. Type the command **nbtstat –r**. This displays NetBIOS name resolution statistics.

14. Type the command **nbtstat –R**. This purges the contents of the NetBIOS name cache table.

15. Type the command **nbtstat –RR**. This releases and refreshes NetBIOS names.

The previous two commands are used in conjunction with Lmhosts and WINS, respectively, and they are not commonly employed in today's networks.

16. Type the command **nbtstat –s**. This displays NetBIOS sessions and attempts to convert the remote IP addresses to names. You might have to make a network connection or two before this command will display any results.

17. Type the command **nbtstat –S**. This displays the same sessions as with the –s parameter. The only difference is that remote computers will be listed by IP address.

Generally, it is wise to use uppercase options such as –A and –S. These provide results by IP address, which is usually preferred by network administrators.

 ANALYZE NETWORK PATHS WITH TRACERT AND PATHPING

GET READY. In this exercise, we analyze network paths with *tracert* and *pathping*. Both show paths to remote destinations, extending beyond one or more routers, but their syntax and results differ. Plus, pathping analyzes the trace after it makes it, further differentiating it from tracert. An Internet connection is required.

1. Type the command **tracert** and view the results. This or **tracert /?** will display the help file for the command. Review the details in the help file. The tracert command shows paths to a destination on another network. It does this by pinging each step along the way three times. The time to live (TTL) for the pings increases with each "hop" to another network.

2. Attempt a trace to google.com by typing **tracert google.com**. The results should be similar to Figure 5-15.

Figure 5-15

Tracert

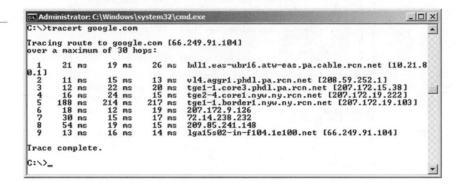

Each step along the way to google.com is referred to as a hop. Each line in the results is a new network that has been hopped to. Notice the name of each router and its corresponding IP address. Usually, you can track geographically where the ICMP packets are going step by step, just by looking at the router name.

3. Type the command **tracert –d google.com**. This runs the same trace, but it does so numerically (as shown in Figure 5-16). This is a significant time saver. Notice how much faster the results are shown without any name resolution to get in the way.

Figure 5-16

Tracert –d

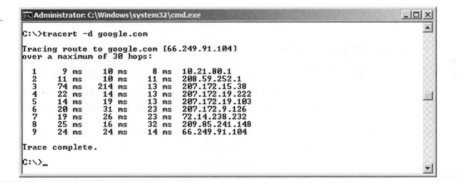

The idea behind this tracert command is that it allows you to find out whether a router has malfunctioned. By comparing the tracert results with your network documentation, you should be able to alert the correct network person to the problem, or perhaps fix the problem yourself. Quite often a router simply needs to be rebooted or turned back on.

4. Type the command **pathping google.com**. Pathping is similar to tracert but it will also compute the degree of packet loss, as shown in Figure 5-17. If there is packet loss, it would show up under the Lost/Sent column and would display a percentage as well.

Figure 5-17

Pathping

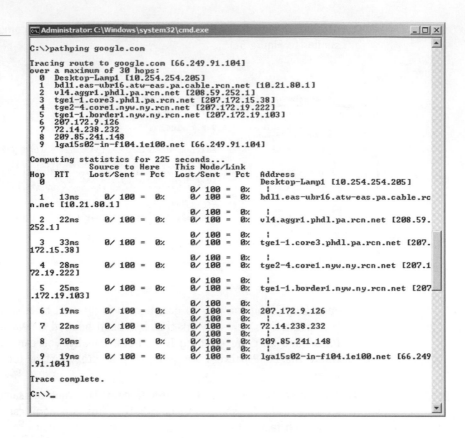

5. Type the command **pathping –n google.com**. This option prevents name resolution in the way that tracert –d does. This can display the results faster than the standard pathping command.

 ANALYZE DOMAIN NAMES WITH NSLOOKUP

GET READY. In this exercise, we will analyze DNS information with the Nslookup command. *Nslookup* displays information about DNS names and their corresponding IP addresses, and it can be used to diagnose DNS servers. An Internet connection is required.

1. Type the command **nslookup google.com** and view the results. You should see google.com's corresponding IP address. Try the command with a few other well-known Web site domain names.

2. Type the command **nslookup**. This should bring you to the nslookup shell where you can enact more commands.

3. Press the **?** key and press **Enter**. This displays the various commands you can use in the nslookup shell.

4. Type **exit** to get out of the nslookup shell. We'll work with this command in more depth during Lesson 6.

MAKE NETWORK CONNECTIONS WITH FTP AND TELNET

GET READY. In this exercise, we will make connections to remote systems with FTP and Telnet. An Internet connection is required.

1. Type the command **ftp /?** and view the results. *FTP* stands for file transfer protocol. It is an application layer protocol as well as an application. The FTP command is used in the command prompt to connect to FTP servers.

2. Connect to an FTP server:

   a. Type the command **ftp ftp6.ipswitch.com**. This should make a connection to the IPswitch FTP server.

   b. When the FTP server prompts for a user (username), type **anonymous**.

   c. When prompted for a password, press the **Enter** key, as no password is necessary. Once logged in, your screen should look similar to Figure 5-18.

   d. Press the **?** key to display a list of commands you can use in the FTP shell.

Figure 5-18

FTP connection

3. Type the **dir** command. This shows a list of folders and files within your current directory, similar to how DOS would display them.

4. Change to the ipswitch directory by typing **cd ipswitch**.

5. Type **dir** again. Examine the folders inside.

6. Change to the manuals directory by typing **cd manuals**. (Of course, longer path names can be used to save time if you know where you are going.)

7. Download one of the manuals, such as by typing **get wsftp80.pdf**. The get command downloads the file and stores it in the working directory in Windows 7. Other versions of Windows store the file in the root of C: by default. This can be changed with the **lcd** command. View the manual in the root of C:. It should be a manual for WS_FTP Pro version 8 written in English.

   You can also use the **mget** command to grab multiple files at once. And, if you want to upload a file, the **put** and **mput** commands can do this one at a time or more than one at a time, respectively.

   Sometimes, this might be your only option for connecting via FTP. However, if you can use a third-party GUI-based program, you will be able to work much faster.

8. When finished, type **quit** to end the FTP session and return to the C:\ prompt.

Although FTP is used to transfer files, *Telnet* is used to take control of a remote computer. Basically, a network administrator connects to a remote computer, server, router, or switch by typing **telnet [IPAddress]**. This would either display the C:\ prompt of the remote system if connecting to a Windows computer, or a menu-based system if connecting to a router or switch. Telnet is an older, out-of-date protocol, and as such, it should be replaced with a more secure program such as SSH. Newer operating systems don't have the Telnet service installed by default, and they do not allow the use of the command in the Command Prompt.

 ANALYZE AND CONFIGURE TCP/IP WITH NETSH AND ROUTE

In this exercise, we will analyze and configure our system with the netsh and route commands.

Netsh is a built-in command-line scripting utility that enables you to display and modify the network configurations of the local computer. Netsh commands tend to be rather long and in depth, so the utility gives you the option to save configuration scripts for later use.

1. Type the command **netsh /?** and view the results. This help file shows the basic syntax for the netsh command and the first-level commands that can be run within the netsh shell.

2. Type the command **netsh**. This allows you to access the netsh shell. From here, if you press the **?** key, you will see a list of first-level commands, essentially the same that were in the help file previously. These are shown in Figure 5-19.

Figure 5-19

Netsh

3. Type the command **interface**. This will bring you to the netsh interface portion of the netsh shell. From here, you can make modifications to network adapter configurations.

4. Type quit to exit out of the netsh shell.

5. Modify, add, and remove IPv4 addresses.

   For the next several portions of this exercise, it is assumed that the name of the network adapter is "Local Area Connection." If you are using a different name, please substitute that name in any of the applicable syntax. If it is easier for you, or if you encounter any problems, consider changing the name of the network adapter from "Local Area Connection" to "LAN" if you have not already done so. Be sure to use the new name "LAN" where necessary in the syntax.

   a. Type the following syntax to *modify* the IPv4 address:

      **netsh interface ip set address name="Local Area Connection"
      static 192.168.1.101 255.255.255.0 192.168.1.1**

      "Local Area Connection" is the name of your network adapter. If you have modified the name to lan or something different, make sure that is what you type within the quotations. This syntax changes the IPv4 address and modifies the gateway address.

b. Type **ipconfig** to see the new address.

c. Type the following syntax to *add* an IPv4 address:

netsh interface ip add address name="Local Area Connection" 192.168.1.102 255.255.255.0 192.168.1.1

d. Type **ipconfig** to see the secondary address. It should be labeled as (tentative), whereas the original IP address is preferred. The results should look similar to Figure 5-20.

Figure 5-20

A secondary (tentative) IP address

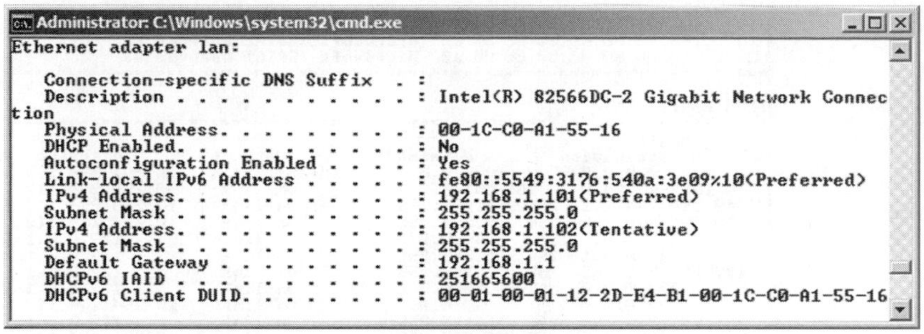

```
Administrator: C:\Windows\system32\cmd.exe                              _ □ ×
Ethernet adapter lan:

   Connection-specific DNS Suffix  . :
   Description . . . . . . . . . . . : Intel(R) 82566DC-2 Gigabit Network Connec
tion
   Physical Address. . . . . . . . . : 00-1C-C0-A1-55-16
   DHCP Enabled. . . . . . . . . . . : No
   Autoconfiguration Enabled . . . . : Yes
   Link-local IPv6 Address . . . . . : fe80::5549:3176:540a:3e09x10(Preferred)
   IPv4 Address. . . . . . . . . . . : 192.168.1.101(Preferred)
   Subnet Mask . . . . . . . . . . . : 255.255.255.0
   IPv4 Address. . . . . . . . . . . : 192.168.1.102(Tentative)
   Subnet Mask . . . . . . . . . . . : 255.255.255.0
   Default Gateway . . . . . . . . . : 192.168.1.1
   DHCPv6 IAID . . . . . . . . . . . : 251665600
   DHCPv6 Client DUID. . . . . . . . : 00-01-00-01-12-2D-E4-B1-00-1C-C0-A1-55-16
```

e. Type the following syntax to remove the secondary IPv4 address:

netsh interface ip delete address name="Local Area Connection" 192.168.1.102 255.255.255.0

f. Type the following syntax to change the primary IP address from static to dynamically assigned:

netsh interface ip set address name="Local Area Connection" source=dhcp

g. Check the new configuration with ipconfig.

h. Reset the preferred IP address back to the original using the syntax from step 5a, substituting the IP address and gateway address with your original correct addresses. Check your changes with ipconfig.

You could type these commands one at a time: netsh > interface > ip and so on, but it would be more time consuming.

6. Add an IPv6 address with the following syntax:

netsh interface ipv6 add address interface=Local Area Connection address=2001:ab1:442e:1323::7

7. Type **ipconfig** to see the new address.

8. Remove an IPv6 with the following syntax:

netsh interface ipv6 delete address interface=Local Area Connection address=2001:ab1:442e:1323::7

9. Type **ipconfig** to verify that the address was removed.

If you wish, you can create batch files using various netsh syntax in an effort to save time in the future.

Now, let's discuss the route command. ***Route*** enables you to display and make changes to the local IP routing table of the computer, which displays IP connections to other networks as well as testing networks. Generally, a client computer does not have routes to other actual networks, mainly because a client computer is not normally intended for that role. Also, most client computers have only one network adapter. In order to create routes to other networks, a second network adapter is required. When a computer has two network adapters, it is known as a multi-homed machine.

If it has two and only two network adapters, it is specifically known as a dual-homed machine.

10. Type the command **route print**. This should display results similar to Figure 5-21. This command gives the same result as netstat –r, but it is more commonly used.

Figure 5-21

Route print

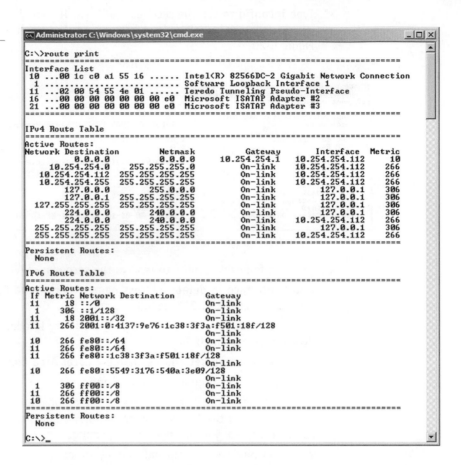

This command shows a list of network adapters (or interfaces) on the local computer, including the MAC address and name of each. Then the IPv4 Route Table is displayed. You will notice several networking connections. The Network Destination column tells you where the computer is trying to connect. The Netmask is the subnet mask for that particular Network Destination. The Gateway is the IP address of the host that is used to gain access to the remote network. The Interface is the IP address of the network adapter that is making the connection to the other network. The Metric column specifies an integer between 1 and 9999; this metric is associated with the speed of the connection, the amount of hops across networks, and so on. Normally, the lowest metric is selected for connections to other networks. This is not an issue if the computer (often a router) only has two or three connections.

You will notice a 0.0.0.0 network destination. This is the local network when no IP address is associated with the computer (for example, when we executed the command ipconfig/release). Then you will see the local network that the computer is a part of; in the figure, it is 10.254.254.0, with a subnet mask of 255.255.255.0. This is the network number for this computer, which has an IP address of 10.254.254.112. Single IP addresses also get a route line item, as you can see in the third line. The local loopback network (127.0.0.0) and the actual local loopback IP address (127.0.0.1) also get route line items, and so on.

There is also an IPv6 Route Table if you are running that protocol. This table shows link-local and global unicast address line items.

11. Add and remove routes. Adding a router requires syntax similar to the netsh command we used to add IP addresses. In the following portion of this exercise, we will add a fictitious route using our local IP address as the interface that makes the connection to the remote network:

   a. Type the command **route add 192.168.1.0 mask 255.255.255.0 [LocalIPAddress]**. An example of this is shown in Figure 5-22.

Figure 5-22

Route add

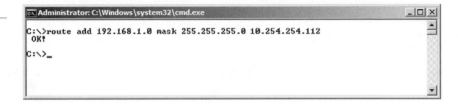

The network we are attempting to connect to is 192.168.1.0, and it has a default Class C subnet mask of 255.255.255.0. The word "mask" takes the place of "subnet mask." Then we used our local IP address, in this case 10.254.254.112, to connect to the remote network. After we pressed **Enter**, a simple **OK!** Message appeared. This means that the route has been added to the local routing table.

   b. Type the command **route print**. You will see the new route in the IPv4 Route Table, as shown in Figure 5-23.

Figure 5-23

Route print with a new route

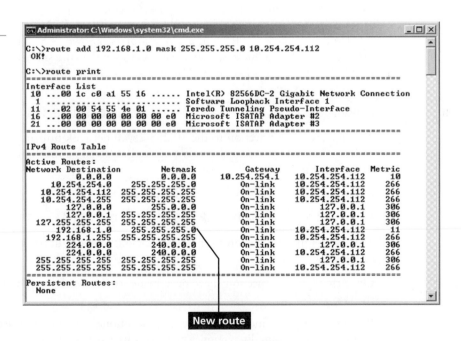

The new route is created for the network address 192.168.1.0, as well as for the broadcast address 192.168.1.255.

   c. Type the command **route delete 192.168.1.0 mask 255.255.255.0**. This should remove the route you added previously. You could also remove all added routes with one command: **route -f**. But be careful with this command. Depending on the operating system and protocols used, as well as the network configuration, this could stop all network connections.

> **d.** Type the command **route print** to view the results. If you start to have any issues with your routing table, consider stopping and restarting TCP/IP, or even restarting the computer. By the way, TCP/IP can be reset in the command line by typing the following command:
>
> **netsh int ip reset c:\resetlog.txt.**

Generally, these added routes will be lost if TCP/IP or the computer is restarted. However, routes can also be added in a persistent manner by using the **–p** option. The p stands for persistent; it preserves the route within the registry even if TCP/IP is restarted.

Again, the idea behind routing is to make connections to remote networks. See Figure 5-24 for some network documentation.

Figure 5-24

Routing documentation

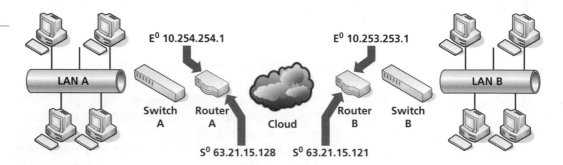

In the figure, there are two LANs, LAN A and LAN B. By default, computers on these LANs would not be able to talk to each other because they are separated by routers and the "cloud" (whatever "the cloud" happens to be). To allow the computers on each LAN to talk to each other, a specific route would have to be created on each LAN's router. Each router has a LAN address (known as E^0) and a WAN address (known as S^0). These are also known as private and public addresses, respectively. Let's say that the subnet mask used on both LANs is 255.255.255.0, just like the CIDR setup we have been using. On router A, we would need the following syntax:

Route add 10.253.253.0 mask 255.255.255.0 63.21.15.121

This makes the connection to the 10.253.253.0 network utilizing the LAN B router's public address. This address is labeled as S^0, or the first serial connection, which is used to connect to different networks.

On router B, we would need the following syntax:

Route add 10.254.254.0 mask 255.255.255.0 63.21.15.128

This makes the connection to the 10.254.254.0 network utilizing the LAN A router's public address.

Once these two connections have been made, communications should be possible between the two LANs.

If the routers are Windows Servers, some additional configuration would be necessary prior to adding these route line items. The servers would need to be equipped with two network adapters, making them multi-homed computers. Then, Routing and Remote Access would have to be configured to allow for IP forwarding. (Alternate software such as ISA could also be used.) After that, the route line items could be added.

If you were using conventional black box routers or appliances, TCP/IP protocols such as RIP and OSPF would be employed to streamline and automate the process:

- ***Routing information protocol (RIP)*** is a distance vector protocol that uses algorithms to decipher which route to send data packets.

• *Open shortest path first (OSPF)* is a link-state protocol that monitors the network for routers that have a change in their link-state, meaning whether they were turned off or on or restarted.

We'll talk more about routing protocols in Lesson 7.

 UTILIZE THE NET COMMAND

GET READY. Although not really considered part of the TCP/IP command set, the *net command* can display all kinds of important networking data, and it allows you to configure various networking options such as services.

1. Type the **net** command. View the results. You will see options such as view, user, session, start, and stop. Each of these options can help you analyze networking configurations and make modifications.

2. Type the command **net view**. This should show the computers on your immediate network, whether they operate as a workgroup or a domain. Each computer listed is preceded by a double backslash. This indicates a UNC or *Universal Naming Convention*. The UNC can be used when mapping drives and connecting to computers for other reasons.

3. Type the command **net time \\[localcomputer]**. For example, type **net time \\ desktop-lamp1**, as shown in Figure 5-25. This displays the current time of the computer. This command can also be used to synchronize time to other computers or time servers.

Figure 5-25

Net time

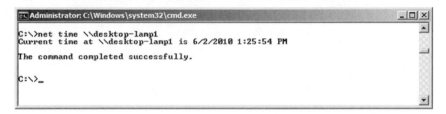

4. Type the command **net user** to display the user accounts on the computer.

5. Type the command **net stop themes**. This will stop the themes service that controls your desktop themes.

6. Type the command **net start themes** to restart the service.

This only scratches the surface of what the net command can do. This command can be incredibly useful to network administrators. Examine some of the other options by typing **net** followed by the option and then **/?** (e.g., **net time /?**).

Table 5-1 reviews the TCP/IP commands we covered in this lesson.

Table 5-1

Summary of TCP/IP commands

COMMAND	DESCRIPTION
Ipconfig	Displays information pertaining to your network adapter, namely TCP/IP configurations.
Ping	Used to test the existence of other hosts on the network.
Netstat	Used to display active TCP (or UDP) connections.
Nbtstat	Displays NetBIOS over TCP/IP statistics for local and remote computers.
Tracert	Shows paths to a destination on another network. It does this by pinging each step along the way three times.

(continued)

Table 5-1 (*continued*)

COMMAND	DESCRIPTION
Pathping	Similar to tracert, but also computes the degree of packet loss.
NSLookup	Displays information about DNS names and their corresponding IP addresses and can be used to diagnose DNS servers.
FTP	Is an application layer protocol as well as an application. The FTP command is used in the command prompt to connect to FTP servers.
Telnet	Used to take control of a remote computer via the command line.
Netsh	A built-in command-line scripting utility that allows you to display and modify network configurations of the local computer.
Route	Lets you display and make changes to the local IP routing table of the computer.

SKILL SUMMARY

IN THIS LESSON, YOU LEARNED HOW TO:

- Work with the command prompt as an administrator and in an efficient manner.
- Use basic TCP/IP commands such as ipconfig and ping to analyze and test a network.
- Use more advanced commands such as netstat, nbtstat, tracert, pathping, route, and netsh to fully examine a computer and configure it in the command line.
- Work with the Net command in an effort to find out more information about a system, start and stop services, and work with the network configuration.

■ Knowledge Assessment

Multiple Choice

Circle the letter that corresponds to the best answer.

1. You are troubleshooting a network connectivity problem and see the command results listed here. What command was typed to acquire these results?

   Request timed out.

   Request timed out.

   Request timed out.

   Request timed out.

   Packets: Sent = 4, Received = 0, Lost = 4 (100% loss),

   a. ipconfig
   b. netstat
   c. ping
   d. nbtstat

2. You are told to determine the MAC address of a Windows computer. Which command should you use to find this information?
   a. ipconfig
   b. ipconfig /all

    c. ipconfig /release

    d. ipconfig /flushdns

3. Proseware, Inc., needs you to decipher the command results listed here. What command was typed to acquire these results?

Active Connections

Proto	Local Address	Foreign Address	State
TCP	0.0.0.0:80	0.0.0.0:0	LISTENING
TCP	0.0.0.0:135	0.0.0.0:0	LISTENING
TCP	0.0.0.0:445	0.0.0.0:0	LISTENING
TCP	10.254.254.205:139	0.0.0.0:0	LISTENING
TCP	127.0.0.1:2804	127.0.0.1:49159	ESTABLISHED
UDP	0.0.0.0:123	*:*	
UDP	0.0.0.0:500	*:*	
UDP	0.0.0.0:2190	*:*	
UDP	0.0.0.0:3702	*:*	
UDP	0.0.0.0:3702	*:*	
UDP	0.0.0.0:4500	*:*	
UDP	0.0.0.0:62038	*:*	
UDP	10.254.254.205:137	*:*	
UDP	10.254.254.205:138	*:*	

    a. netstat

    b. nbtstat

    c. netstat —an

    d. nbtstat —an

4. A coworker asks for your help in analyzing the table shown here. What kind of table is this?

Network

Destination	Netmask	Gateway	Interface
0.0.0.0	0.0.0.0	10.254.254.1	10.254.254.205
10.254.254.0	255.255.255.0	On-link	10.254.254.205
10.254.254.205	255.255.255.255		10.254.254.205
127.0.0.0	255.0.0.0	On-link	127.0.0.1

    a. ARP table

    b. DNS table

    c. Local ARP table

    d. Local routing table

5. The IT director has asked you to ping a computer continuously. Which of the following is the best command to use?

    a. ping -n

    b. ping -t

    c. ping -1

    d. ping 127.0.0.1

6. You are troubleshooting a computer that cannot obtain the proper IP address from a DHCP server. Of the following commands, which should you try first?

    a. ipconfig /release

    b. ipconfig /renew

    c. ipconfig /displaydns

    d. ipconfig /source=dhcp

7. You see the following results in the command prompt. What command did you just type?

Resolved By Broadcast   = 0

Resolved By Name Server = 0

Registered By Broadcast   = 9

Registered By Name Server = 0

   a. nbtstat –r

   b. nbtstat –RR

   c. nbtstat –R

   d. nbtstat –s

8. Your boss's computer can ping other computers, but it cannot connect to Web sites. Examine the following ipconfig results and select the best answer to explain why this has occurred.

IPv4 Address. . . . .: 10.254.254.1

Subnet Mask . . . .: 255.255.255.0

Default Gateway. . . . .: 10.254.254.255

DNS Servers. . . . .: 127.0.0.1

   a. The subnet mask is incorrect.

   b. The IP address is incorrect.

   c. The default gateway is incorrect.

   d. The DNS server is incorrect.

9. A user cannot connect to the 192.168.1.0 network. Review the ipconfig results that follow and select the best answer to explain why this has occurred.

Windows IP Configuration

   Host Name . . . .: Computer1

   Primary Dns Suffix . . . .:

   Node Type. . . . .: Hybrid

   IP Routing Enabled. . . . .: No

   WINS Proxy Enabled . . . .: No

Ethernet adapter LAN:

   Connection-specific DNS Suffix.:

   Description . . . .: Intel(R)
     82566DC-2 Gigabit Network Connection

   Physical Address . . . .: 00-1C-C0-A1-55-16

   DHCP Enabled . . . .: No

   Autoconfiguration Enabled . . . .: Yes

   IPv4 Address. . . . .: 10.254.254.105(Preferred)

   Subnet Mask . . . .: 255.255.255.0

   Default Gateway. . . . .: 10.254.254.1

   DNS Servers. . . . .: 10.255.254.1

   a. The MAC address is incorrect.

   b. The DNS server address is incorrect.

   c. The default gateway address is incorrect.

   d. The IP address is incorrect.

10. You are troubleshooting a network connectivity problem and see the command results listed here. What command was typed to acquire these results?

1	15 ms	19 ms	19 ms	10.21.80.1
2	12 ms	22 ms	12 ms	208.59.252.1

3	152 ms	216 ms	149 ms	207.172.15.38
4	14 ms	24 ms	37 ms	207.172.19.222
5	21 ms	16 ms	25 ms	207.172.19.103
6	17 ms	23 ms	30 ms	207.172.9.126
7	15 ms	14 ms	15 ms	72.14.238.232
8	15 ms	35 ms	18 ms	209.85.241.148
9	30 ms	23 ms	44 ms	66.249.91.104

a. ipconfig
b. netstat
c. tracert
d. pathping

Fill in the Blank

Fill in the correct answer in the blank space provided.

1. The manager of IT asks you to explain to her what command issued the following results:

   Reply from 10.254.254.1: bytes=32 time=1ms TTL=64
   Reply from 10.254.254.1: bytes=32 time<1ms TTL=64
   Reply from 10.254.254.1: bytes=32 time<1ms TTL=64
   Reply from 10.254.254.1: bytes=32 time<1ms TTL=64
   Reply from 10.254.254.1: bytes=32 time<1ms TTL=64
   Reply from 10.254.254.1: bytes=32 time<1ms TTL=64
   Reply from 10.254.254.1: bytes=32 time<1ms TTL=64
   Reply from 10.254.254.1: bytes=32 time<1ms TTL=64
   Reply from 10.254.254.1: bytes=32 time<1ms TTL=64
   Reply from 10.254.254.1: bytes=32 time<1ms TTL=64

   The command typed was _____.

2. A coworker cannot finish troubleshooting a computer before the end of the day. Before leaving, your coworker tells you the following results took over three minutes to acquire, and he asks you not to delete them from his screen:

   Tracing route to google.com [66.249.91.104]

   over a maximum of 30 hops:

   0 Desktop-Lamp1 [10.254.254.205]

   1 bdl1.eas-ubr16.atw-eas.pa.cable.rcn.net [10.21.80.1]

   2 vl4.aggr1.phdl.pa.rcn.net [208.59.252.1]

   3 tge1-1.core3.phdl.pa.rcn.net [207.172.15.38]

   4 tge2-4.core1.nyw.ny.rcn.net [207.172.19.222]

   5 tge1-1.border1.nyw.ny.rcn.net [207.172.19.103]

   6 207.172.9.126

   7 72.14.238.232

   8 209.85.241.148

   9 lga15s02-in-f104.1e100.net [66.249.91.104]

   Computing statistics for 225 seconds . . .

   Source to Here This Node/Link

```
Hop  RTT    Lost/Sent = Pct Lost/Sent = Pct Address
 0                             Desktop-Lamp1
   [10.254.254.205]
                       0/ 100 = 0% |
 1  14ms  0/ 100 = 0% 0/ 100 = 0% bdl1.eas-ubr16.atw-eas.
   pa.cable.rc
n.net [10.21.80.1]
                       0/ 100 = 0% |
 2  25ms 0/ 100 = 0% 0/ 100 = 0% vl4.aggr1.phdl.pa.rcn.net
   [208.59.
252.1]
                       0/ 100 = 0% |
 3  33ms 0/ 100 = 0% 0/ 100 = 0% tge1-1.core3.phdl.pa.rcn.
   net [207.
172.15.38]
                       0/ 100 = 0% |
 4  38ms 0/ 100 = 0% 0/ 100 = 0% tge2-4.core1.nyw.ny.rcn.
   net [207.1
72.19.222]
                       0/ 100 = 0% |
 5  32ms 0/ 100 = 0% 0/ 100 = 0% tge1-1.border1.nyw.
   ny.rcn.net [207
.172.19.103]
                       0/ 100 = 0% |
 6  21ms 0/ 100 = 0% 0/ 100 = 0% 207.172.9.126
                       0/ 100 = 0% |
 7  23ms 0/ 100 = 0% 0/ 100 = 0% 72.14.238.232
                       0/ 100 = 0% |
 8  22ms 0/ 100 = 0%     0/ 100 = 0%
```

The command that was typed to produce these results is _____.

3. You need to add the IP address 192.168.1.1 to the network adapter via the command line. It also needs to have a gateway address of 192.168.1.100. The command you should type is _____.

4. You are troubleshooting a computer that is making strange connections to the Internet on its own. The _____ command will show you the network sessions to various computers on the Internet.

5. Your boss wants you to download some manuals from an FTP site. He wants you to do so via the command line. The _____ command will allow you to accomplish this goal.

6. A coworker has determined the IP address of a domain name as shown in the following results:

```
DNS request timed out.
    timeout was 2 seconds.
Server: UnKnown
Address: 10.254.254.1

Non-authoritative answer:
Name: google.com
Address: 66.249.91.104
```

Your coworker typed the _____ command to acquire these results.

7. You are troubleshooting a server and decide to refresh the NetBIOS names. You type a command that yields the following results:

   The NetBIOS names registered by this computer have been refreshed.

   You typed the _____ command.

8. You are simulating network traffic to a remote host. Examine the following results of a TCP/IP command:

   Reply from 10.254.254.1: bytes=1500 time=2ms TTL=64

   Reply from 10.254.254.1: bytes=1500 time<1ms TTL=64

   Reply from 10.254.254.1: bytes=1500 time<1ms TTL=64

   Reply from 10.254.254.1: bytes=1500 time<1ms TTL=64

   Ping statistics for 10.254.254.1:

       Packets: Sent = 4, Received = 4, Lost = 0 (0% loss),

   Approximate round trip times in milli-seconds:

       Minimum = 0ms, Maximum = 2ms, Average = 0ms

   The exact command that was issued was _____.

9. You are told by your boss to empty the DNS cache of a computer and reconnect to the nearest DNS server. You need to type the _____ and _____ commands.

10. You are troubleshooting a client's network. The client is using the following IP network scheme:

    IP network: 10.254.254.0

    Subnet mask: 255.255.255.0

    The client cannot access the 10.253.253.0 network. You go to the server that is also acting as the router between the two networks and type a command. You see the following results:

Network Destination	Netmask	Gateway	Interface
0.0.0.0	0.0.0.0	10.254.254.1	10.254.254.205
10.254.254.0	255.255.255.0	On-link	10.254.254.205
10.254.254.205	255.255.255.255		10.254.254.205
127.0.0.0	255.0.0.0	On-link	127.0.0.1

    You typed the _____ command. The reason the client cannot access the 10.253.253.0 network is because _____.

■ Case Scenarios

Scenario 5-1: Connecting to an FTP Server

Proseware, Inc., needs you to download several files from an FTP server. Here are the details:

Server name: ftp.proseware.com

File names: manual1.txt, manual2.txt, manual3.txt, manual4.txt

List the commands you would use in the command line to connect to the fictitious FTP server and download the files.

Scenario 5-2: Troubleshooting TCP/IP Results

The ABC Company wants you to figure out what is happening on its network. The company complains that it cannot connect a particular computer to the 10.253.253.0 network, to the 10.253.253.1 router, or to any other host on that network.

One of the company's technicians managed to get the following results within two different command-line windows:

Results #1:

IPv4 Address . . . . : 10.254.254.205

Subnet Mask . . . . : 255.255.255.0

Default Gateway . . . . : 10.254.254.1

Results #2:

Pinging 10.253.253.1 with 32 bytes of data:

Request timed out.

Request timed out.

Request timed out.

Request timed out.

Packets: Sent = 4, Received = 0, Lost = 4 (100% loss),

1. What commands were issued?
2. What is the problem here?
3. How can this problem be resolved?

Scenario 5-3: Documenting a Basic Wide Area Network

A client wants you to design a basic WAN with two LANs that can communicate with each other. The client would like the following configuration:

LAN A

- 192.168.1.0 network
- 255.255.255.0 subnet mask
- A router with the following configurations:
  a. LAN address: 192.168.1.250
  b. WAN address: 18.52.197.1

LAN B

- 192.168.2.0 network
- 255.255.255.0 subnet mask
- A router with the following configurations:
  a. LAN address: 192.168.2.199
  b. WAN address: 18.52.197.2

Create network documentation that shows the LANs, their central connecting device (such as a switch), and the router. Then show the command syntax you would use in the command line to make the routed connections between the LANs.

Scenario 5-4: Advanced Pinging

Proseware, Inc., wants you to set up a baseline to a server. You decide to implement the ping command and its various options. Proseware wants you to do the following:

1. Set up daily ping tests to a server with the IP 10.254.254.1 that will consist of 1,000 ICMP echoes.

2. Set up daily ping tests to a server with the same IP that will consist of one hundred 1,500 byte ICMP packets.

3. Configure these so that they run every day and are output to a text file.

 Workplace Ready

TCP/IP Command Table

TCP/IP commands are a huge part of a network administrator's life. The ability to use them quickly and efficiently depends on the knowledge of the user. Memorization of the commands, and especially the various command options, is imperative. Proper and smart use of the command prompt is also vital.

Research the commands listed after the following table and create your own table that describes them and each of their options (e.g., ping –t). In your table, include a column that describes why the command (and its option) would be used.

EXAMPLE SOLUTION			
Ping	–t	Pings a remote computer continuously.	Used to determine long-term connectivity. Works well with cabling tests.
Ipconfig	/all	Shows in-depth information about a network adapter.	Can help find details such as the MAC address, DNS server, and so on.

FTP

Ipconfig

Nbtstat

Net command

Netsh

Netstat

Nslookup

Pathping

Ping

Route

Telnet

Tracert

Note that navigation in Windows can be slightly different in different versions. Once you are finished assembling your table, spend some time working with each of the commands on as many of the following operating systems that you can:
-Windows 7
-Windows Vista
-Windows XP
-Windows Server 2008 or 2003

6 LESSON

Working with Networking Services

OBJECTIVE DOMAIN MATRIX

SKILLS/CONCEPTS	MTA EXAM OBJECTIVE	MTA EXAM OBJECTIVE NUMBER
Setting Up Common Networking Services	Understand networking services.	3.5
Defining More Network Services	Understand networking services.	3.5
Defining Name Resolution Techniques	Understand names resolution.	3.4

KEY TERMS

acknowledge

APIPA

authentication header (AH)

discovery

domain name system (DNS)

DORA

Dynamic Host Configuration Protocol (DHCP)

encapsulating security payload (ESP)

IP forwarding

Internet Protocol Security (IPsec)

offering

Remote Access Service (RAS)

Remote Desktop Protocol (RDP)

Remote Desktop Services

request

Routing and Remote Access Service (RRAS)

security association (SA)

Terminal Services

Windows Internet Name Service (WINS)

Network engineers love networking services. Services busy at work, such as DHCP and DNS, are equal to the beautiful sound of a hammer to a building contractor. These services are what make the networking world go round.

Proseware, Inc., expects you, as a network engineer, to set up a smart, efficient set of networking services, including DHCP, DNS, terminal services, and even WINS for the company's older devices.

It is important to understand how to configure servers to run these services, as well as how to configure clients to connect appropriately to those services. This should be understood from both a theory standpoint and a hands-on one. In addition, testing, troubleshooting, and performance baselining are all important aspects of network services.

In this lesson, we will explore how to install and configure DHCP, DNS, WINS, and Terminal Services, and we'll discuss other technologies such as RAS and IPSec as well. By mastering these skills and concepts, you will gain another level of experience on your way to being a network engineer.

Setting Up Common Networking Services

THE BOTTOM LINE

Networking services, such as DHCP and Terminal Services, are common in Microsoft networking environments. These help automate processes that would otherwise be done manually by a network administrator. They also allow greater connectivity for a much broader group of computing solutions. In this section, we will demonstrate the basics of DHCP and Terminal Services in action.

Working with DHCP

CERTIFICATION READY
How would you set up a DHCP network?
3.5

DHCP is the Dynamic Host Configuration Protocol. It sends IP information to clients automatically, making configuration of IP addresses on the network easier and automated. This protocol uses a four-step process known as DORA when disseminating IP addresses, and it employs ports 67 and 68.

In order to better understand how to work with DHCP on the server and on the client side, you must have a basic idea of how DHCP works.

Dynamic Host Configuration Protocol (DHCP) allows properly configured client computers to obtain IP addresses automatically from a DHCP server. This is done so that a network administrator does not have to manually configure IP addresses on all the computers on a network individually. The DHCP server takes care of this task quickly and automatically. This protocol therefore reduces the amount of system administration, allowing devices to be added to the network with little or no manual intervention.

The IP information obtained might include the following:

- IP addresses
- Subnet masks
- Gateway addresses
- DNS server addresses
- Other advanced options

A server or appliance runs the DHCP service and is configured to send the IP information to the clients. Usually, client computers benefit from this service; however, sometimes servers also obtain IP information automatically. This depends on the type of server and, as far as DHCP goes, the server acquiring the IP address automatically also becomes a client. For example, a file server may host files, but it may also be a client of a DHCP server. There are a few types of hosts that can be excluded from the scope of DHCP, including routers, firewalls, and some servers such as domain controllers. The beauty of a DHCP device is that it is fast, efficient, and should not cause an IP conflict.

Now, let's talk about how DHCP works. DHCP sessions use a four-step process known as **DORA**. The four steps are in this process are as follows:

- ***Discovery:*** The client computer broadcasts out to the network in order to find a DHCP server.
- ***Offering:*** The DHCP server sends out a unicast "offering" of an IP address to the client computer.
- ***Request:*** The client broadcasts to all servers that it has accepted the offer.
- ***Acknowledge:*** The DHCP server sends a final unicast to the client that includes the IP information the client will use.

Normally, when a computer first tries to obtain an IP address, it goes through all four stages. However, if a client already has an address and wants to renew it (within certain time parameters), only the last two steps are necessary. So, for example, if the client computer ran an ipconfig /release and an ipconfig /renew, only the request and acknowledge steps would occur. This is because the computer retains information about the IP address within the registry. If the IP address's lease hasn't run out, this information can be taken from the registry, and as long as the server agrees to the computer reusing the address, everything will work the same as it did previously.

DHCP works on two ports, 67 and 68. Servers run inbound port 67 to listen to client requests in order to hand out IP addresses. Clients run inbound port 68 to accept the data from the server.

TAKE NOTE*

DHCP utilizes ports 67 and 68.

 CONFIGURE DHCP

GET READY. In this exercise, you will learn how to configure DHCP on the server and on the client side. Here, we will be using Windows Server 2008 as the DHCP server. This server will have a static IP address assigned to the network adapter. Installing a DHCP server consists of the following actions:

- Installing the DHCP service
- Configuring an IP scope
- Activating the scope
- Authorizing the server
- Configuring advanced IP options (optional)

1. Go to your Windows Server. Configure the DHCP server statically with the following IP address: 192.168.1.100.

2. Install and configure the DHCP service:

   a. Go to the Server Manager console window. You can get to this in various ways, such as by clicking **Start > Administrative Tools > Server Manager.**

   b. On the left side, click **Roles.**

   c. On the right side, click **Add Roles.** This displays the Add Roles Wizard.

   d. Click **Next.** This displays the Select Server Roles window.

   e. Check **DHCP Server** and click **Next.**

   f. Read the Introduction. Note that this local server should have a static IP address assigned. This is a general rule of DHCP; DHCP servers should use a static IP. Click **Next.**

   g. In the Network Connection Bindings step, verify that the static IP is check marked and click **Next.**

   h. In the IPv4 Settings step, leave the information blank and click **Next.** This step refers to DNS and domain controllers that we have not set up yet. Without this information, the DHCP server will simply hand out IP addresses, subnet masks, and gateway addresses.

   i. In the IPv4 WINS settings step, click **Next.** Again, we haven't set this up yet. You can always return to your DHCP server later to configure such things as WINS and DNS.

j. Add a DHCP scope by clicking the **Add** button. A scope is a range of IP addresses that can be handed out to clients. Add the following information:

- **Scope name:** Proseware Scope1
- **Starting IP address:** 192.168.1.150
- **Ending IP address:** 192.168.1.199
- **Subnet mask:** 255.255.255.0
- **Default gateway:** 192.168.1.1
- **Subnet type:** Wired

An example of this is shown in Figure 6-1.

Figure 6-1

Adding a DHCP scope

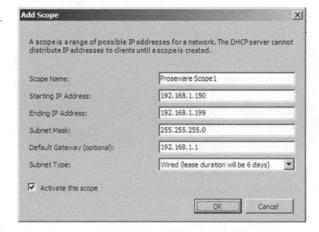

Of course, this information will vary depending on the configuration you want for your network. Also, you have the option to select wireless as the Subnet type. Note that Wired has a lease duration of six days by default, whereas Wireless has a duration of eight hours. Wireless connections should always have a shorter lease equal to the duration of one work day or less.

Make sure that "Activate this scope" is checkmarked and click **OK**. That adds the scope to the list. You can add more in the future if you wish, but for now, we will leave it as is. Click **Next** to continue.

k. In the Configure DHCPv6 Stateless Mode window, select **Disable**. We are focusing on IPv4 for this exercise, but IPv6 could always be configured later if necessary. Click **Next**.

l. For the IPv6 DNS Settings window, simply click **Next**. We will not be configuring this feature.

m. You should now see a Confirmation window (Figure 6-2). Review the information in this window and make sure it is correct before clicking **Install**. In the figure, we left DHCPv6 Stateless Mode enabled because our particular server needs to have it running.

Figure 6-2

DHCP Confirmation window

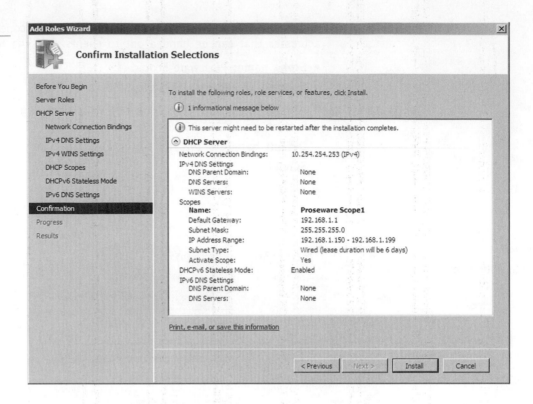

When complete, the Results should show that the installation succeeded. Click **Close** to finish. This will authorize the server.

At this point, the DHCP server is ready to hand out IP addresses to client computers.

3. Go to a Windows client computer and obtain an IP address automatically:

   a. Access the IPv4 Properties dialog box for the wired network adapter.

   b. Select the **Obtain an IP address automatically** radio button.

   c. Click **OK** for all dialog boxes.

   d. Open the command prompt and type **ipconfig /all**. You should obtain an IP address automatically from the list of IP addresses in the DHCP server's IP scope. Most likely, it will be the first one on the list: 192.168.1.150.

   e. If, for some reason, you cannot obtain an IP address, check your configuration settings on the server. Also, on the client, you can attempt an **ipconfig/release** and **ipconfig /renew** to retry obtaining an IP address. In some cases, you might obtain an IP address from another DHCP device or server. If this is the case, remove that device from the network. If your client has obtained an address on the 169.254.0.0 network, then APIPA has intervened and self-assigned an IP address. See the next exercise for information about how to disable APIPA.

   f. Test your new IP address by pinging the IP address of the DHCP server and another client on the network. Disable any firewalls that might block pings.

4. When you are finished, return the client computers to normal. If necessary, access the server and stop the DHCP service.

⊙ **DISABLE APIPA**

GET READY. Sometimes, *APIPA* can get in the way of a client obtaining an IP address properly (e.g., when a client attempts to obtain an IP address from a DHCP server, but the DHCP server is too busy). At that point, APIPA would self-assign an IP address to the client computer, and the computer would be stuck with that address until an ipconfig / release and /renew was run from the command line. Depending on the version of Windows and the configuration, this still might not be enough. If you see an IP address of 169.254. x.x, then you know that the client has self-assigned an IP address with the help of APIPA. This shouldn't happen often, but you never know. Just in case, here's how to disable APIPA in the Registry:

1. Access the Registry by pressing **Windows + R** on the keyboard and typing **regedit.exe**.

2. Navigate the following path:

    Computer > HKEY_LOCAL_MACHINE > SYSTEM > CurrentControlSet > Services > Tcpip > Parameters > Interfaces

3. In the Interfaces subkey, find the network adapter on which you wish to disable APIPA. The best way to do this is to find the current IP address of the network adapter with an ipconfig, then locate that adapter in the registry by searching through each of the interfaces one at a time and examining the IPAddress entry.

4. Right click the right pane and select **New > DWORD**.

5. Name the new dword **ipautoconfigurationenabled**.

6. Then, make sure the entry is set to zero. This is the disabled setting. An example of this is shown in Figure 6-3.

Figure 6-3

Disabling APIPA

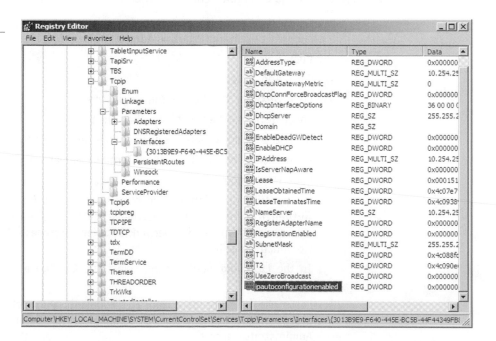

Once APIPA is disabled, it will not interfere with the client's particular network adapter attempting to obtain an IP address. However, this does not ensure that the client will receive an IP address. Always verify that the DHCP server is configured properly and connected to the network.

Working with Terminal Services

Terminal Services allows client computers to control a server remotely or use applications that have been loaded on the server. It uses port 3389. In order for clients to connect to a server running Terminal Services, they must run the Remote Desktop Protocol or be thin-client computers.

Terminal Services, also known as *Remote Desktop Services*, is a type of thin-client terminal server computing. It allows client computers to access and use applications loaded on the server, as well as to connect to and take control of a server. Thin-client computers *and* PCs can connect to servers running Terminal Services. The service uses port 3389 and is also known as Microsoft WBT Server. WBT stands for Windows-Based Terminal.

You can configure a set of applications that thin-clients are allowed to access, or you can set up Terminal Services to allow full administrative access to the server.

When clients connect, they do so with the Remote Desktop program, which is based on the *Remote Desktop Protocol (RDP)*.

⊙→ CONFIGURE TERMINAL SERVICES

GET READY. In this exercise, you will learn how to configure Terminal Services on a Windows Server for administrative access. You will also learn how to connect to the server and control it from a client computer.

1. Go to your Windows Server. In this exercise, we are using a Windows Server 2008 computer as our Terminal Services server.

2. Install and configure Terminal Services:

   a. Go to the Server Manager console window. You can get to this in various ways, such as by clicking **Start > Administrative Tools > Server Manager**.

   b. Click **Roles**.

   c. Click **Add Roles**.

   d. Click **Next** for the Before You Begin screen.

   e. Check **Terminal Services** and click **Next**.

   f. Read the Terminal Services introduction and click **Next**.

   g. In the Role Services screen, check **Terminal Server** and **TS Licensing**. Then click **Next**.

   h. Click **Next** again.

   i. In the Authentication Method screen, select the **Do not require Network Level Authentication** radio button. Then click **Next**. Keep in mind that many network environments will require Network Location Awareness (NLA), but for this exercise, we will disable it.

   j. In the Licensing Mode screen, select the **Configure later** radio button, then click **Next**.

   k. Leave the User Groups screen as the default and click **Next**. You can add groups of users at any time to Terminal Services. For now, we will just allow Administrator access.

   l. Leave the default setting for the TS Licensing Configuration screen. By default it is **This workgroup**, but if you are part of a domain, you can add the server to that as well. Click **Next**.

   m. Review the Confirmation screen. Your results should be similar to Figure 6-4. Then click **Install**.

Figure 6-4

Terminal Services Confirmation
screen

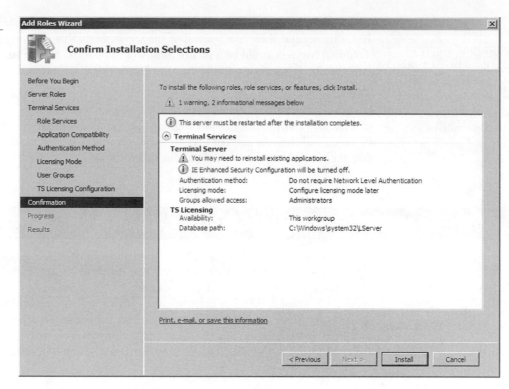

Terminal Services will take a moment to install. When it is finished, move on to step 3.

3. Connect to the server with the Remote Desktop program:

   a. Go to the Windows client computer.

   b. Open Remote Desktop by navigating to **Start > All Programs > Accessories > Remote Desktop Connection**.

   c. Type in the IP address of the server on which you configured Terminal Services.

   d. Type in the username **administrator**. An example is shown in Figure 6-5.

   e. Click **Connect**.

Figure 6-5

Remote Desktop Connection
login dialog box

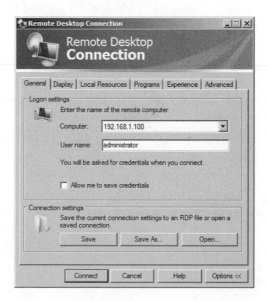

TAKE NOTE

Modifications might be necessary to the Remote Desktop settings on the client computer. Make sure that outbound remote connections are allowed.

This makes the connection to the server and prompts for the server's username and password. Enter those, and then take control of the server. Note that opening port 3389 for use with Terminal Services could be a security vulnerability, so be sure to use Terminal Services only if it is absolutely necessary, and always use Network Level Authentication to secure it further.

There are two ways to leave a session. The first is to log off, which ends the user's session and closes all programs associated with that session. The second is to disconnect. This stops the connection, but the user session still runs on the server, programs still run, resources can still be used, and the user can connect later and resume that session. If you have full administrative access, you can also restart or shut down the server.

■ Defining More Networking Services

THE BOTTOM LINE

Remote Access Service (RAS) is grouping of different hardware and software platforms to allow remote access to another computer or network device. Originally used with dial-up services, Microsoft RAS has morphed into RRAS, or Routing and Remote Access Service. This powerful service allows clients to connect remotely to a central network using dial-up and high-speed Internet connections. It also allows connectivity through VPNs. IPsec is an encrypting and authenticating protocol that helps secure VPN and other types of network transactions.

Defining RRAS

CERTIFICATION READY
How would you define RRAS?
3.5

Microsoft's RRAS is built into Windows Server and offers a variety of functions, including dial-in service and the ability to create virtual private networks.

Routing and Remote Access Service (RRAS) is a network service in Windows Server 2008, Windows Server 2003, and Windows Server 2000. It permits an administrator to configure dial-up remote access servers, VPN servers, and IP routing, as well as NAT.

For a long time, the standard way to telecommute to work was to utilize a direct dial-up connection. This is illustrated in Figure 6-6. Although this allowed for connectivity, it was often slow, and users suffered from noisy and dropped lines.

Figure 6-6

Dial-up connection

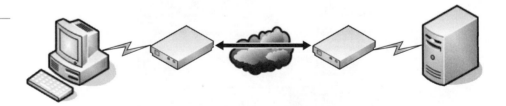

Today, the standard is to utilize a Virtual Private Network or VPN. With VPNs (Figure 6-7), the inherent power of the Internet is exploited, and direct IP connections are made from clients to a VPN server or router. Dial-up connections via modems that connect to the Internet are still supported, but more commonly, high-speed connections like DSL, cable, and fiber optic are preferred.

Figure 6-7

VPN connection

VPN
Client

ISP

VPN
Server

 ENABLE ROUTING AND REMOTE ACCESS SERVICES

GET READY. In this exercise, you will learn how to load up and enable RRAS by performing the following actions:

1. Go to your Windows Server. In this exercise, we are using a Windows Server 2008 computer.

2. Create a new MMC by going to **Start > Run** and typing **MMC**.

3. Add the Routing and Remote Access snap-in:

   a. Click **File > Add/Remove Snap-in**.

   b. Scroll down and click **Routing and Remote Access**.

   c. Click **Add**.

   d. Click **OK**.

   If you wish, you can add the Server Manager to your MMC as well so that you have most of the tools you will need in one window.

   At this point, RRAS is not configured or running. Your MMC should look similar to Figure 6-8.

Figure 6-8

MMC with RRAS and Server Manager snap-ins added

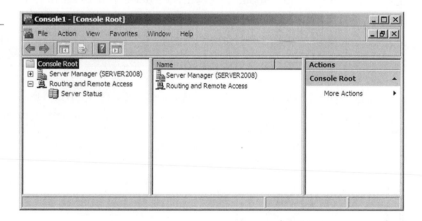

4. Right-click **Routing and Remote Access**, and select **Add Server**.

5. In the Add Server window, leave the default as **This computer** and click **OK**. This adds the server to the RRAS list in the MMC.

6. Right click the server name and select **Configure and Enable Routing and Remote Access**.

7. Click **Next** for the welcome window.

   The welcome window is where you can select whether you want to have remote access, a VPN, or set up the server as a router. In this exercise, we will make a basic router.

8. Select the **Custom configuration** radio button and click **Next**.

9. Select the **LAN routing** check box and click **Next**.

10. Click **Finish** for the summary screen.

Now RRAS is configured and can be modified further depending on what network adapters and IP addresses the server has. By enabling LAN routing, the concept known as *IP forwarding* has been turned on, but only if the server has two or more network adapters. IP forwarding bridges the gap between the two network adapters even if they are on two different IP networks.

11. Be sure to save the MMC for use later on. You might also want to disable RRAS in case you will be using other services that might conflict with it in the future. To do this, just right click the server in the MMC and select **Disable**.

Defining IPsec

Internet Protocol Security (IPsec) is a protocol within the TCP/IP suite that encrypts and authenticates IP packets. It is designed to secure any application traffic because it resides on the network layer (or Internet layer, as TCP/IP programmers refer to it). This protocol is used in conjunction with virtual private networks and is an integral part of IPv6. There are three main protocols that IPsec uses to perform its necessary functions:

- *Security association (SA):* This generates the encryption and authentication keys that are used by IPsec.

- *Authentication header (AH):* This provides connectionless integrity and the authentication of data. It also provides protection versus replay attacks.

- *Encapsulating security payload (ESP):* This provides the same services as AH but also provides confidentiality when sending data.

The particular IPsec protocol that is used is determined by the application utilizing IPsec. We will talk more about IPsec when we delve into VPNs in Lesson 8.

■ Defining Name Resolution Techniques

THE BOTTOM LINE

Computers work best when communicating by IP address. However, humans work best when they communicate with words. Something has to give. Therein lies the purpose of name resolution. Names can be resolved or translated to IP address by services such as DNS and WINS.

Defining DNS

The *Domain Name System (DNS)* is a worldwide service that resolves host names to IP addresses. This facilitates proper communication between computers. DNS servers communicate with each other in a hierarchy in an effort to teach each other their name resolutions. DNS servers are also implemented in today's LANs (e.g., Microsoft domains), although DNS can be used on any operating system that runs TCP/IP. The LAN DNS servers do the same thing as their Internet counterparts, just on a smaller scale (although sometimes not so small!). DNS servers use inbound port 53 to accept name resolution requests. Microsoft DNS servers run the DNS service, and clients can connect to and use that service as long as their IP properties pages are configured properly.

INSTALL DNS AND CREATE A ZONE

GET READY. In this exercise, we will install DNS to a Windows Server 2008.

1. Open the previous MMC or create a new one.
2. Navigate to **Server Manager > Roles**.
3. Click the **Add Roles** link.
4. Click **Next**.
5. Check the **DNS Server** option as shown in Figure 6-9 and click **Next**.

Figure 6-9

Adding the DNS service

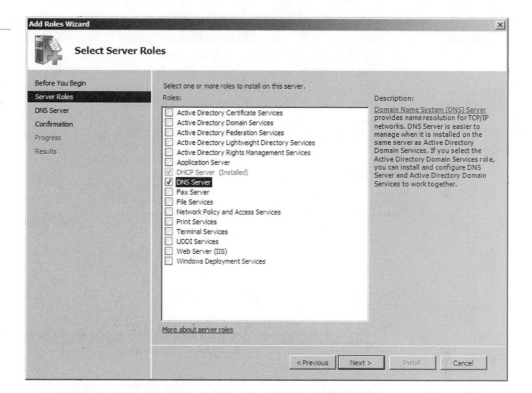

6. Click **Next** for the introduction.
7. Click **Install** at the confirmation window. Installation will take a few moments. A restart of the computer might be necessary depending on the configuration.
8. The installation should succeed. Click **Close** at the results screen.
9. DNS should now be added to the Roles list under Server Manager. However, let's go ahead and add it as a snap-in as well.

   Now we'll add a zone. Zones are areas of the DNS namespace, such as Microsoft.com or dmz.Proseware.com.
10. Access the DNS snap-in and navigate to Forward Lookup Zones.
11. Right click **Forward Lookup Zones** and select **New Zone**.
12. Click **Next** for the welcome window.
13. Select the **Primary Zone** radio button and click **Next**.
14. Give the zone a name (e.g., **dnstest.com**). Then click **Next**.
15. In the Zone File window, leave the default name (e.g., dnstest.com.dns) and click **Next**.
16. Leave the default selection of **Do not allow dynamic updates** and click **Next**.

17. Review the summary and click **Finish**.

You should now have a zone called **dnstest.com** inside the Forward Lookup Zones folder. This is where DNS records will be stored, such as hostnames and their corresponding IP addresses. Some zones allow for these records to be created automatically (e.g., in a domain). Otherwise, records can be added manually. If client computers want to use this DNS server, their IP Properties pages need to be updated by adding the IP address of the server to the preferred or alternate DNS server field.

Defining WINS

Windows Internet Name Service (WINS) is a service that resolves NetBIOS names to IP addresses. It is Microsoft's version of the NetBIOS Name Service (NBNS) combined with a name server. A Windows computer name (e.g., Computer1), can be considered a host name and interact with DNS, and/or a NetBIOS name either working alone or in concert with a WINS server. Most companies opt to use DNS, but sometimes you will find WINS-enabled devices and WINS servers on less common and older devices. Whereas DNS can have hosts added statically or dynamically, WINS only works in a dynamic fashion. No configuration of a WINS server is necessary once it is installed, other than database replication.

 INSTALL WINS

GET READY. In this exercise, we will install WINS to a Windows Server 2008. Note that this is done in the Add Features section and not the Add Roles section.

1. Open the previous MMC or create a new one.
2. Navigate to **Server Manager > Features**.
3. Click the **Add Features** link.
4. Check the **WINS Server** option as shown in Figure 6-10 and click **Next**.

Figure 6-10

Adding the WINS server

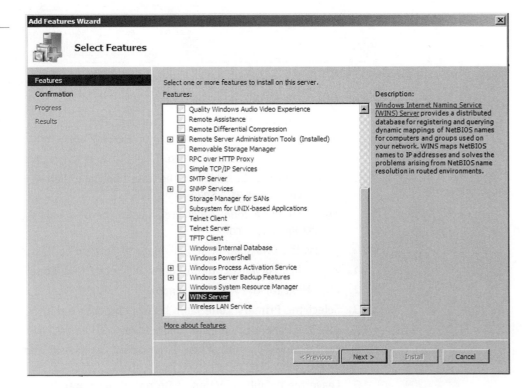

5. Click **Install** at the Confirmation window. No other configuration is necessary.

6. The installation should succeed. Click **Close** at the results screen.

7. At this point, if you click on the Features option, you should see several features installed, including WINS server as shown in Figure 6-11.

Figure 6-11

Server 2008 features list

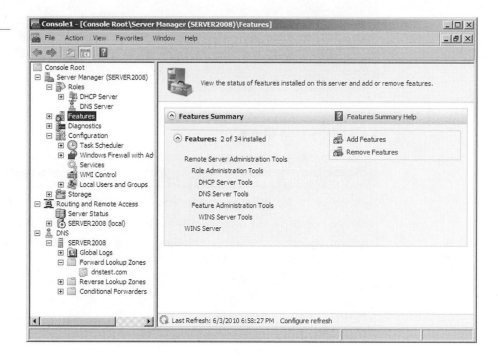

8. To have the WINS server take care of name resolution for Windows clients, go to the IP Properties window of the client computer, then click the **Advanced** button and click the **WINS** tab. From there, one or more WINS servers can be added.

Table 6-1

Networking services

COMMAND	DESCRIPTION
DHCP	Short for Dynamic Host Configuration Protocol. It allows properly configured client computers to obtain IP addresses automatically from a DHCP server.
Terminal Services	A type of thin-client terminal server computing. It allows client computers to connect to and take control of a server. Thin-client computers *and* PCs can connect to servers running Terminal Services.
Routing and Remote Access Service (RRAS)	A network service in Windows Server 2008, Windows Server 2003, and Windows Server 2000. It allows an administrator to configure dial-up remote access servers, VPN servers, and configure IP routing, as well as NAT.
IPsec	A protocol within the TCP/IP suite that encrypts and authenticates IP packets. It is designed to secure any application traffic because it resides on the network layer.

(continued)

Table 6-1 *(continued)*

COMMAND	DESCRIPTION
DNS	A worldwide service that resolves host names to IP addresses. This facilitates proper communication between computers. A hierarchy of DNS servers communicates with each other in an effort to teach one another their name resolutions.
WINS	A service that resolves NetBIOS names to IP addresses. It is Microsoft's version of the NetBIOS Name Service (NBNS) combined with a name server.

SKILL SUMMARY

IN THIS LESSON, YOU LEARNED:

- How to install and configure DHCP to hand out IP addresses to client computers.
- The four-step DHCP process known as DORA.
- How to install and configure Terminal Services so that client computers can connect remotely to a server and take control of it in the GUI.
- How to install and configure Routing and Remote Access Service (RRAS) as a LAN router.
- To define IPsec and the various types, including SA, AH, and ESP.
- How DNS and WINS function and how to install them in Windows Server 2008, as well as how to create forward lookup zones.

Knowledge Assessment

Multiple Choice

Circle the letter that corresponds to the best answer.

1. Your Windows client failed to broadcast to all servers that it has accepted an IP address offer. What step is this in the four-step DORA process?
   a. Discovery
   b. Offering
   c. Request
   d. Acknowledge

2. You are in charge of setting up a DHCP server to hand out IP addresses and other IP-related information. Which of the following cannot be obtained from a DHCP server?
   a. IP address
   b. MAC address
   c. DNS server address
   d. Gateway address

3. Proseware, Inc., wants you to scan servers for DHCP activity. Which ports should you be looking for?
   a. 53 and 54
   b. 80 and 443
   c. 20 and 21
   d. 67 and 68

4. A coworker asks for your help in analyzing a problem with a DHCP server. The server's scope has been created and the IP range appears to be valid, yet no clients are obtaining IP addresses. What could be the reason for this? (Select the best answer.)
   a. The server was not authorized.
   b. The scope was not activated.
   c. The scope was not authorized.
   d. The server is down.

5. The IT director has asked you set up a computer to acquire an IP address from a newly configured DHCP server. Which of the following is the best command to use?
   a. ping -n
   b. ipconfig /renew
   c. ipconfig /release
   d. ping -renew

6. You are troubleshooting a computer that cannot obtain the proper IP address from a DHCP server. When you run ipconfig, the address 169.254.25.53 shows up in the results. What service is assigning the IP address to the client?
   a. DHCP
   b. WINS
   c. APIPA
   d. DNS

7. You have just scanned the ports of your server and see that port 3389 is open. What can you deduce from this?
   a. The WINS service is running.
   b. The DNS service is running.
   c. Terminal Services is running.
   d. RRAS is running.

8. Your boss asks you to take control of a server remotely from within the GUI of the client OS. What is the proper tool to use?
   a. Remote Desktop
   b. Telnet
   c. FTP
   d. SSH

9. You have been asked by a client to install a VPN server. Which of the following services should be chosen in order to accomplish this?
   a. DNS
   b. RRAS
   c. WINS
   d. IPsec

10. Which protocol generates encryption and authentication keys that are used by IPsec?
    a. ESP
    b. AH
    c. SA
    d. IPv6

Fill in the Blank

Fill in the correct answer in the blank space provided.

1. The _____ service resolves host names to IP addresses.

2. The _____ service resolves NetBIOS names to IP addresses.

3. The _____ step in the DORA four-step process is when a client broadcasts out to the network in order to find a DHCP server.

4. When renewing a DHCP assigned IP address, usually _____ steps of the DORA process are involved.

5. To install the DHCP service on a Windows Server 2008 computer, you would use the _____ section of the Server Manager.

6. By default, wired DHCP leases last for _____ days.

7. The _____ and _____ commands are useful when troubleshooting a client that is having difficulty obtaining an IP address from a DHCP server.

8. A client that has obtained an IP address of 169.254.10.175 is getting the IP address from _____.

9. _____ enables clients to connect to and take control of a server.

10. _____ networks take the place of direct dial-up connections by using the inherent power of the Internet.

■ Case Scenarios

Scenario 6-1: Selecting the Appropriate Services

A client wants you to install a service or services that will allow him to do the following:

1. Enable NetBIOS name to IP address resolution.
2. Allow virtual connectivity to the LAN from remote clients in a secure manner.

What two services will enable this functionality?

Scenario 6-2: Selecting the Appropriate Services

The ABC Company wants you to install a service or services that will allow it to do the following:

1. Enable host name to IP address resolution internally in the company.
2. Enable client computers to obtain IP information automatically.
3. Allow administrators to access servers to control them remotely.

What three services will enable this functionality?

Scenario 6-3: Setting Up a DHCP Server

Proseware, Inc., needs you to set up a DHCP server on a D-Link DIR-655 router. The following are details for the IP configuration:

- IP scope: 10.254.254.1–10.254.254.199
- DHCP lease time: 480 minutes
- Always broadcast: Enabled
- NetBIOS announcement: Enabled
- NetBIOS node type: Broadcast only
- Primary WINS address: 10.254.254.250

Access the DIR-655 emulator at the following link and configure the DHCP server appropriately: http://support.dlink.com/emulators/dir655/133NA/login.html

Scenario 6-4: Setting Up a New DHCP and Migrating Old Computers

Proseware, Inc., currently uses the 192.168.1.0 Class C network for 225 computers. The company wants to add another 200 new computers and install a new DHCP server. Specifically, Proseware wants you to:

1. Select a classful IP network number that can support the total number of computers, old and new.

2. Obtain new addresses from the new DHCP server on the original 225 computers.

✳ **Workplace Ready**

DHCP Is Everywhere!

IP addresses that are obtained from a DHCP server can be found everywhere. Most computers on a LAN get their IP information, including IP address, subnet mask, gateway address, DNS server address, and more, from a DHCP server. Home users' computers usually get their IP information from the DHCP server in their four-port SOHO router. And the router gets its WAN address from an Internet Service Provider (ISP). Equipment such as gaming consoles and digital video recorders also get dynamically assigned IPs. PDAs and some cell phones, as well as other handheld computers and gaming equipment, are also in the DHCP group.

Take a look around your house, work, school, library, and so on and make a list of devices and computers that obtain IP addresses automatically from a DHCP server. Then, use the Internet to research the major ISPs that hand out IP addresses and what IP network numbers they use.

Understanding Wide Area Networks

OBJECTIVE DOMAIN MATRIX

SKILLS/CONCEPTS	MTA EXAM OBJECTIVE	MTA EXAM OBJECTIVE NUMBER
Understanding Routing	Understand routers.	2.2
Defining Common WAN Technologies and Connections	Understand wide area networks (WANs).	1.3

KEY TERMS

asynchronous transfer mode (ATM)

basic rate ISDN (BRI)

Border Gateway Protocol (BGP)

broadband cable

Committed information rate (CIR)

CSU/DSU

digital subscriber line (DSL)

dynamic routing

fiber distributed data interface (FDDI)

Frame Relay

header

hops

Integrated Services Digital Network (ISDN)

Interior Gateway Routing Protocol (IGRP)

leased lines

Open Shortest Path First (OSPF)

overhead

packet switching

packet switching exchange (PSE)

permanent virtual circuit (PVC)

POTS/PSTN

primary rate ISDN (PRI)

Routing Information Protocol (RIP)

Synchronous Optical Network (SONET)

static routing

synchronous

T1

T3

T-carrier

trailer

virtual circuit

X.25

Your client Proseware, Inc., needs to expand its network. Previously, you set up local area networks for Proseware, but now the company wants a wide area network (WAN) with all the routers necessary to make those connections.

You must give Proseware several wide area networking options, along with the different types of routers that will work best for each of those options. The skills required for this task include the ability to document wide area networks and the know-how to install various networking services and protocols.

Developing these skills requires a lot of knowledge, so this lesson defines the most common WAN technologies available and increases your understanding of routing protocols and routing devices.

■ Understanding Routing

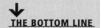
THE BOTTOM LINE

Routing is the process of moving data across networks or internetworks between hosts or between routers themselves. Information is transmitted according to the IP networks and individual IP addresses of the hosts in question. A router is in charge of maintaining tables of information about other routers on the network or internetwork. It also utilizes several different TCP/IP protocols to transfer the data and to discover other routers. IP routing is the most common kind of routing, just as TCP/IP is the most common protocol suite. IP routing occurs on the network layer of the OSI model.

Identifying Static and Dynamic Routing

A static route is one that has been manually configured. A dynamic route is one that has been implemented dynamically with special routing protocols. In this section, we will configure RRAS statically and then add the Routing Information Protocol (RIP) to allow for dynamic routing.

CERTIFICATION READY
How can you differentiate between static and dynamic routing?
2.2

Static routing refers to the manual configuration of a router. For example, when a routing entry is manually entered into the routing table with the **route add** command, this is known as static routing. We demonstrated a basic example of this in Lesson 5. An example of a static router is a Windows Server 2008 computer with two network adapters and IP routing (IP forwarding) enabled, as shown in Lesson 6. This is a basic type of router that does not change with the network and is not fault tolerant. Statically entered routes do not "know" what is happening on the network; they cannot sense new routers or the modified state of a particular router. Accordingly, there is a great deal of maintenance required with a static router. Because of this, the better solution is to utilize dynamic routing.

Dynamic routing is implemented by dynamically configuring routing tables. This is done with dynamic routing protocols such as RIP and OSPF, as mentioned in Lesson 5. Both of these are part of the TCP/IP suite of protocols, and they both work on layer 3 of the OSI model. It is important to be able to distinguish between routable protocols and routing protocols. NetBEUI is an example of a nonroutable protocol. An example of a routable protocol would be TCP/IP or RIP. Let's talk further about RIP and some other routing protocols:

- *Routing Information Protocol (RIP):* A dynamic protocol that uses distance-vector routing algorithms to decipher which route to send data packets. In packet-switched networks, a distance-vector routing protocol uses the Bellman-Ford algorithm to calculate where and how data will be transmitted. The protocol calculates the direction or interface that packets should be forwarded to, as well as the distance from the destination. RIPv1 and RIPv2 are common among today's networks.

- **Open Shortest Path First (OSPF):** A link-state protocol that monitors the network for routers that have a change in their link state, meaning they were turned off, turned on, or restarted. This is perhaps the most commonly used interior gateway protocol in large networks. Interior gateway protocols are used to determine connections between autonomous systems.

- **Interior Gateway Routing Protocol (IGRP):** A proprietary protocol used in large networks to overcome the limitations of RIP.

- **Border Gateway Protocol (BGP):** A core routing protocol that bases routing decisions on the network path and rules.

When it comes to larger networks and the Internet, routing tables can become cumbersome. A router requires a lot of fast, efficient memory to handle these tables. Older routers simply cannot cope with the number of entries, and some protocols such as BGP might not work properly on these routers. Because the Internet is growing so quickly, ISPs collectively utilize CIDR in an attempt to limit the size of routing tables. Network congestion and load balancing are also issues. Depending on the scenario, you might need to use newer routers with more memory and faster network connections, and you should carefully consider which protocols you use. Generally, a small to mid-sized company can make do with RIP. Let's show this in action.

 CONFIGURE RRAS AND ADD RIP

GET READY. In this exercise, you will configure RRAS as a NAT server and install RIP on a Windows server. We will be using Windows Server 2008 Standard.

1. Go to the server and access the MMC created previously. If you do not have one, create a new one and add the RRAS snap-in.

2. Expand the Routing and Remote Access snap-in, then right click the server name and select **Configure and Enable Routing and Remote Access**.

3. Click **Next** for the welcome window.

4. Select the **Network address translation** (NAT) radio button and click **Next**.

5. In the NAT Internet Connection screen, leave the default **Create a new demand-dial interface to the Internet** option selected and click **Next**. (Your options might be slightly different depending on the type and amount of network adapters present on the server.)

6. Click **Next** to apply the selections.

7. Click **OK** for the Routing and Remote Access pop-up window.

8. Click **Next** to start RRAS. This will bring up the Demand Dial Interface wizard.

9. Click **Next** for the welcome screen.

10. Leave the default Interface name and click **Next**.

11. Leave the default radio button **Connect using VPN** and continue by clicking **Next**.

12. In the VPN Type window, leave the current selection and click **Next**.

13. Enter a destination address of **192.168.1.100** and click **Next**.

14. Leave the defaults for Protocols and Security and click **Next**.

15. For the Dial-Out credentials, enter the following:

    Username = administrator

    Leave the rest of the information blank and click **Next**.

16. Click **Finish** for the completion window.

17. Click **Finish** for the RRAS completion window.

    At this point, you should see your RRAS server modified. It should also have a green arrow pointing upward, signifying that it is running. An example is shown in Figure 7-1.

Figure 7-1

Configured RRAS server

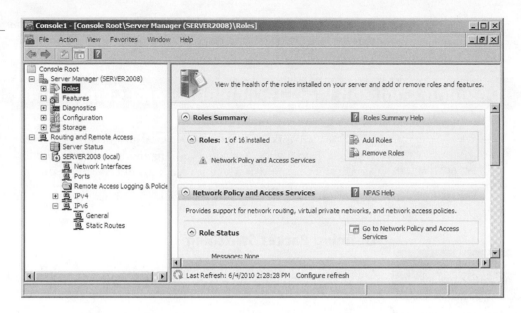

If you encounter any problems, consider removing unnecessary services, such as the previously installed DHCP and DNS. Also make sure those roles have been completely removed in the Server Manager.

 INSTALL RIP

GET READY. Now, install RIP by performing these actions:

1. In the Routing and Remote Access snap-in, navigate to:

   Servername > IPv4 > General

2. Right click General, then select New Routing Protocol.

3. In the New Routing Protocol window, select **RIP version 2 for Internet Protocol** and click **OK**. This should install RIP into the IPv4 portion of RRAS, as shown in Figure 7-2.

4. Save and close the MMC.

Figure 7-2

RIP installed

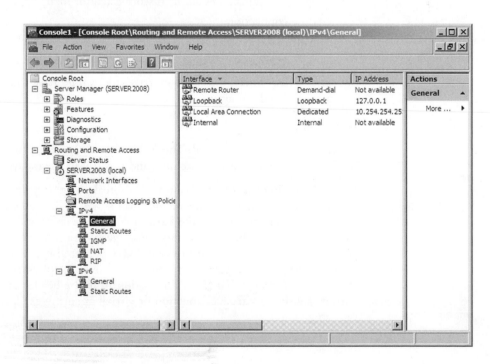

RIP can now take care of what we did with static routes in previous lessons. Keep in mind that for much bigger networks, other protocols are more desirable.

■ Defining Common WAN Technologies and Connections

THE BOTTOM LINE

Wide area networks connect multiple local area networks together. If an organization wishes to have a wide area connection to another office, it needs to decide on a networking service and the speed at which it wishes to connect. Budgeting plays a significant role in these types of decisions.

Defining Packet Switching

CERTIFICATION READY
How would you define
X.25 and Frame Relay?
1.3

Packet switching is how data packets are moved over switched wide area networks. Types of packet switching services include X.25 and Frame Relay. This section defines those two services.

Most WANs utilize some type of packet switching technology. Let's discuss the technology world prior to packet switching and talk about why packet switching is a superior solution.

Packet switching services include X.25 and Frame Relay. Before packet switching, there were direct dial-up connections and other archaic forms of communication. Some of the problems associated with these included the following:

- Until the early 1970s, data transfer was analog with much static and noise. It was also primarily asynchronous and conducted by dial-up modems.
- Data transfer could be as much as 40% overhead and only 60% actual information. Overhead included the allowance for noise, error checking, flagging, stop/start bits, parity, and so on.
- Longer data transfers could be disconnected for many reasons, including:
  - ○ Poor connection
  - ○ Network degradation
  - ○ Loss of circuits
- After a disconnect, the entire message (file) would have to be resent, usually after the person dialed out again.

DEFINING X.25

Then packet switching arrived. The *X.25* communications protocol was one of the first implementations of packet switching, and it is still in use today.

Packet switching was originally created to break down large messages into smaller, more manageable segments for transmission over a WAN. Basically, the sending computer sends its message over the LAN to the hardware/software component known as the router. The router then breaks the file into more manageable pieces (known as packets). Every packet gets a portion of the original message. Every packet also gets a segmentation number and address info. Each packet is then transmitted over the physical link to the switching system (telco), which picks a wire for transmission from the header information of the packet. This establishes a virtual connection or virtual circuit. Next, packets are re-assembled at the receiving router.

Here are the X.25 packet switching steps:

1. A computer sends data to the router as normal through the OSI model over the LAN.

2. Data is gathered by the router (as the message), but the router then disassembles the entire lot into jumbled packets. Thus, the router is known as a PAD (packet assembler/disassembler).

3. The PAD sends the packets to a ***CSU/DSU*** (high-speed digital data interchange device) as serial information. The CSU/DSU is the equivalent of the modem for the entire LAN. It is known as a DCE, or data communications equipment. In this scenario, the PAD (or router) is known as the DTE, or data terminating equipment.

4. The CSU/DSU sends the packets to the demarcation point (demarc) in the office or company. Quite often, the CSU/DSU is the demarc, otherwise known as the point where your responsibility as an administrator ends and the telecommunications or data communications provider's responsibility begins. The demarc could also be a network interface device or simple networking jack.

Figure 7-3 illustrates the process up to this point.

Figure 7-3

X.25 packet switching process

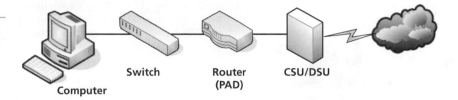

Computer · Switch · Router (PAD) · CSU/DSU

5. This then leads to the central office of the phone company that is supporting the X.25 service.

6. The central office (C.O.) picks a wire and transmits to the switching office, which then continues to the power lines, and so on. When the central office does this, it is known as a virtual circuit.

7. The information ends up at the receiving central office, which sends the data over another virtual circuit to the correct line that leads to the other office.

8. This then leads to their demarcation point (demarc), to a CSU/DSU, and then to their receiving router (PAD).

9. The receiving PAD then buffers the info, checks it, recounts, and puts the packets in sequence.

10. It then sends over the LAN in regular OSI model fashion to the correct receiving computer.

The "cloud" is the area of the telephone company's infrastructure that is in between the demarcation point of your office and the receiving office. All central offices, switching offices, telephone poles, and lines are part of the cloud.

The cloud is represented in Figure 7-4.

Figure 7-4

X.25 "cloud"

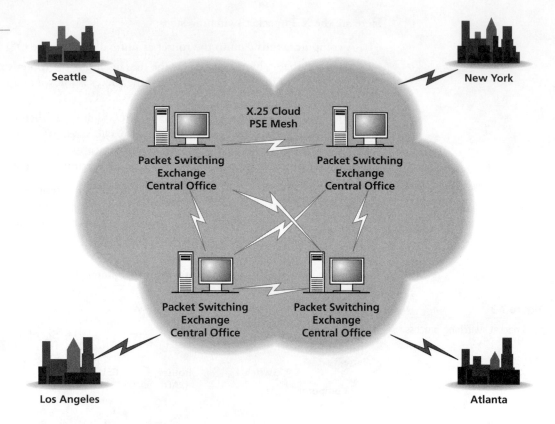

Characteristics of X.25 include the following:

- It is usually digital.
- It is usually synchronous. This means that the connection is controlled by a clocking circuit so that both X.25 devices know when to transmit data without having collisions.
- It involves a 56K or 64K max line.
- It is also known as variable length packet switching.
- A PAD decides which circuit the information is going to take as part of the virtual circuit concept.
- Packets usually have 128 bytes of actual data, but some configs go up to 512 bytes.

Now, let's cover the X.25 components. Basically, an X.25 packet is made of overhead and data. *Overhead* is the packet's header and trailer information combined. Therefore, if someone asks what the *two* parts of a packet are, you would answer the overhead and the data. However, if someone asks about the *three* parts of a packet, you would say the header, data, and the trailer. Overhead is not real data. It is information sent as additional electrical impulses, but it is not part of the original message. The *header* information includes items such as the packet flag, HDLC (high-level data link control), the from address, information with error detection, and so on. The *trailer* includes items such as the cyclic redundancy check (CRC), which checks the size of the packet for accuracy at the destination computer. An entire X.25 packet can be seen in Figure 7-5.

Figure 7-5

X.25 packet

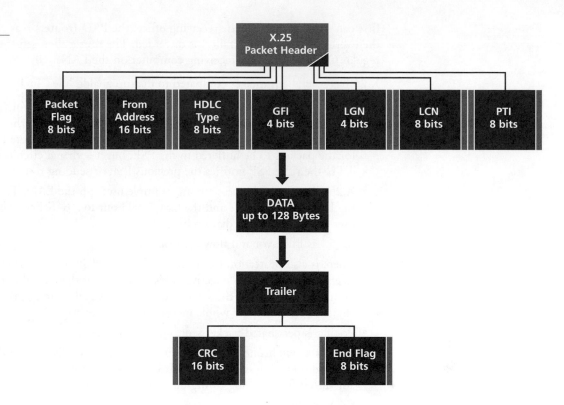

Generally, an X.25 packet will be a maximum of 128 bytes, but remember that a packet's data can be up to 512 bytes and is always of variable length. Some packets have no data at all; they are informational only to the X.25 system.

Now, let's move on to PSEs and switching to virtual circuits. A PSE is a ***packet switching exchange***. These are located in the central offices just inside the cloud, and they are really mega switching computers that handle huge numbers of packets and decide which circuit (out of tens of thousands) each packet will take. Quite often, these PSEs are UNIX powered. Immense amounts of processing power are required for the task of sending X.25 packets.

The PSE reads the address and framing information of the packet and then *routes* it in the correct direction. This is another example of the fact that computers can be routers as well; in fact, they are the original routers. These computers act as routers because they can decide multiple paths for the packet. The PSE chooses a circuit (out of thousands) that is used least, is most direct, or is most available. The PSE then orders up a leased line from the local exchange carrier (LEC). It uses this line as the circuit for the packets. In the old days, this was an analog line (2400 bps). Today, it is a digital line, usually at the speed of 64K. It is also ***synchronous***, which means that there is a clocking circuit that controls the timing of communications between the different routers.

Remember, the PSE has thousands of circuits from which to choose. These are known as a circuit set. The chances of the entire message of packets taking one circuit are slim, because so many different users and companies are utilizing the bandwidth. Therefore, a typical message of ten packets could be spread over five circuits. Because multiple circuits are being used (and not just one), the entire circuit set is known as the ***virtual circuit***.

There could be several PSE stops along the way. These PSEs are also PADs, and they disassemble and reassemble the packets. These stops are also known as ***hops***. For every hop along the way, the PSE buffers the packets into RAM and holds them there until the next PSE gets the packet and acknowledges it. This way, if a packet is lost between two PSEs, then the first can send it again. At the receiving office, the PAD (router) reassembles the packets and the overhead (header and trailer) is discarded. The router then sends the information in the regular OSI format to the receiving computer on the LAN.

X.25 has several advantages compared to dial-up analog lines, including the following:

- If any data fails, X.25 automatically recovers and sends it again. This is assuming that there are circuits available in the virtual circuit. If this is not the case and all circuits are being used by others, then other arrangements are made. There is a TTL (time to live) for the packets to be buffered in the PSE, but if a virtual circuit is not available past the TTL, then the PSE notifies the previous PSE or sending router.
- X.25 allows shared access among multiple users on the LAN. They share access through the LAN via the router and the CSU/DSU out to a 64K line. This is as opposed to each user having a separate dial-up line.
- X.25 has full error and flow control.
- There is also protection from intermediate link failure. X.25 is not completely fault tolerant, but it is 70% effective. This is because of the virtual circuit, whereas, on a dial-up line, you are using the same circuit to move a file through the whole transfer. If that circuit is lost, then the whole message must be sent again.
- Pricing is per shared packet sent, not per minute.
- X.25 is a synchronous, digital transmission. Digital is inherently better and faster because there is less noise, and also because the information does not have to be converted from analog to digital and back. So, this is less overhead in the form of conversion.
- There is less overhead per file. For dial up, there can be as much as 40% overhead per file, but with X.25, it can be as little as 8%.

DEFINING FRAME RELAY

Frame Relay is the advancement of X.25 packet switching. It is a newer form of packet switching designed for faster connections. With this system, the packets are now referred to as *frames*. Like X.25, Frame Relay uses transmission links only when needed. It also uses a virtual circuit, but one that is more advanced. Frame Relay created the "virtual network" that resides in the cloud. Many customers use the same groups of wires or circuits (known as shared circuits). Like private connections (T1 and so on), Frame Relay transmits very quickly. It might use a T1 connection, but not in a private manner. The T1 is a trunk carrier, a physical connection that has a data transfer rate of 1.544 Mbps. Unlike X.25, much less processing is needed in Frame Relay. Inside the switches or PSEs, most overhead is eliminated. The network only looks at the address in the frame. Unlike dedicated T1 private connections, Frame Relay uses a public leased line.

Frame Relay was created to take advantage of the low-error, high-performance digital infrastructure now in place and to better service synchronous transmissions only. It is a much simpler network compared to a private line network.

Figure 7-6 offers an example of a T1 mesh network. Connections are between each city. This is similar conceptually to the mesh topology.

Figure 7-6

T1 mesh network

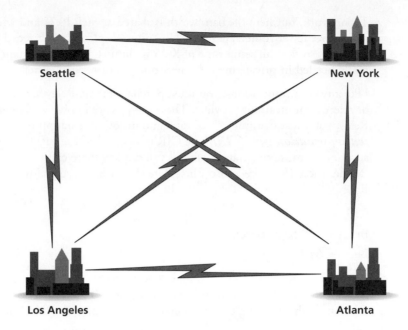

Figure 7-7 offers an example of a Frame Relay WAN. Only one connection is needed to the cloud per city.

Figure 7-7

Frame Relay network

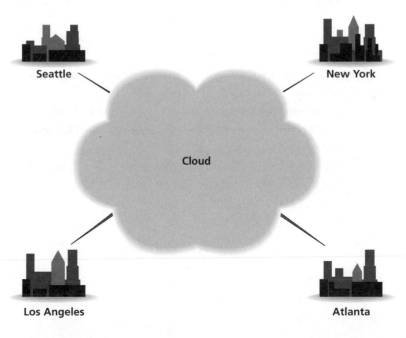

Disadvantages of Frame Relay are decreased speed and privacy as compared to a private T1 internetwork. Advantages include lower costs and the need for less equipment.

Now, let's discuss some of the characteristics of Frame Relay. With Frame Relay, multiple sessions can run simultaneously on the same link. These connections to the cloud are known as permanent logical links or ***permanent virtual circuits (PVCs)***, not to be confused with the plastic casing on a category 5 cable. The PVC links the sites together in the cloud, and this is accomplished, once again, by the PSE (packet switching exchange). This is just like a Private

T1 network, but here the bandwidth is shared at each PVC and with other customers as well. Therefore, fewer routers, CSU/DSUs, and multiplexors are needed per site. A PVC is always available, so the call setup time of X.25 is eliminated. The constant fine-tuning that is normally needed in private mesh T1 networks is not needed either.

Like any communications, you must purchase Frame Relay service from an Internet services or telecommunications provider. These services are known as *leased lines*. Also with Frame Relay, you must commit to a certain amount of information over time. This is the ***committed information rate (CIR)***. The CIR is assigned to each PVC that services the organization's account. Because this transmission is full duplex, there can be two CIRs for each PVC. Besides the CIR, there is also Burst Rate (Br), which is equal to the CIR, and Burst Excess Rate (Be), which is 50% above the Br. For example:

CIR = 128 Kbps

Br = 128 Kbps beyond CIR

Be = 64 Kbps beyond Br

Burst Rates are for two seconds max. The aggregate throughput in this example is 320 Kbps. So, if you purchase a 128 Kbps Frame Relay leased line, then you get temporary 320 Kbps. Obviously, this is going to save money because it provides bandwidth when we need it.

The frame format in Frame Relay consists of the following:

- **Flag:** Usually 126 or 127 (01111110 or 01111111 in binary). Marks the beginning and end of the Frame.
- **DLCI** (Data Link Control ID): 1024 LCNs (Logical Channel Numbers) maximum. Marks the PVC addressing scheme.
- **FECN** (Forward Explicit Congestion Notification): For congested CIRs and order of priority.
- **BECN** (Backward Explicit Congestion Notification): For congested CIRs and order of priority.
- **CR** (Command Response Rate): Usually not in Frame Relay.
- **EA** (Extension bit): If this is 0, it extends the DLCI address to the address extension in the optional fourth byte.
- **DE** (Discard Eligibility bit): Denotes whether a frame is eligible or whether the CIRs are congested.
- **Second EA:** If this is 1, it ends the DLCI.
- **FCS** (Frame Check Sequence): This offers 2 bytes of error checking, similar to the CRC.

Figure 7-8 shows the components of a frame in Frame Relay.

Figure 7-8

Frame Relay frame

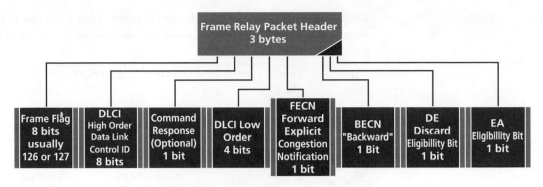

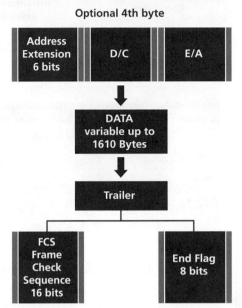

Circuit switching is another WAN switching method in which a dedicated physical circuit through a carrier network is established, maintained, and terminated for each communication session. Used extensively in telephone company networks, it operates much like a normal telephone call. It may be used in PSTN data connections.

Defining T-Carriers

T-carriers are interfaces implemented in mid-sized and large organizations that carry data at high speeds, generally 1.544 MB/s or higher. This section defines a few of the common T-carrier lines.

A *T-carrier* or telecommunications carrier system is a cabling and interface system designed to carry data at high speeds. The most common of these is the T1. The basic data transfer rate of the T-carrier system is 64 Kbps, which is known as DS0, which is the digital signaling scheme. Correspondingly, DS1 would be the digital signaling scheme for the T1-carrier. The two most common T-carrier systems are as follows:

- *T1:* An actual trunk carrier circuit that is brought into a company. Can run as a dedicated high-speed link or have other shared technologies running on top of it, like Frame Relay and ISDN. It is considered 1.544 Mbps, but only 1.536 Mbps of that is for data. The remaining 8 Kbps is for T1 trimming/overhead. The 1.536 Mbps is broken into 24 equal 64 Kbps channels and can be used with a multiplexor.

- *T3:* Stands for trunk Carrier 3. This is the equivalent of 28 T1s. It is considered 44.736 Mbps, using 672 64 Kbps B channels. T3 will come to a company as 224 wires or thereabouts and must be punched down to a DSX or like device.

T1 and T3 are the names used in the United States. In Japan, they are also known as J1/J3, and in Europe, they are denoted E1/E3.

Different services can run on a T-carrier system. They might be Frame Relay, ISDN, or other services. Otherwise, a T-carrier can be a dedicated private connection between LANs to form a completely private WAN.

Figure 7-9 shows a typical T1 connection and service.

Figure 7-9

Typical T1 configuration with Frame Relay

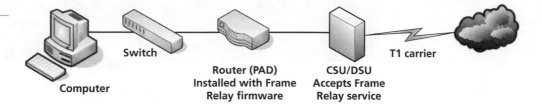

Switch

Computer

Router (PAD)
Installed with Frame
Relay firmware

CSU/DSU
Accepts Frame
Relay service

T1 carrier

Table 7-1 summarizes the main types of T-carrier systems and their equivalents.

Table 7-1

Common T-carriers, their speeds, and their equivalents

CARRIER SYSTEM	UNITED STATES	JAPAN	EUROPE
Level 0–DS0	64 Kbps	64 Kbps	64 Kbps
Level 1–DS1	1.544 Mbps–T1	1.544 Mbps–J1	2.048 Mbps–E1
Level 3–DS3	44.736 Mbps–T3	32.064 Mbps–J3	34.368 Mbps–E3
Level 4–DS4	274.176 Mbps–T4	97.728 Mbps–J4	139.264 Mbps–E4

CERTIFICATION READY
How would you define WAN technologies such as ISDN, ATM, and SONET?
1.3

Defining Other WAN Technologies and Internet Connectivity

Although Frame Relay and T-carriers are common WAN connectivity technologies, there are also other types of connections that a company might opt for, such as ISDN, ATM, SONET, cable, or DSL. This section defines those other WAN technologies.

The *Integrated Services Digital Network (ISDN)* is a digital technology developed to combat the limitations of PSTN. Users that have ISDN can send data, fax, or talk on the phone, all simultaneously from one line. ISDN can be broken down into two major categories:

- *Basic rate ISDN (BRI):* This is 128 Kbps with two equal B channels at 64 Kbps each for data, and one 16 Kbps D channel for timing. Generally, devices that connect to BRI lines can handle eight simultaneous connections to the Internet.
- *Primary rate ISDN (PRI):* This is 1.536 Mbps, and it runs on a T-1 circuit. PRI has 23 equal 64 Kbps B channels for data, along with one 64 Kbps D channel for timing.

Many companies still use this for video conferencing or as a fault tolerant secondary Internet access connection. Video conferencing requires a PRI line, because BRI does not have enough bandwidth. Data commuters will use BRI connections if DSL or cable Internet is not available.

Asynchronous transfer mode (ATM) is a cell-based switching technology as opposed to a packet switching technology. The cells involved in ATM are a fixed length, normally 53 octets (or 53 8-bit bytes). ATM is used as a backbone for ISDN.

OCx is the standard for data throughput on *SONET* connections. SONET is an abbreviation of Synchronous Optical Network. It transfers multiple digital bit streams over optical fibers. The rates presented in the following list are known as synchronous transport signal rates:

OC Level	Transmission Rate
OC-1	51.84 Mbps
OC-3	155.52 Mbps
OC-12	622.08 Mbps
OC-24	1.244 Gbps
OC-48	2.488 Gbps
OC-192	9.953 Gbps

Fiber distributed data interface (FDDI) is a standard for transmitting data on optical fiber cables at a rate of around 100 Mbps. It uses the ring topology.

Digital subscriber line (DSL) is a family of technologies that provides data transmissions over local telephone networks. Variations of DSL include the following:

- **xDSL** is the standard for the various digital subscriber lines.
- **ADSL** (asymmetrical digital subscriber lines) can run on your home telephone line so that you can talk on the phone and access the Internet at the same time. However, some versions limit you to 28,800 bps upload speed, and the download speed is variable, spiking as high as 7 Mbps. It is usually not as fast as cable Internet.
- **SDSL** (symmetrical digital subscriber line) is installed (usually to companies) as a separate line and is more expensive. SDSL data transfer rates can be purchased at 384 K, 768 K, 1.1 M, and 1.5 M. The upload and download speed are the same or symmetrical.

Broadband cable is used for cable Internet and cable TV. It operates at a higher speed than DSL and it can usually get up to an average of 5 to 7 Mbps, although the serial connection has the theoretical ability to go to 18 Mbps. DSLreports.com commonly shows people connecting with cable at 10 Mbps.

POTS/PSTN stands for plain old telephone system/public switched telephone network. This is what we use now for "regular" phone lines, and it has been around since the 1940s. POTS/PSTN is now digital at the switching office and some central offices, but there analog lines run to people's homes.

Table 7-2 offers a summary of the WAN technologies and connections that have been discussed in this lesson.

Table 7-2

WAN technologies and connections

WAN Technology	Description
X.25	One of the first implementations of packet switching. Usually 64 Kbps with a 128 byte payload per packet.
Frame Relay	The advancement of X.25 packet switching. It is a newer form of packet switching designed for faster connections.
T-carrier	A cabling and interface system designed to carry data at high speeds. The most common of these is the T1.
ISDN	A digital technology developed to combat the limitations of PSTN. Users that have ISDN can send data, fax, and talk on the phone simultaneously from one line.
ATM	A cell-based switching technology (as opposed to a packet switching technology). The cells are a fixed length, normally 53 octets.

(continued)

Table 7-2 *(continued)*

WAN Technology	Description
SONET	Abbreviation of synchronous optical network, it transfers multiple digital bit streams over optical fibers.
FDDI	A standard for transmitting data on optical fiber cables at a rate of around 100 Mbps.
DSL	A family of technologies that provides data transmissions over local telephone networks.
Broadband cable	High-speed cable Internet allowing for connections up to 5 to 7 Mbps.
POTS/PSTN	Plain old telephone system/public switched telephone network

SKILL SUMMARY

IN THIS LESSON, YOU LEARNED:

- The differences between static and dynamic routing.
- How to install and configure RRAS to function as a network router and how to install the Routing Information Protocol.
- How to define packet switching types, such as X.25 and Frame Relay.
- What T-carrier lines are, the different types of lines, and their Japanese and European counterparts.
- The basics about various other wide area networking technologies, such as ATM, SONET, FDDI, and so on.
- An introduction to different personal and small business Internet connectivity types.

■ Knowledge Assessment

Multiple Choice

Circle the letter that corresponds to the best answer.

1. You have been hired to install several routing protocols to a group of routers. Which one of the following is not an example of a dynamic routing protocol?
   a. RIP
   b. IGRP
   c. RRAS
   d. OSPF

2. You need to install the latest version of RIP on Windows Server 2008. Which version should you select?
   a. Version 1
   b. Version 2
   c. Version 3
   d. RIP does not have multiple versions

3. Proseware, Inc., has hired you to install a PAD (router) that will enable a packet switched connection to the Internet. Which of the following is an example of packet switching technology?
   a. T1
   b. Frame Relay
   c. 802.1X
   d. ATM

4. A coworker asks for your help installing a NAT server. What is the best tool to use for this?
   a. DNS
   b. RIP
   c. ATM
   d. RRAS

5. The IT director has asked you to install a new demarc device. What is he referring to? (Select the best answer.)
   a. A router
   b. A CSU/DSU
   c. A switch
   d. A server

6. You have been asked to troubleshoot a wide area networking technology that has a maximum data transfer rate of 64 Kbps. What technology will you be troubleshooting?
   a. Frame Relay
   b. ATM
   c. X.25
   d. SONET

7. The manager of IT has instructed you to install a PAD. To which of the following devices is a PAD most similar?
   a. Hub
   b. Switch
   c. Router
   d. CSU/DSU

8. Your boss asks you to have the organization's ISP install a T1 line. What is the total speed or throughput of that line?
   a. 1.536 Mbps
   b. 1.544 Mbps
   c. 1.5 Mbps
   d. 15.35 Mbps

9. A customer wants to install an ISDN line for video conferencing. Which of the following should you install?
   a. BRI
   b. ATM
   c. PRI
   d. OC3

10. A small business wants to ensure that its DSL Internet connection uploads and downloads the same amount of information per second. Which type of DSL should you install?
    a. xDSL
    b. ADSL
    c. SDSL
    d. DSL Lite

Fill in the Blank

Fill in the correct answer in the blank space provided.

1. You must install a routing protocol that monitors the network for routers that have changed their link state. The _____ protocol will allow you to accomplish this.

2. The _____ is a protocol that bases routing decisions on the network path and rules.

3. To enable dynamic routing, you have been instructed to install RIPv2. You should install this in the _____ snap-in.

4. A customer requires a high-speed packet switching alternative to X.25. In this situation, you should install _____.

5. X.25 connections utilize a clocking circuit. This makes them _____.

6. You are analyzing Frame Relay frames and find that a message consisting of ten separate packets was sent over five different circuits. These five circuits together form a _____ circuit.

7. Your company just purchased a leased line that runs the Frame Relay service. The standard data rate for this service is known as _____.

8. A client wishes to upgrade her remote users from dial-up to a faster service. However, cable Internet and DSL are not available in the users' respective areas. Another valid alternative is to use _____.

9. A customer wants a WAN technology that does not use variable length packets but instead uses fixed length cells. You should recommend _____.

10. A client with eight computers needs a cost-effective Internet solution that can transmit 128 Kbps. You should recommend _____.

■ Case Scenarios

Scenario 7-1: Selecting the Appropriate Service and Protocol

A client wants you to install a service that will allow network connections from Windows Server 2008. She wants you to select a well-known routing protocol that utilizes distance-vector algorithms. What should you recommend?

Scenario 7-2: Selecting the Appropriate WAN Technology

The ABC Company wants you to install a WAN technology that will allow high-speed access to the company's satellite office. ABC wants it to be a private, dedicated connection. What technology should you recommend?

Scenario 7-3: Recommending the Right Service

Proseware, Inc., requires that you set up an extremely fast wide area connection that can communicate at 2.4 Gbps over fiber optic lines. What service should you recommend?

Scenario 7-4: Setting Up Several Routes to Other Networks

Proseware, Inc., wants you to set up several routes to other networks. The company gives you the following documentation:

Route #1

- Network: 192.168.1.0
- Subnet mask: 255.255.255.0
- Gateway: 65.43.18.1

Route #2

- Network: 10.10.1.0
- Subnet mask: 255.255.255.0
- Gateway: 128.52.67.101

Route #3

- Network: 172.16.0.0
- Subnet mask: 255.255.0.0
- Gateway: 84.51.23.132

Access the DIR-655 emulator at the following link and configure the routing options appropriately: http://support.dlink.com/emulators/dir655/133NA/login.html.

✳ Workplace Ready

Find the Path—With Routing

IP routing is one of the most important pieces of TCP/IP. Without it, companies would not be able to communicate, and home offices wouldn't be able to get on the Internet. In short, the virtual world would come crashing down. IP routing (also known as IP forwarding) makes the connection between a router's two or more network adapters on different IP networks. There are many types of routers that allow connections from one network to another.

Use the Internet to research different types of routers, from SOHO four-port routers to business level routers and on to the enterprise routers that an ISP would use. Make a list of your findings, including manufacturer, model, price, and, if possible, who uses them. Try to find at least three routers for each of the following categories:

Small office/home office (SOHO)

Business level (small to mid-sized business)

Enterprise level

Analyze your findings and state your case for the best router in each category. Back up your argument with information regarding pricing, functionality, speed, and the number of routes and data transactions each device can handle.

Defining Network Infrastructures and Network Security

OBJECTIVE DOMAIN MATRIX

SKILLS/CONCEPTS	MTA EXAM OBJECTIVE	MTA EXAM OBJECTIVE NUMBER
Understanding Networks outside the LAN	Understanding the concepts of the Internet, intranet, and extranet.	1.1
Understanding Security Devices and Zones	Understanding the concepts of the Internet, intranet, and extranet.	1.1

KEY TERMS

3-leg perimeter configuration

application-level gateway (ALG)

back-to-back configuration

caching proxy

circuit-level gateway

demilitarized zone (DMZ)

extranet

firewalls

Internet

Internet content filter

Internet Engineering Task Force (IETF)

intranet

IP proxy

Layer 2 Tunneling Protocol (L2TP)

NAT filtering

network intrusion detection system (NIDS)

network intrusion prevention system (NIPS)

packet filtering

perimeter network

Point-to-Point Tunneling Protocol (PPTP)

proxy server

stateful packet inspection (SPI)

virtual private network (VPN)

Web 2.0

World Wide Web (WWW)

Proseware, Inc., is a growing, dynamic company that not only needs fast connections on its LAN and WAN, but also requires various network infrastructures so that it can communicate properly with customers, sister organizations, and partners.

As the network engineer, you are in charge of setting up secure connections for remote users and clients. You are also responsible for private connectivity to partners' Web sites and other corporate networks.

By using network infrastructure concepts such as VPNs, intranets, and extranets, and by employing security devices like firewalls and proxy servers, you can develop a secure method of connecting everything together while limiting access to only those users who require it.

■ Understanding Networks Outside the LAN

↓
THE BOTTOM LINE

The biggest wide area network of them all is the Internet. The Internet is well known for the World Wide Web, but it is not as well known for the other services that reside on it, or for its inner workings.

Other technologies such as intranets and extranets enable organizations to communicate and share data with each other in a secure manner using the inherent properties of the Internet in a privatized way. Virtual private networks often come into play when it comes to intranets and extranets. They are used to create secure connections that can cross over public networks.

Defining the Internet

CERTIFICATION READY
How do you define the
Internet?
1.1

The Internet is the largest WAN in the world. It is a public domain available to everyone in the United States, and it is available to most other countries as well. This section defines the Internet and the way it functions.

The *Internet* is a worldwide system of connected computer networks. Computers that connect to the Internet use the TCP/IP protocol suite. It is estimated that there currently are 2 billion Internet users and an estimated 650 million computers connected to the Internet, although it is difficult to estimate this due to NAT and other similar services. The origins of the Internet can be traced back to ARPANET, which was developed by the U.S. government for security purposes; however, ARPANET was a disjointed group of networks using outmoded or non-uniform protocols. By using TCP/IP to join different types of networks together, the Internet was created.

The Internet is not controlled by any one governing body—except for two technical aspects. First, the IP classification system is defined by the IANA (Internet Assigned Numbers Authority). Second, DNS is defined by the *Internet Engineering Task Force (IETF)*. Otherwise, the Internet is "controlled" by various ISPs and network providers depending on the location. These companies define how the Internet is accessed.

Companies use the Internet for many reasons, including:

- To communicate messages such as email.
- To gather information, often through the usage of web pages.
- To share information, often through the use of a web server.

- For e-commerce.
- To collaborate with other companies, organizations, and users.

Individuals use the Internet for these reasons as well as for social networking, shopping, file sharing, gaming, and other multimedia use.

Though the World Wide Web is a big part of the Internet, it is not the entire Internet. However, users quite often use the terms interchangeably. Technically, the Internet is the entire data communications system that connects the world, including hardware and software. Meanwhile, the *World Wide Web (WWW)* is an enormous system of interlinked hypertext documents that can be accessed with a web browser. The World Wide Web Consortium defines standards for how these documents are created and interlinked. Currently, the World Wide Web is in a stage known as *Web 2.0* (with Web 3.0 just under way). Web 2.0 is an interactive type of web experience compared to the previous version 1.0. Web 2.0 allows users to interact with each other and act as contributors to Web sites as well. Currently, when most people access the Internet, they do it through a web browser, but there are many other tools that can also be used to access the Internet, including instant messaging programs, FTP clients, third-party media programs, and more.

Defining Intranets and Extranets

CERTIFICATION READY
How do you define intranets and extranets?
1.1

> Intranets and extranets are used by organizations to share data with select individuals. Whereas an intranet is used by an organization to share data with its employees, an extranet is used to share data with sister companies or other partnered organizations.

An *intranet* is a private computer network or single Web site that an organization implements in order to share data with employees around the world. User authentication is necessary before a person can access the information in an intranet; ideally, this keeps the general public out, as long as the intranet is properly secured.

Generally, a company refers to its intranet as its private Web site, or perhaps the portion of the company Web site that is private. However, intranets use all of the inherent technologies characteristic of the Internet. For instance, within an intranet, TCP/IP protocols such as HTTP and FTP and email protocols like POP3 and SMTP are all employed just the same way as they are on the Internet. Again, the only difference is an intranet is a privatized version of the Internet, and any company can have one.

An *extranet* is similar to an intranet except that it is extended to users outside a company, and possibly to entire organizations that are separate from or lateral to the company. For instance, if a company often needs to do business with a specific organization, it might choose to set up an extranet in order to facilitate information sharing. User authentication is still necessary, and an extranet is not open to the general public.

Figure 8-1 illustrates both an intranet and extranet. Users can connect to intranets and extranets by simply logging in to a Web site or by using a virtual private network.

Figure 8-1

Intranet and extranet

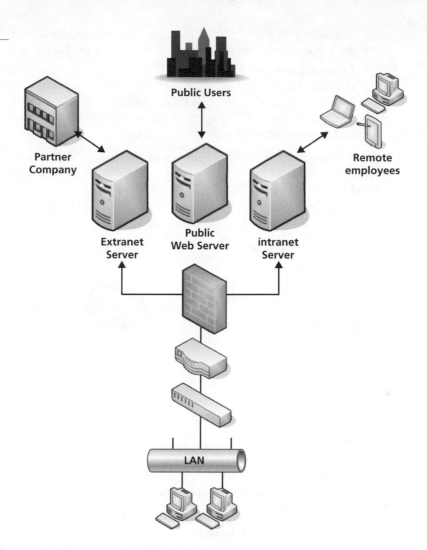

Understanding VPNs

> A VPN is a virtual private network that allows connectivity between two remote networks. It can also be used locally, but that implementation is much less common.

In order to better understand virtual private networks, let's discuss them a bit further and show how to set up a basic VPN.

A *virtual private network (VPN)* is a connection between two or more computers or devices that are not on the same private network. In fact, there could be LANs or WANs in between each of the VPN devices. In order to ensure that only the proper users and data sessions cross to a VPN device, data encapsulation and encryption are used. A "tunnel" is created, so to speak, through the LANs and WANs that might intervene; this tunnel connects the two VPN devices together. Every time a new session is initiated, a new tunnel is created. Some technicians refer to this as tunneling through the Internet, although some VPN tunnels might go through private networks as well.

VPNs normally utilize one of two tunneling protocols:

- *Point-to-Point Tunneling Protocol (PPTP)* is the more commonly used protocol, but it is also the less secure option. PPTP generally includes security mechanisms, and no additional software or protocols need to be loaded. A VPN device or server that allows incoming PPTP connections must have inbound port 1723 open. PPTP works within the point-to-point protocol (PPP), which is also used for dial-up connections.

- *Layer 2 Tunneling Protocol (L2TP)* is quickly gaining popularity due to the inclusion of IPsec as its security protocol. Although this is a separate protocol and L2TP doesn't have any inherent security, L2TP is considered the more secure solution because IPsec is required in most L2TP implementations. A VPN device or server that allows incoming L2TP connections must have inbound port 1701 open.

An illustration of a basic VPN is shown in Figure 8-2. Note that the VPN server is on one side of the cloud and the VPN client is on the other. The VPN client will have a standard IP address to connect to its own LAN. The IP address shown in the figure is the IP address it gets from the VPN server. The computer has two IP addresses; in essence, the VPN address is encapsulated within the logical IP address.

Figure 8-2

A basic VPN connection

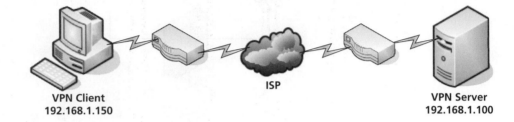

VPN Client
192.168.1.150

ISP

VPN Server
192.168.1.100

CREATE AND CONNECT TO A VPN

GET READY. In order to set up a VPN, you first need to configure a VPN appliance or server. Then, the clients need to be configured to connect to it. In this exercise, we will use Windows Server 2008 for our VPN server and Windows 7 as our VPN client. Here, we are setting up a mock VPN. Although both computers are on the same LAN, this exercise simulates what it is like to set up a real VPN.

1. Configure the VPN server:
   a. Access the previously made MMC, or access **Routing and Remote Access** from **Administrative Tools**.
   b. View the server within RRAS and check the configuration. If it is already configured (with a green arrow pointing upward), then right click it, select **Disable Routing and Remote Access**, click **Yes**, and move on to step 1c. If it isn't configured, move on to step 1c.
   c. Right click the server and select **Configure and Enable Routing and Remote Access**.
   d. Click **Next** for the Welcome screen.
   e. Select the third radio button named **Custom configuration**, as shown in Figure 8-3. Then click **Next**.

Figure 8-3

Selecting Custom configuration

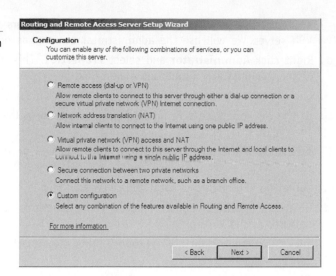

Normally, you would select the third radio button called **Virtual private network (VPN access and NAT)**; however, that will only work if your server has two or more network adapters. For this exercise, we will assume that the server only has one adapter.

f. In the Custom Configuration screen, check **VPN access** and click **Next**.

g. Click **Finish** to complete the configuration.

This might create a new policy automatically. If the system asks you to do so, restart the service. When finished, the server within RRAS should have a green arrow pointing upward. The VPN server is now ready to accept incoming VPN connections.

By default, the VPN server will hand out IP addresses to the clients. However, you can have a DHCP server hand out addresses as well.

2. Configure user accounts:

a. Access the Computer Management console window. You can do this by navigating to **Start > Administrative Tools > Computer Management** or by adding the Computer Management snap-in to the MMC.

b. Navigate to **System Tools > Local Users and Groups > Users**, as shown in Figure 8-4. By default, this will display the Administrator and the Guest

Figure 8-4

Accessing the Users folder

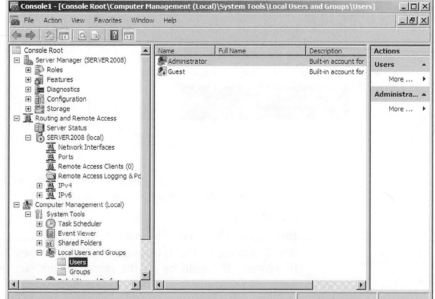

TAKE NOTE*

If you do not wish to use the administrator account, make sure you use another account that has administrative rights on the server.

account. From here, you can give permissions to users to allow access to the VPN server. We will use the administrator account as our example.

c. Right click **Administrator** and select **Properties**. This displays the General tab of the Administrator Properties dialog box.

d. Click the **Dial-in** tab.

e. In the Network Access Permission box, select the **Allow access** radio button. Then click **OK**.

f. Make note of the administrator password; you will need it to connect from the client.

3. Configure the VPN client by installing a VPN adapter:

a. Go to the Windows client computer. Verify that it is connected to the same network as the server.

b. Click **Start**, then right click **Network**. This displays the Network and Sharing Center window.

c. Click the **Set up a new connection or network** link.

d. Click **Connect to a workplace** and click **Next**.

e. Select the **Use my Internet connection (VPN)** option.

f. In the Internet address field, type the IP address of the server.

g. Give a name to the VPN connection in the Destination name field. Then click **Next**.

h. Type in the user name and the password of the administrator account on the server. Click **Next**.

At this point, the VPN adapter should connect to the VPN server. The adapter in the Network Connections window should read **VPN Connection** on the second line, as shown in Figure 8-5, which tells you that it is connected. If it was disconnected, the VPN adapter would be grayed out, and it would read **Disconnected**. By the way, the third line should read **WAN Miniport (PPTP)**. This tells us that we have made a PPTP connection, which is the default type of connection. To make L2TP connections, you would have to do a bit more configuring on the server and the client side.

TAKE NOTE*

If Windows asks you to set up an Internet connection, select the option to set up one later.

Figure 8-5

A VPN connection in its connected state

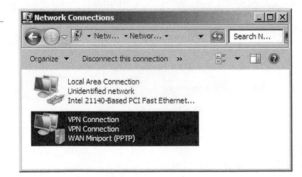

i. You can also tell whether you are connected to a VPN server using the command prompt. Access the command prompt and type the following command:

ipconfig /all

This should show the VPN connection and the Local Area Connection. Note the IP address of the Local Area Connection. Then note the VPN connection IP address. It should be on the same network, and it was applied by the VPN server. An example is shown in Figure 8-6.

Figure 8-6

Ipconfig showing results of VPN adapter

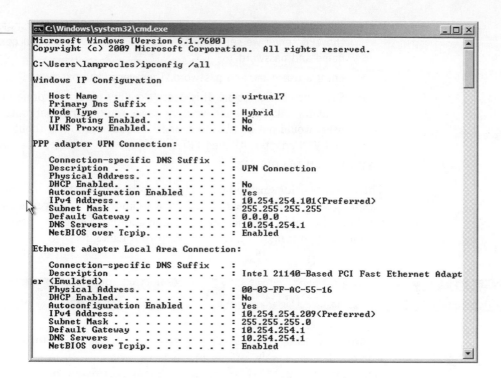

There you have it: a basic VPN connection. What we did is a simulation because we only did it on a LAN between computers. Still, if the Internet were involved, the process would work the same way. Some companies actually implement LAN VPN connections for added security. Keep in mind that every time you encrypt, encapsulate, or otherwise change data, it slows down the network and uses more resources.

When you are finished with the exercise, reset all systems back to normal.

SHOW VPN FUNCTIONALITY ON A ROUTER

GET READY. VPN devices can also come in the form of appliances and routers. For example, the D-Link DIR-655 router we used previously can be set up to accept incoming VPN connections with the PPTP or L2TP protocols. Let's examine where to go on the router to set this up.

1. Access the D-Link DIR-655 router at the following link:
   http://support.dlink.com/emulators/dir655/133NA/login.html
2. Log in (no password is required).
3. Click the **Setup** link at the top of the screen.
4. Click the **Manual Internet Connection** setup button.
5. In the Internet Connection Type drop-down menu, select **PPTP (Username/ Password)**. This will modify the rest of the details of the page. Note that you can also select **L2TP** from this list.
6. Scroll down to PPTP Internet Connection Type.
7. From here, you need to select either static or dynamic IP. If you have received a static IP address from your ISP, select the **Static IP** radio button and enter the IP information. If you are receiving a dynamic IP from the ISP, select the **Dynamic IP** radio button. This will gray out the PPTP IP Address, PPTP Subnet Mask, and PPTP Gateway IP Address fields.

At this point, you can have the router forward PPTP requests to a server (for example, the VPN server we set up in the previous exercise). Or, you could simply enter a user-name and password.

8. Enter a username and password. Then verify the password.

9. Save the configuration. This doesn't really save any information because it is an emulator, but this would work the same way on an actual router. At this point, external users would not be able to connect to your network without a username, password, and VPN adapter utilizing PPTP.

10. Log off the DIR-655.

This is one way for small offices and home offices to create an intranet of their own. By only accepting secure connections from users who know the proper username and password, you weed out the public Internet users. This, in addition to security devices and zones on the perimeter of your network, can help keep your data safe.

■ Understanding Security Devices and Zones

THE BOTTOM LINE

Security devices such as firewalls are the main defense for a company's networks, whether they are LANs, WANs, intranets, or extranets. Perimeter security zones such as demilitarized zones (DMZs) help keep certain information open to specific users or to the public while keeping the rest of an organization's data secret.

Defining Firewalls and Other Perimeter Security Devices

CERTIFICATION READY
How do you define and configure a firewall?
1.1

Firewalls are used to protect a network from malicious attack and unwanted intrusion. They are the most commonly used type of security device in an organization's perimeter.

Firewalls are primarily used to protect one network from another. They are often the first line of defense in network security. There are several types of firewalls; some run as software on server computers, some run as stand-alone dedicated appliances, and some work as just one function of many on a single device. They are commonly implemented between the LAN and the Internet, as shown in Figure 8-7.

Figure 8-7

A firewall

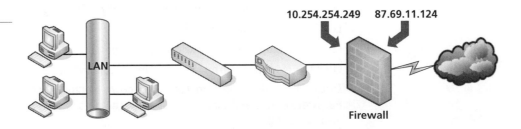

Generally, there is one firewall, with the network and all associated devices and computers residing "behind" it. By the way, if a device is "behind" the firewall, it is also considered to be "after" the firewall, and if the device is "in front of" the firewall, it is also considered to be "before" the firewall.

In Figure 8-7, you can see that the firewall has a local address of 10.254.254.249, which connects it to the LAN. It also has an Internet address of 87.69.11.124, which allows connectivity for the entire LAN to the Internet. The firewall also hides the LAN IP addresses. By default, the IP address 87.69.11.124 should be completely shielded. This means that all inbound ports are effectively closed and will not allow incoming traffic, unless a LAN com-puter initiates a session with another system on the Internet. Regardless, you should check this with third-party applications such as Nmap or with a web-based port scanning utility like ShieldsUP!. We will show these in upcoming exercises. If any ports are open, or unshielded, they should be addressed immediately. Then, the firewall should be rescanned for vulnerabilities.

Many of today's firewalls have two types of firewall technologies built into them: SPI and NAT. However, there are a couple other types of firewall methodologies of which you should be aware:

- *Packet filtering* inspects each packet that passes through the firewall and accepts or rejects it based on a set of rules. There are two types of filtering: stateless packet inspec-tion and *stateful packet inspection (SPI)*. A stateless packet filter, also known as pure packet filtering, does not retain memory of packets that have passed through the firewall. Because of this, a stateless packet filter can be vulnerable to IP spoofing attacks. However, a firewall running stateful packet inspection is normally not vulnerable to this because it keeps track of the state of network connections by examining the header in each packet. It should be able to distinguish between legitimate and illegitimate packets. This function operates at the network layer of the OSI model.

- *NAT filtering*, also known as NAT endpoint filtering, filters traffic according to ports (TCP or UDP). This can be done in three ways: using basic endpoint connections, by matching incoming traffic to the corresponding outbound IP address connection, or by matching incoming traffic to the corresponding IP address *and* port.

- *Application-level gateway (ALG)* supports address and port translation and checks whether the type of application traffic is allowed. For example, your company might allow FTP traffic through the firewall, but it may decide to disable Telnet traffic. The ALG checks each type of packet coming in and discards those that are Telnet packets. This adds a layer of security; however, it is resource intensive.

- *Circuit-level gateway* works at the session layer of the OSI model when a TCP or UDP connection is established. Once the connection has been made, packets can flow between the hosts without further checking. Circuit-level gateways hide information about the private network, but they do not filter individual packets.

Examples of network firewalls include the following:

- The D-Link DIR-655 SOHO router/firewall used previously
- Cisco PIX/ASA firewalls
- Juniper NetScreens
- Microsoft's Internet Security and Acceleration Server (ISA) and Forefront

 CONFIGURE A SOHO FOUR-PORT FIREWALL

GET READY. Let's explore where to go on a SOHO router to turn on SPI and NAT filtering firewalls. To do so, perform these steps:

1. Access the D-Link DIR-655 router at the following link:
   http://support.dlink.com/emulators/dir655/133NA/login.html
2. Log in (no password is required).
3. On the main **Device Information** page, click the **Advanced** link near the top of the window. This should bring up the Advanced page.
4. On the left side, click the **Firewall Settings** link. This should display the Firewall Settings window.

5. Take note of the first setting: **Enable SPI**. This is stateful packet inspection. It should be selected by default, but if not, select it and move on to the next step.

6. View the NAT Endpoint Filtering section directly under the Firewall Settings. Increase the security of UDP Endpoint Filtering by clicking the radio button **Port and Address Restricted**.

7. Next, enable anti-spoofing by clicking the **Enable anti-spoofing checking** check box.

8. Finally, scroll down and view the Application Level Gateway (ALG) Configuration. **PPTP, IPSec (VPN), RTSP**, and **SIP** should all be selected.

➔ SCAN HOSTS WITH Nmap

GET READY. In this exercise, we will scan a computer with Nmap. This vulnerability scanner is best known for its port scanning abilities. We will use this tool to scan for open ports on a computer.

1. Download and install the command-line version of the Nmap program. You will also be prompted to install the WinPCap program.

2. Extract the contents to a folder of your choice.

3. Write down the IP address of a Windows host on your network. For this example, we will use a host with the IP address 10.254.254.208.

4. Scan the ports of that host with the –sS parameter (for example, **nmap –sS 10.254.254.208**).

5. If there are non-essential ports open, turn off their corresponding unnecessary services, such as FTP or HTTP. This can be done in a variety of places, including Computer Management. If there are no services that you wish to turn off, enable one and then rescan the ports with Nmap (to show that the service is running), turn off the service, and move on to the next step.

6. Scan the ports of that host a second time, once again with the –sS parameter. This time, you are verifying that the services are turned off by identifying that the corresponding ports are closed.

7. If possible, scan the ports of a four-port SOHO router/firewall or a computer with a firewall running. Use the –P0 parameter (for example, **nmap –P0 10.254.254.208**). This may take up to five minutes. Doing this will verify whether the firewall is running properly by displaying that all of the ports are filtered. The –sS option we used previously will not work on a fully firewalled device because the initial ICMP packets from the ping will not be accepted. –P0 does not use ICMP packets, but it takes longer to complete.

➔ SCAN THE INTERNET CONNECTION WITH ShieldsUP!

GET READY. There are several online port scanners available. This exercise requires an Internet connection in order to access one of them. This exercise will scan the ports of whatever device is facing the Internet. This could be the local computer if it connects directly to the Internet or a four-port router, or perhaps a more advanced firewalling device. It all depends on your network scenario.

1. With a web browser, connect to www.grc.com.

2. Click on the **ShieldsUP!** picture.

3. Scroll down and click the **ShieldsUP!** link.

4. Click the **Proceed** button.

5. Select the **Common Ports** scan. This will initiate a scan of the computer or device that is being displayed to the Internet. If you access the Internet through a router/

firewall, then this will be the device that is scanned. If your computer connects directly to the Internet, then the computer will be scanned.

6. Make note of the results. It should show the public IP that was scanned. Then it will list the ports that were scanned and their status. The desired result for all ports listed is "Stealth," all the way down the line for each of the listed ports. If there are Open or Closed ports, you should check to make sure that the firewall is enabled and operating properly.

7. Try a few other scans, such as **All Service Ports** or **File Sharing**.

A *proxy server* acts as an intermediary between a LAN and the Internet. By definition, proxy means "go-between," acting as such a mediator between a private and a public network. The proxy server evaluates requests from clients, and if they meet certain criteria, forwards them to the appropriate server. There are several types of proxies, including the following:

- *Caching proxy* attempts to serve client requests without actually contacting the remote server. Although there are FTP and SMTP proxies among others, the most common caching proxy is the *HTTP proxy*, also known as a *web proxy*, which caches web pages from servers on the Internet for a set amount of time. This is done to save bandwidth on the company's Internet connection and to increase the speed at which client requests are carried out.

- *IP proxy* secures a network by keeping machines behind it anonymous; it does this through the use of NAT. For example, a basic four-port router will act as an IP proxy for the clients on the LAN it protects.

Another example of a proxy in action is Internet content filtering. An *Internet content filter*, or simply a content filter, is usually applied as software at the application layer and it can filter out various types of Internet activities, such as access to certain Web sites, email, instant messaging, and so on.

Although firewalls are often the device closest to the Internet, sometimes another device could be in front of the firewall, making it the closest to the Internet—a network intrusion detection system, or perhaps a more advanced network intrusion prevention system.

A *network intrusion detection system (NIDS)* is a type of IDS that attempts to detect malicious network activities (e.g., port scans and DoS attacks) by constantly monitoring network traffic. The NIDS will then report any issues that it finds to a network administrator as long as it is configured properly.

A *network intrusion prevention system (NIPS)* is designed to inspect traffic, and, based on its configuration or security policy, it can remove, detain, or redirect malicious traffic in addition to simply detecting it.

Redefining the DMZ

CERTIFICATION READY
How would you define a DMZ?
1.1

A *perimeter network* or *demilitarized zone (DMZ)* is a small network that is set up separately from a company's private local area network and the Internet. It is called a perimeter network because it is usually on the edge of a LAN, but DMZ has become a much more popular term. A DMZ allows users outside a company LAN to access specific services located on the DMZ. However, when the DMZ set up properly, those users are blocked from gaining access to the company LAN. Users on the LAN quite often connect to the DMZ as well, but without having to worry about outside attackers gaining access to their private LAN. The DMZ might house a switch with servers connected to it that offer web, email, and other services. Two common DMZ configurations are as follows:

- *Back-to-back configuration:* This configuration has a DMZ situated between two firewall devices, which could be black box appliances or Microsoft Internet Security and Acceleration (ISA) Servers.

- *3-leg perimeter configuration:* In this scenario, the DMZ is usually attached to a separate connection of the company firewall. Therefore, the firewall has three connections—one to the company LAN, one to the DMZ, and one to the Internet.

SET UP A DMZ ON A SOHO ROUTER

GET READY. In this exercise, we demonstrate how to enable the DMZ function of a typical four-port SOHO router:

1. Access the D-Link DIR-655 router at the following link:

   http://support.dlink.com/emulators/dir655/133NA/login.html

2. Log in (no password is required).
3. Click the **Advanced** link at the top of the screen.
4. Click the **Firewall Settings** link at the right.
5. Scroll down to the **DMZ Host** section.
6. Check the **Enable DMZ** option.
7. Type the IP address of the host that will be connected to the DMZ.

   At this point, you would also physically connect that host to a port on the router. Or, you could connect an entire layer 3 switch to the port and enter that switch's IP address in this field. This would allow you to connect multiple hosts to the switch while only using one port on the router.

■ Putting It All Together

THE BOTTOM LINE

Building an entire network for an organization can take months or even years! The concepts covered in these lessons only scrape the surface of the gigantic networking world. However, what we covered up until now is still a lot of information. Let's try to complete the Proseware, Inc., scenario by combining the various technologies we learned about into one efficient, well-oiled network.

In this scenario, Proseware, Inc., wants just about every component and technology possible for its network. Let's list what they require and follow it up with some network documentation that will act as the starting point for our network plan. Here are the basic components that Proseware, Inc., desires for its for their network:

- Client-server local area network with the following:
  - 300 client computers, some of which are laptops and tablet PCs
  - 1 master switch and 4 other secondary switches (1 per department) set up in a hierarchical star fashion
- 5 LAN Windows Servers connected directly to the master switch:
  - 2 Domain Controllers
  - 1 DNS server
  - 1 DHCP server
  - 1 RRAS server
- Wired and wireless considerations:
  - Category 6 twisted-pair cable for the client desktop PCs
  - Wireless 802.11n connections for laptops and tablet PCs

- ○ 1000BASE-SX fiber optic connections for the servers and switches
- ○ 10GBASE-SR fiber optic connection for the master switch
- 3-leg perimeter DMZ with the following equipment and zones:
  - ○ Switch with 1000BASE-SX fiber optic connection
  - ○ 3 DMZ Windows Servers:
    - Web server
    - FTP server
    - Email server
  - ○ Intranet for remote users with authentication server
  - ○ Extranet for connection to partner company utilizing the same authentication server as the intranet

Figure 8-8 shows an example of how this network documentation might start out.

Figure 8-8

Network documentation

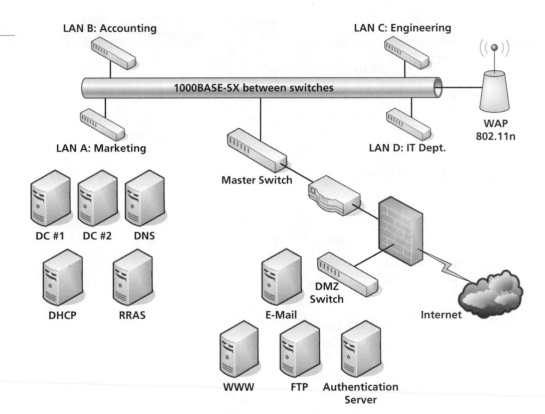

Take some time to think about exactly what would be entailed when installing this network. For example, what kind of network adapters would the LAN servers require in order to take advantage of the 10 Gbps fiber connection that the master switch provides? What type of firewall should be used in order to facilitate all the different connections necessary, such as intranet, extranet, LAN connectivity to the Internet, and so on.?

This type of network documentation is just a starting point, of course. More documents will be necessary to define how and where cables will be installed, determine an IP addressing scheme and list of static IP addresses, and much more. However, this type of planning gives the basis for all of the configurations and planning yet to come.

SKILL SUMMARY

IN THIS LESSON, YOU LEARNED:

- How to differentiate between the Internet, intranets, and extranets.

- How to set up a virtual private network with Windows Server 2008 and with a typical SOHO four-port router.

- About firewalls and how to initiate port scans on them to see whether they are locked down.

- About other perimeter devices and zones, such as proxy servers, internet content filters, NIDS, NIPS, and the DMZ.

■ Knowledge Assessment

Multiple Choice

Circle the letter that corresponds to the best answer.

1. You have been tasked to set up an authentication server on a DMZ that will allow only users from a partner company. What kind of network are you configuring?
   a. Internet
   b. Intranet
   c. Extranet
   d. World Wide Web

2. You are in charge of setting up a VPN that allows connections on inbound port 1723. What tunneling protocol are you going to use?
   a. PPTP
   b. PPP
   c. L2TP
   d. TCP/IP

3. Proseware, Inc., wants you to set up a VPN server. What service in Windows Server 2008 should you use?
   a. FTP
   b. DNS
   c. RRAS
   d. IIS

4. The IT director has asked you to install a firewall. Which of the following is not a type of firewall?
   a. NAT filtering
   b. DMZ
   c. ALG
   d. Stateful packet inspection

5. You suspect an issue with one of the ports on the firewall. You decide to scan the ports. Which of the following is the appropriate tool to use?
   a. PPTP
   b. Protocol analyzer
   c. NMAP
   d. NIDS

6. Your client wants a server that can cache web pages in order to increase the speed of commonly accessed Web sites. What type of server does the client require?
   a. Proxy
   b. DNS
   c. Firewall
   d. VPN

7. The customer you arc working for wants a device that can detect network anomalies and report them to an administrator. What type of device is the customer looking for?
   a. Internet content filter
   b. Proxy server
   c. WINS server
   d. NIDS

8. Your boss asks you to set up an area that is not on the LAN but not quite on the Internet. This area will house servers that will serve requests to users who are connecting to your intranet. What type of zone does your boss want you to set up?
   a. DMZ
   b. Extranet
   c. FTP
   d. VPN

9. You have been asked by a client to install a VPN server that can offer unencrypted tunnels by default, or encrypted tunnels by using IPSec. Which of the following services should you choose in order to accomplish this?
   a. DNS
   b. L2TP
   c. WINS
   d. IPsec

10. You have set up a default VPN in Windows Server 2008. However, your boss is not happy with the level of security. She would rather have L2TP combined with IPsec. What tunneling protocol is running currently on the server?
    a. RRAS
    b. L2TP without IPsec
    c. PPTP
    d. VPNv2

Fill in the Blank

Fill in the correct answer in the blank space provided.

1. _____ allows users to interact with each other and contribute to Web sites.

2. The _____ defines DNS.

3. The _____ is an enormous system of interlinked hypertext documents.

4. You have set up a network zone that allows remote access for employees of your company. This is known as a _____.

5. You install a VPN server that uses inbound port 1701. The server is utilizing the _____ protocol.

6. You installed a VPN server and configured a VPN adapter on a client computer. However, the connection cannot be completed from the client to the server. This is because you skipped the _____ step.

7. The VPN server has been configured and is running properly. However, it has not been configured to hand out IP addresses to clients. When a VPN server is configured this way, the clients obtain their IP addresses from a _____ server.

8. A firewall normally has a private and a _____ IP address.

9. You have installed a firewall that accepts or rejects packets based on a set of rules. This firewall keeps track of the state of the network connection. It is running a type of packet filtering known as _____.

10. You have configured a firewall so that all ports are closed. Now you are attempting to scan the firewall's ports to verify that there are no open ones. You should use the _____ option within the Nmap port scanning program.

■ Case Scenarios

Scenario 8-1: Setting Up a DMZ

A client wants you to set up a DMZ with two servers. Each server will service a different set of people:

1. Server #1 will service employees who work from home.
2. Server #2 will service two partner companies.

What two types of network zones will enable this functionality?

Scenario 8-2: Selecting the Appropriate Services

The ABC Company wants you to install a solution that will allow it to do the following:

1. Enable remote client computers to connect via tunneling.
2. Allow for a high level of security during remote connections.

What solution and protocol will enable this functionality?

Scenario 8-3: Setting Up a PPTP Server

Proseware, Inc., requires that you set up a PPTP server on a D-Link DIR-655 router. The following are details for the IP configuration:

- IP address: 10.254.254.50 (static)
- Subnet mask: 255.255.255.0
- Gateway address: 10.254.254.1
- PPTP server IP address: 10.254.254.199
- Username: administrator
- Password: 123PPTPABC##

Access the DIR-655 emulator at the following link and configure the DHCP server appropriately: http://support.dlink.com/emulators/dir655/133NA/login.html

Scenario 8-4: Creating a WAN with VPN

This activity will require two Windows Server 2008 computers, each with two network adapters.

The purpose of this case scenario is to connect two separate networks together over a simulated WAN and then implement a VPN between the two. Normally, a client on one IP network cannot connect to or ping a client on another IP network. Here, the goal is to have the clients on both networks pinging each other through a routed connection. Each city is considered its own separate LAN, yet New York City and London will connect to make this WAN. You will need the following at your disposal:

- Two Windows Server 2008 computers with two network adapters each; because these will have two network connections, they will be known as multi-homed machines or computers
- Two client computers minimum
- Crossover cable

You will need to change the IP addresses on all machines.

Servers should be set up as IP .1.

Clients' IP addresses should ascend from there. Make sure to also set the gateway address to the Server's LAN IP.

When all IPs are configured, make sure that all clients can ping the server on the LAN.

Table 8-1

IP chart

City	LAN Networks	WAN IP (Second NIC)
New York City	192.168.1.0	152.69.101.50
London	192.168.2.0	152.69.101.51

TAKE NOTE *

Tip: Remember that you can make a crossover cable. Just make sure to use the 568A wiring standard on one end and the 568B standard on the other. Wiring was covered in Lesson 3, "Understanding Wired and Wireless Networks."

1. Try to ping any host on the other city. You should not be able to. The results should say Destination Host Unreachable or Request Timed Out. You should, however, be able to ping all hosts, including the server in your city.
2. Verify that your servers have the second NIC set up and functioning with the proper IP address. Label it WAN card.
3. Connect your crossover cable from WAN card on the NYC server to the WAN card on the London server.

Create your own internetwork now, and afterward, set up the VPN connection from one city to the other so that clients on one city (your choice) can log in to the VPN server in the other city.

✳ Workplace Ready

Examine Various Levels of Firewalls

Firewalls are extremely important in network security. Every network needs to have one or more of these in order to have any semblance of safety.

Even if your network has a firewall, individual client computers should be protected by a software-based firewall as well. Most versions of Windows come with a built-in firewall program. Some versions such as Windows 7 also include the Windows Firewall with Advanced Security. This can be accessed by going to **Start > Control Panel > System and Security > Windows Firewall**. Then click the **Advanced settings** link. From here, custom inbound and outbound rules can be implemented, and the firewall can be monitored as well. Check it out!

When you are done, access the Internet and research the firewalls offered by the following companies:

- Check Point
- Cisco
- D-Link
- Linksys
- Microsoft (ISA)

Describe the pros and cons of each of these vendors' solutions. From your analysis, define which solution would be best for the following scenarios:

- Home office with four computers
- Small office with 25 computers
- Mid-sized company with 180 computers
- Enterprise-level company with 1,000 computers

In your argument, prove your point by showing devices that can support the appropriate number of users.

Index

Exam Objective	Skill Number	Lesson Number
Understanding Network Infrastructures		
Understand the concepts of Internet, intranet, and extranet.	1.1	8
Understand local area networks (LANs).	1.2	1
Understand wide area networks (WANs).	1.3	7
Understand wireless networking.	1.4	3
Understand network topologies and access methods.	1.5	1
Understanding Network Hardware		
Understand switches.	2.1	2
Understand routers.	2.2	7
Understand media types.	2.3	3
Understanding Protocols and Services		
Understand the OSI model.	3.1	2
Understand IPv4.	3.2	4
Understand IPv6.	3.3	4
Understand names resolution.	3.4	6
Understand networking services.	3.5	6
Understand TCP/IP.	3.6	5